The World Book of Math Power

THE
WORLD BOOK OF
MATH
POWER

Volume 2

Using Math

World Book, Inc.
Chicago

Staff

Publisher

William H. Nault

President

Tom Murphy

Editorial

Vice-president
Dominic J. Miccolis

Administrative director
Roberta Dimmer

Managing editor, print
Maureen Mostyn Liebenson

Associate editor
Karen Zack Ingebretsen

Editors
Suzanne B. Aschoff
Cynthia Fostle
Kathy Klein
Judith A. Witt

Director of research
Mary Norton

Permissions editor
Janet T. Peterson

Writers
Bryan H. Bunch
Everett T. Draper
William F. Keefe

Art

Art director
Wilma Stevens

Assistant art director
Joe Gound

Senior editorial artist
Deirdre Wroblewski

Photography director
John S. Marshall

Designers
Randi Brill
Image House

Illustrations
ANCO/Boston
Bill Anderson
Trudy Rogers

Art production
Mitchell Gound
Kelly Shea
Brenda Tropinski

Copyright © 1983 by
World Book Encyclopedia, Inc.,
525 West Monroe Street,
Chicago, Illinois 60661

1991 Revised Printing
All rights reserved. This volume may not be reproduced in whole or
in part in any form without written permission from the publishers.

Printed in the United States of America

ISBN 0-7166-3224-1
Library of Congress Catalog Card
No. 90-70044
g/ia

Product production

Vice-president
Daniel N. Bach

Director, manufacturing
Sandra Van den Broucke

Vice-president, pre-press services
Jerry Stack

Product manager, pre-press services
Janice Rossing

Advisers

Lola J. May, Ph.D.
Mathematics Consultant
Winnetka Public Schools
Winnetka, Illinois

Peter Pereira, M.A.
Associate Professor
School of Education
DePaul University
Chicago

Photo credits
cover: NASA
587, 637: Steve Hale
793: Editorial Photocolor Archives Inc.

Contents

Volume 2   Using Math

Introduction

There's no question about it: whether you are a child or an adult, you use math in some way every day of your life. Math, if you know how to use it properly, can help you solve all sorts of problems quickly and accurately. But if you don't know math, these problems can frustrate and confuse you.

Volume 1, *Learning Math,* has provided you with the skills necessary to solve ordinary—and extraordinary—mathematical problems. Now Volume 2, *Using Math,* will put those skills to practical use.

Part IV, "Relaxing with Math," is designed to help you feel at ease with math by showing how math is a natural part of the way you think. You are also shown how to do "quick math," or mental arithmetic, to speed up the computation process and make your math more accurate.

Part V, "Putting Math to Work," will show you how to use math to make home repairs and remodeling jobs easier, as well as cooking and traveling. Managing money, whether in personal or business affairs, is a mathematical activity. In Part V, you will learn how math can make your money work for you.

Part VI, the "Math Powerhouse," is a rich source of mathematics information compiled as a reference you can use for a variety of purposes. It presents a history of mathematics, plus a glimpse of the most famous mathematicians and their contributions to the field of mathematics. Next, you will learn about mathematics competitions that are ongoing in schools across the nation. And, if you would like to read even more about math, there is a list of useful and entertaining math books, all described so that you will know which to pick for independent math reading.

Math symbols, vocabulary, operations, formulas, and tables come next. Organized in one place, they will be easy to find throughout your mathematics study. Finally, an index to Volumes 1 and 2 completes *Using Math,* just as it completed *Learning Math.* This detailed source will show you where to find all the information in *Math Power.*

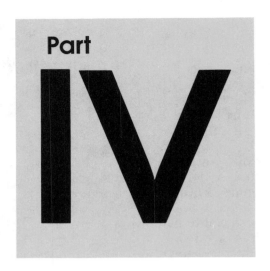

Part

IV

Relaxing with Math

Many people, especially those who have "always had trouble with math," think that it is impossible to relax with mathematics. What they probably don't know is that math is a part of every life. People come by math understandings very early and very naturally. In other words, everyone relaxes with math quite often.

Math is much more than adding up long columns of figures and working algebra formulas. These exercises merely sharpen math skills that you already have, just as speaking and writing develop language skills. Mathematics includes so many different subjects that it is hard to define. One definition that fits most of the mathematics you learn in school is that mathematics is the study of quantities and relations through the use of numbers and symbols. Does that sound difficult? Then think of it this way. Whenever you rush to be on time, take two aspirins, or select the "biggest piece of fudge," you are using math. See how mathematically inclined you are?

You are about to explore your everyday world with mathematics as a lively companion instead of a silent partner, as it may have seemed until now. First, you will learn how math is not only part of you, but of animals about you, as well. Then, you will see how you can "touch" math. Finally, you will find out how you can speed up math operations—or skip them entirely—and still arrive at correct or usable solutions to mathematical problems, perhaps without even using pencil and paper. Sound impossible? Relax, you've got what it takes. You see, the math is already in your mind. ■

(Preceding photo) Math games are a favorite pastime for many families.

The Math in Your Mind

From an early age, all human beings use some mathematics, even in cultures that have no written language. Other animals also use mathematics. Crows have been known to keep track of up to thirty persons. Bees can measure angles and lengths. And almost all animals learn to recognize shapes and sizes. (Yes, shapes and sizes are a part of math.) Rabbits must learn, for example, the shape of a flying hawk so that they can take cover. They must also learn the shapes of edible leaves. For animals, mathematics means survival.

Humans are probably born with some very basic mathematical abilities. With no teaching whatsoever, almost anyone can tell the difference between one object and two objects, know that one object is much larger than another, and recognize the difference between a circle and a triangle. But higher levels of mathematics require training. You must learn special techniques to tell the difference between 137 sheep and 141 sheep, or between a liter of water in a pail and a quart of water in a carton. The purpose of mathematics education is to build on inborn abilities and gradually take them to higher levels.

Counting

How can you be sure that crows count? In farming areas, crows can be a nuisance because they eat young plants. Scarecrows sometimes help keep crows away, but often the only way to get rid of crows is to shoot them. Crows are smart, however. If they see a person with a shotgun, they won't invade the field until the person leaves. You see, crows recognize the shape of a shotgun. So to shoot crows, a farmer may build a hiding place in the field, called a *blind*. Even then the crows are hard to fool. If they see a farmer enter the blind, they won't attack the corn until the farmer leaves.

One farmer had an "easy" solution to this problem. Two people would enter the blind, but only one would come out. The person who was left would shoot the crows when they flew into the field. But when the plan was tried, the crows did not come into the field until the second person left the blind.

More help was needed. Three people went into the blind and two came out. The crows were not fooled. Four people going in and three coming out did not fool the crows either. At this point, everyone became very curious about how high the crows could count. So the farmer in charge asked more people to enter the blind. It was not until thirty people entered the blind and twenty-nine came out that the crows were fooled into the field. That is, the crows had finally "lost count."

What is counting? Adult human beings can usually count up to five objects without any special technique. A person can look at a stack of four or five books and tell how many there are without actually counting. If a stack contains six or seven books, however, the person must count in order to tell their exact number. Counting is done by matching each book in the stack with a number name. People learn different number names and rules for combining the names to form numbers in order from one upward. A person may count the books by saying, "One, two, three, four, five, six, seven." The person matches each number name with one of the books in the stack. If seven is matched with the last book in the stack, it tells how many books there are.

Crows, however, probably "count" by the mental technique that humans use for five or fewer objects. Since crows cannot use language, they have developed the ability to judge larger quantities by sight.

The number-name method was probably not the first way that humans used to count. Long ago, humans probably used sets of objects to match things they wanted to count. For example, a shepherd who wanted to make sure that all the sheep were safe for the night could match each sheep with a pebble and keep the pebbles in a bag. Each night, the shepherd could check to see if there was a sheep for each pebble and a pebble for each sheep. In that way, the sheep were counted, even though no number name was used. The matching process was more important than the use of number names.

Along trade routes in the Middle East, archeologists have found hollow clay balls filled with markers. The archeologists believe that ancient merchants used these balls to tell buyers how many items they had sent. For example, if seventeen bars of copper were shipped from Cyprus to Turkey, a ball containing seventeen markers would be shipped, too. When the shipment got to Turkey, the buyer could break open the ball, match the markers with the bars of copper, and know if the proper amount had arrived safely.

Eventually, the markers were shown as dents on the outside of the ball, so people could check the number along the way without breaking the ball open. The clay was baked hard after the dents were made so no new dents could be added or old dents removed. The dents became the first system of writing numbers, the *cuneiform* system. In fact, people developed ways to write numerals before they developed ways to write words. About five thousand years ago, Babylonians used numerals that looked like this:

1	2	3	4	5	6	7	8	9	10

The counting process results in a whole set of numbers—1, 2, 3, 4, 5, and so forth—that can go on indefinitely. These numbers are often called the *counting numbers* or the *natural numbers*. The counting numbers are the basis of all numbers, but they are not enough to solve all the mathematical problems that might arise.

Measurement

Suppose, for example, that the merchant in Cyprus had more than enough copper to make 16 bars but not enough to make 17 bars. If the merchant wanted to ship all the copper, he would need a way to show that he was sending sixteen whole bars and one partial bar. How could he relate this information to the buyer? The answer is to use what today are called fractions.

Fractions are numbers but they are different from the counting numbers. If two partial bars make one whole bar, then each partial bar is a half, or $\frac{1}{2}$, of a whole bar. If three partial bars make one whole, then the size of each partial bar is a third, or $\frac{1}{3}$. In each case, a *measurement* takes place. The merchant is *measuring* the size of the partial bar in terms of the whole number 1. Fractions thus allow the merchant to measure the partial quantity against the whole quantity.

Things may become a bit more complicated for the merchant. Perhaps the amount of leftover copper he wishes to send will not "go evenly" into one bar. For example, it will take three partial copper bars to make up two (not one) whole bars. The easy solution is to use the fraction $\frac{2}{3}$.

A fraction is always a way of showing a relationship between two numbers—the number of parts and the number of wholes. If you had any difficulty following the example of the merchant, try this: You divide a candy bar and give your friend one-half. He has half of the whole bar. You just split the whole down the mid-dle, in other words. Neither one of you is confused be-cause fractions are a natural part of the way you think. You share via fractions.

One number in a fraction tells how many parts the whole was divided into. The other number tells how many parts are in the piece being measured. Here is a new way of thinking about the merchant's copper bars using fractions to split the bars mentally.

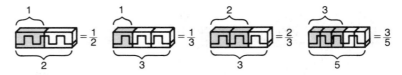

Can you split a candy bar into halves? Thirds? Fifths? Then you can use fractions correctly, and you understand the mathematical concept ratio. A *ratio* between two quantities is the number of times one contains the other. Since fractions show a ratio of two numbers, mathematicians call fractions the *rational numbers*. You don't need mathematicians to explain this concept to you. You've been using it for years.

Shape

Shape is an important concept in mathematics. Shape can be defined in terms of numbers. Can you think of a shape that has three sides? Four sides? Five sides? Did you think of these?

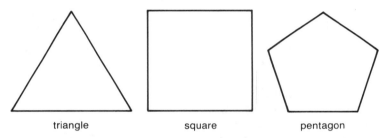

triangle   square   pentagon

All of these shapes are associated with numbers. A figure made with three straight lines has to be a triangle; it cannot be a square. Four straight lines of equal length can make a square, but never a pentagon. The five sides of the pentagon cannot be put into the shape of a triangle. Each figure has its own characteristics, which mathematicians call *properties*. The properties can be defined in terms of the numbers 3, 4, and 5. The properties vary from figure to figure.

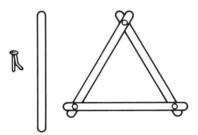

Take three sticks from a frozen dessert and fasten them at the ends. (Note that the sticks are of equal length.) You have just made a triangle. You can try pushing it into different forms, but it doesn't change. It is rigid. Now add a fourth stick. Push the sticks into different positions. Do you always have a square? No, sometimes you have what's called a *parallelogram*. What does this mean in terms of numbers? It means that if you have a shape made of three straight lines, you are going to have a triangle no matter how you try to move the sides around. If you have a shape made of four straight lines of equal length, you may have more than one type of four-sided figure. This difference in properties between the triangle and the four-sided figure is intricately interwoven with the numbers 3 and 4 that are associated with the figure.

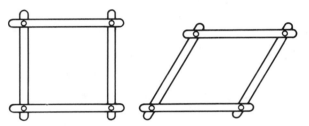

Measurement enters into shape as well. If all sides of a four-sided figure made from straight lines are the same length, as above, the shape has one set of properties. Otherwise, the shape has another set of properties. The same goes for triangles. Here are some more examples of three- and four-sided shapes.

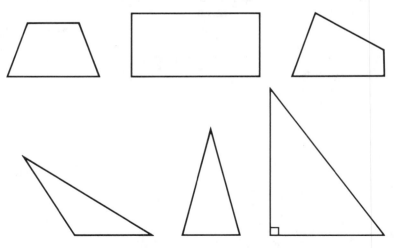

Look at the third triangle more closely. It is a very important shape in mathematics. The sides of this triangle have the measurements 3 cm, 4 cm, and 5 cm. Any triangle whose sides have the measurements 3, 4, 5—no matter what the measurement *units* are—always makes an angle of the same size between the three-unit side and the four-unit side. This angle is the one called a *right angle*. This triangle is a *right triangle*.

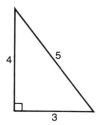

The right triangle can also have sides of different lengths, as shown here.

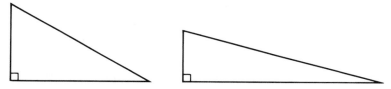

The properties of the right triangle have interested many mathematicians for thousands of years, Pythagoras among them. You can read more about the right triangle and Pythagoras in Section 10 of Part III in the first volume of *Math Power*.

Patterns

Through the ages, people didn't have to go to school to see that number and measurement were closely related. They saw that there were patterns in counting and measuring physical objects. For example, ancient peoples recognized that everyone had two feet and two eyes, but only one nose.

Still, language shows that numbers have not always been used for measurement. Sometimes, *number words* are used. For example, a *pair* of shoes and *twin* engines both mean two objects, but no one ever says "a twin of shoes." In one North American Indian language, different number words are used for living things, for round things, for long things, and for days. The Fiji language uses one word for ten coconuts and another word for ten boats. These words developed without the basic pattern involved in "twoness," "tenness," "hundredness," or number in general.

Similarly, people began to see that the properties that triangles made from sticks shared with triangles made from gold rods also formed a pattern. The important idea was the triangular shape, not what the triangle was made from—just as twoness did not depend on whether the objects were shoes or engines. In fact, people began to think that a triangle, like a number, was a pattern.

This observation led to a major conclusion. Mathematics deals with both number and shape because both follow patterns. In other words, mathematics is the study of patterns, and the study of patterns is mathematics.

Logic and Proof

While some patterns of mathematics are fairly obvious, others are less so. Consider a pattern such as the following:

$$2 + 3 = 3 + 2 \qquad\qquad 9 + 5 = 5 + 9$$
$$27 + 58 = 58 + 27 \qquad 132 + 6 = 6 + 132$$

You can observe that this pattern holds true for a great many pairs of counting numbers. But no matter how many pairs of numbers you check, there will always be pairs that you have not checked. If you want to be sure that the pattern holds true for all pairs of counting numbers, you must go beyond simply seeing that the pattern is true for a great many pairs.

One way to convince yourself that the pattern is true for all pairs of counting numbers is to use *logic*. Logic is also called *reasoning*. In its simplest form, logic is the argument that because one set of conditions is true, a given result must follow. For example, if you know that

All men are mortal.
Socrates is a man.

then you also know that

Socrates is mortal.

This example is a famous *syllogism,* a kind of logical scheme of formal argument. But the arguments of logic can be less formal than that. For example, suppose that an addition problem such as 9 + 5 is shown as two sets of dots, with nine dots on the left and five dots on the right.

• • • • • • • • •   • • • • •

You can also show the problem 5 + 9 with five dots on the left and nine dots on the right. If you turn this book upside down, you get the second problem. Obviously, turning the book upside down does not change the total number of dots, so you have reasoned that 9 + 5 = 5 + 9. The same reasoning would apply to twenty-seven dots, to fifty-eight dots, and, in fact, to any number of dots on the left and any number on the right. This line of thinking is a *proof* of the following: For counting numbers, called *n* and *m* here, it is always true that

$$n + m = m + n$$

no matter which two counting numbers *n* and *m* are.

Logic is not the same as mathematics, but it is the main tool for finding patterns. Logic by itself, however, does not go far enough. Since the time of the ancient Greeks, more than 2000 years ago, mathematicians have tried to set up perfect rules for logic and math, rules that everyone could agree on. Then it would be possible to say what really was a proof and what was not. For example, how do you know that turning the book upside down does not change the number of dots? Should turning the book upside down be accepted as a proof—a legitimate way to solve problems in math?

The Greeks believed that there were a few simple rules of logic and math that everyone could accept. They called the rules of logic *axioms* and the rules of math *postulates*. This idea turned out to be extremely useful. When applied to the study of shapes, for example, the Greek mathematician Euclid (305–285 B.C.) was able to show that about five axioms and five postulates were enough to prove everything that was known. (Later mathematicians improved on his system, but not on the basic idea.) This approach to mathematics is called an *axiomatic system*. As a result of Euclid's success, it became common to think of proof as something that happened only in axiomatic systems. But in reality, early mathematicians proved results in whatever ways they could. You can read more about Euclid's system and other approaches to proof in Section 10 of Part III in the first volume of *Math Power*.

Counting, measurement, shape, patterns, logic and proof—these are all parts of math that are basically easy to think about. Now get ready to reach out and actually touch math.

Math You Can Touch

People usually think of mathematics as a mental process. But this is not exactly so. Math in many ways represents the physical part of your life. An example from the ancient Greeks will show you how this is true.

Although the Greeks had a system of writing numbers based on letters of the alphabet (similar to Roman numerals), the ordinary people found it too complicated to work with. But they needed to use math just as much as the mathematicians. So, instead of using the "bulky" letters, they computed with small stones, or counters, on a board. They were literally able to move their numbers around on the board.

The Greek mathematicians didn't find the letter system very efficient, either. But they went beyond using stones for counting and instead used pictures of stones drawn in the sand. It was a bit more convenient for them to work with a clean board covered with sand than with a board and a bag of stones. They showed their numbers as holes in the sand—dots, in other words. The Greeks had developed a method of picturing numbers as arrangements of dots. They merely had to touch the sand in a certain way and the numbers (dots) would appear. They could just as easily remove them.

The ordinary Greek people's stones and the mathematicians' pictures in sand are two examples of mathematical *models*. Stones on a board are a good model of counting numbers because they can be combined in the same way that counting numbers are. An example of a poor mathematical model would be to try to use drops of water on a board. The drops might run together, making this model an unreliable method of counting. But if you have three stones on a board and put four more on, you will always get seven stones.

Models are used by modern educators to help students learn math. The educators have several names for the models they use. One, the *concrete model,* is like the stone-and-board method. This model, like the ancient one, makes it possible to put objects into *one-to-one correspondence* with the objects to be counted. For example, stones are concrete models. If you want to represent three pairs of sandals, you can use three stones to do so. In modern schoolrooms, students may represent three apples with three blocks, instead.

Sometimes a single stone or other marker is used to represent two, ten, one hundred, or some other number. It is still a physical object that can be touched and manipulated, but it is less concrete than using exactly as many markers as the number of objects to be counted. A model that uses single objects to stand for collections of objects is called *semiconcrete.*

Concrete and semiconcrete models help people visualize numbers, but they are not always practical to use. Imagine a teacher taking home a class's homework made up of individual counting boards with loose stones for every problem from every student. In such a case, it would be easier to work with pictures of the counting boards and stones. The pictures would be considered *semiabstract models*.

The semiabstract model shows what physical operations are supposed to have taken place. For example, a lesson may show pictures of blue dots, each representing one object. Maybe the children were asked to circle the number of fingers the teacher held up. By circling the right number of dots, the children have "grouped" them. A lesson may also have different-colored dots. If the blue dots represent one object and the red dots represent two, and there are three windows in the classroom, the students can show how many windows there are by circling one blue and one red dot.

Mathematical Models

The next level of model is the *abstract* level. *Abstract models* represent numbers and operations on numbers with actual numerals and mathematical signs. For example, both the symbols $3 + 4 = 7$ and

$$\begin{array}{r} 3 \\ +4 \\ \hline 7 \end{array}$$

are abstract models for numbers.

There is yet another model, but it is one you cannot reach physically. This model is the idea of the numbers themselves: no objects, no pictures, no numerals, just the thought of "one," "two," and other numbers. This model has no name.

Understanding the first four kinds of math models—concrete, semiconcrete, semiabstract, and abstract—is important to understanding the discussion that follows. If you don't have a clear understanding of these four models, review the previous discussion before reading on.

Concrete Counting Numbers

You already know one way that counters can be used for counting. That is, if you match a set of counters with another set of objects so that there is one counter for each object and one object for each counter, you know the number of objects you have.

Now suppose that you are counting people entering a store through a turnstile. As each person passes through the turnstile, you place a counter on a board. At the end of the day, the number of counters is the same as the number of people who passed through the turnstile. This matching process suggests an important model for the counting numbers. The empty board represents 0, which is not a counting number. (The counting numbers and 0 taken together are called the *whole numbers*). Put a counter on the board and you have the first counting number, 1. Add another and you have the second, which is $1 + 1$, or 2. Add another, and you have $2 + 1$, or 3. Each counting number is formed from the one before it in the same way. This provides a model of the counting numbers that does not depend on one-to-one correspondence. In fact, it is the *plus-one model* that is generally used to teach the counting numbers to small children, often combined with the idea of one-to-one correspondence.

The next level of dealing with the counting numbers includes the four familiar operations of addition, subtraction, multiplication, and division. Each operation combines two counting numbers to get a third. Each also has a model at the concrete level.

Keep in mind as you read that concrete models help you understand the nature of the mathematical computations you perform every day. Some of the examples may seem far-fetched, but concentrate on them anyway. Get some counters, like pennies, and work through appropriate examples. The physical process will show an interrelationship of mathematical operations you may not know exists.

Addition

Suppose that you are counting people entering a store, but there is no turnstile. Instead of entering the store one at a time, people can enter in groups of any size. If you are using stones on a board to keep track of the number entering, you have to change your strategy. As each group (or individual person) enters, you quickly model the group with stones using one-to-one correspondence. When a group of three people enters, you grab three stones as a group and place them on the board. When a group of four people enters, you add four stones to the board in one handful. At this point, the number of stones on the board is the same as if seven people had entered one by one through a turnstile. This grouping can replace counting one at a time. Manipulating stones or other counters in this way is the basic concrete model of addition.

There is another way that addition can be modeled. Let's say that it's getting late in the day, and you already have 217 stones on the board. A large group of people comes in, and you do not have time to match them with a group of stones. So instead of matching the whole group and putting all the stones on the board at once, you take a random handful of stones from the pile and, one-by-one, put a stone on the board for each person in the group. You get the same result either way. This represents the *counting-on model* of addition. If you said the numbers aloud, you would say 218, 219, 220, 221, 222, 223, 224, 225. It is the same as putting stones on the board in one handful.

The counting-on model is an important tool in learning addition and in finding a number when you have forgotten how to add abstractly. It always works for counting numbers. If you have 6 and want to add 5, you can always think "7, 8, 9, 10, 11," counting the numbers you are thinking until you have five of them. Notice that it is necessary to start counting on with the number just after the number that is being added to.

The numbers that are combined in an addition problem are called *addends,* and the number that is obtained as a result is called the *sum.* It is not practical to use a concrete model every time you need to add. For the smaller counting numbers, through nine at least, you must memorize the sums of each possible pair of addends. These sums, which include all possible combinations from $0 + 0$ to $9 + 9$, are called the *basic addition facts.* There are one hundred of them. You'll find the addition facts and other mathematics facts soon to be mentioned in Part VI, the "Math Powerhouse." You may want to refer there before going on.

One hundred addition facts are a lot for children to remember at first. So they need strategies to learn all the facts and to recall the ones that they forget. One strategy is to return to the concrete model, using counters. Often the handiest counters are their fingers, which they can use either in one-to-one correspondence for sums less than ten, or in the counting-on strategy for larger sums. For efficient computation, however, youngsters must pass beyond the finger-counting stage and memorize all the basic addition facts.

Subtraction

Suppose that your job at the store includes making sure that all customers have left at the end of the day. You can also use a concrete model to determine this. As each group of people leaves the store, you simply remove from the board the number of counters that matches one-to-one with that group. If, at the end of the day, there are no counters on the board, you know that everyone who has entered has also left. In fact, at any time during the day, the number of counters on the board represents the number of persons in the store. Say that there are thirty-eight customers in the store and six of them leave in a group. You remove six counters from the board. There are thirty-two counters left, so you know that there are now thirty-two customers left in the store. This is the *take-away model* for subtraction.

Another model for subtraction is just as useful. It is similar to the counting-on model for addition. As the six customers leave the store, instead of removing six counters all at once, you can remove one counter at a time. This is the *counting-back model* for subtraction. Like the counting-on model of addition, it is a useful way to learn or to recall the answers to subtraction problems.

Here is another concrete model for subtraction. The store hopes to attract 500 customers to a big sale. Late in the day, not subtracting for people who have left the store, you have 437 counters on the board. How many more people need to come into the store to reach 500? This is the subtraction problem $500 - 437$, but the answer cannot be found by removing counters from the board. Instead, it is necessary to *add* counters. If you do not know the answer, you can add one counter at a time until you reach 500, keeping track of how many counters you have added. The number you added will be the answer to $500 - 437$. This is sometimes called the *missing-addend* or *difference model* of subtraction.

Like the addition facts, the *basic subtraction facts* must be memorized. One hundred facts are generally labeled basic. These include all the whole-number facts from $0 - 0 = 0$ to $18 - 9 = 9$. In subtraction, the number you are subtracting from is generally called the *minuend,* although sometimes—thinking of the missing-addend model—it is called the *sum.* The number you subtract is called the *subtrahend.* The answer is most often called the *difference*—thinking of the missing-addend model—or the *remainder*—thinking of the take-away model. The 100 basic subtraction facts are those for which both the subtrahend and the difference is 9 or less.

Multiplication

One concrete model for multiplication is simply *repeated addition.* For example, assume you want to count the people riding a roller coaster. Each car holds 8 passengers and there are 6 cars. One way to find the answer using counters is to add 8 counters to a board 6 times. This is the same as $8 + 8 + 8 + 8 + 8 + 8$, but it is also the same as 6×8.

In another concrete model, if you want to multiply 6 × 8, you can arrange your counters in a rectangle that has 6 rows with 8 counters in a row.

While this is essentially the same as repeated addition, this model, called the *array model*, is often easier to use. Furthermore, the array model can be used to make discoveries about multiplication that are hard to see using the repeated-addition model. For example, since a 6-by-8 array and an 8-by-6 array have the same number of counters, 6 × 8 = 8 × 6.

A third physical model for multiplication is quite different from the other two in that its relation to addition is not at all obvious. Place 6 counters on one side of the board. Place 8 counters opposite those 6. Now connect each counter in one set to every other counter in the other set, using pieces of string as the connectors. You get 48 connectors, which is the same number as 6 × 8.

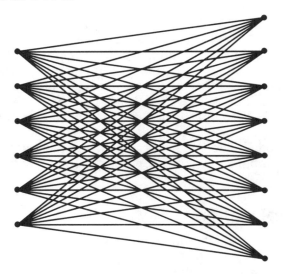

This model is the *Cartesian-product*, or *matching* model. The matching model is not very useful for learning the multiplication facts, but it is handy for understanding certain kinds of problem situations, such as "If Sarah has 3 blouses and 4 skirts that all match, how many different outfits can she put together?" The answer is 3 × 4, or 12, which is a direct result of the matching model.

Two numbers that are multiplied are sometimes called *factors*. The answer is always called the *product*. If you want to make a distinction between the two factors—based on the addition model for multiplication—the number of addends is called the *multiplier* and the addend that is repeated is called the *multiplicand*. A peculiarity of the way people write multiplication is that the order of the factors is changed when going from the horizontal form 6 × 8 = 48 to the vertical form

$$\begin{array}{r} 8 \\ \times 6 \\ \hline 48 \end{array}$$

In both the horizontal and vertical forms, 6 is the multiplier and 8 is the multiplicand.

Like the basic addition and subtraction facts, it is important to memorize the 100 *basic multiplication facts*. They are the facts for which both factors are 9 or less. In fact, it is even more important to memorize the multiplication facts because it is harder to use concrete models to get the products than it is for addition or subtraction.

Division

Just as one model for subtraction is a missing-addend model, suggesting the relationship between addition and subtraction, one model for division is the *missing-factor model,* which indicates the relationship between multiplication and division. The name for this kind of relationship is *inverse operation.* Subtraction and addition are inverse operations, and division and multiplication are inverse operations. Therefore, if you need to find 48 ÷ 6, you can use your memorized multiplication fact 6 × 8 = 48 to find the answer. This model can be made into a concrete model by using the array model for multiplication. If you have 48 stones that you want to divide into 6 groups, you can put the 48 stones into an array that has 6 stones on one side. The number of stones on the other dimension of the array is the missing factor.

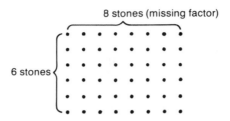

8 stones (missing factor)

6 stones

There is also a subtraction model for division. You can find the answer to 48 ÷ 6 by subtracting 6 from 48 until you have subtracted all the 6s you can. There will be 8 of them. Note that this is not identical to 6 × 8 = 48, which would be to subtract groups of 8 from 48.

Here's another method to find 48 ÷ 6. Make a picture of 48 dots. Then, circle 6 dots at a time until all dots are circled. Count the rings. Or use only 6 rings, so that the same number of dots is in each ring. Count the dots inside a ring.

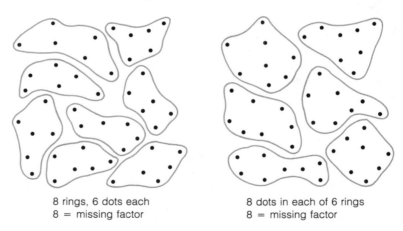

8 rings, 6 dots each
8 = missing factor

8 dots in each of 6 rings
8 = missing factor

How, you may well ask, can you circle the dots when you don't know how many dots to put into each circle? There is a physical model for doing this that you probably know. Suppose that you have 48 cents that you want to divide equally among 6 friends. You give the first friend a penny, then the next friend a penny, and so on until you reach the sixth friend. Then you start all over. You keep repeating the process until you run out of pennies. When you are finished, each of

your 6 friends has 8 pennies: the missing factor. If you
have ever used this technique, you were dividing via
a model of the concrete counting numbers without
knowing it.

For the problem here, to translate into circles and
dots, you may begin by drawing six circles and placing
48 dots to the side. Then start moving the dots into the
circles, crossing out a dot each time you move it. First
you move one dot into each circle, then another dot
into each, and so forth until all the dots have been
moved. There will be eight dots per circle.

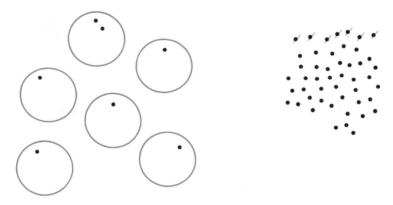

In division, the number you are dividing by is
called the *divisor,* the number you are dividing into is
called the *dividend,* and the answer is called the *quotient.* So in 48 ÷ 6 = 8, 48 is the dividend, 6 is the
divisor, and 8 is the quotient.

The answers to the division problems used thus far
have "come out even." Answers that do not come out
even are a problem with division that does not occur
with the other whole-number operations. For example,
if you divide 50 by 6, you end up with 2 counters left
over. The number of leftover counters is called the
remainder.

In the concrete models of division based on subtraction, the remainder emerges naturally. For example, if you subtract 6 from 50 over and over, you will
end up with 2 left over. In the concrete models based
on multiplication, however, the remainder requires a
bit of extra work.

Every number has a relatively small number of factors. For example, 2 and 5 are factors of 10 because
2 × 5 = 10; 1 and 10 are also factors of 10. The fac-

tors of 48 are 1, 2, 3, 4, 6, 8, 12, 16, 24, and 48. If 48 is divided by any number other than one of its factors—5, for example—there will be a remainder. The missing-factor approach involves asking the question "5 times what number is equal to 48?" When you are restricted to the whole numbers, there is no answer. Therefore, the missing-factor model must be modified to become "5 times what number *plus what number* is equal to 48?" In that case the answer can be determined to be $(5 \times 9) + 3 = 48$. (The parentheses mean that you multiply 5×9 before you add the 3.)

By combining multiplication and addition, you can almost always find an answer to division problems involving whole numbers. No physical model works for division by zero, however, so division by zero is undefined. For example, if you have nine dots and try to circle zero of them and then count the circles, you will never have any circles to count. Or, if you start out with zero circles and move one dot at a time into the circles, you won't have any place to put your dots.

Because division by 0 is ruled out, there are only 90 *basic division facts*. They correspond to the situations in which the divisor is a counting number from one through nine and the quotient is a whole number from zero through nine. (Note that while a divisor cannot be 0, a dividend can. When the dividend is 0, the quotient is 0.) When there is a remainder, the problem is not counted as a basic fact.

Now that you have learned the many ways you can "touch" math, you should go back and review each model. If you haven't already done so, set up your own models of the different problems. Change the problems, too, using different numbers. If you take the time to practice with the models, you will have a firm foundation for the next section. It will explain how you can do math more quickly than you had ever thought possible.

Quick Math: Mental Arithmetic

There is little doubt that everyone would like to perform mathematical operations as quickly and as accurately as possible. In this section, you will learn many techniques for achieving the ability to do "quick math." One caution, however, is that there are times when you are expected to "show your work" in arriving at a mathematical answer. This is true both in the classroom and outside. When the situation is appropriate, using quick math is rewarding; it is also fun. But never use quick math when your instructions do not permit you to do so.

One

One certainly is a useful number. If you add 1 to any counting number, you get the next counting number: $2 + 1 = 3$; $7 + 1 = 8$. If you subtract 1, you get the previous counting number: $10 - 1 = 9$; $5 - 1 = 4$. If you multiply by 1, you get a product that is equal to the multiplicand: $1 \times 3 = 3$; $1 \times 15 = 15$. Similarly, if you divide by 1, the quotient is the same as the dividend: $6 \div 1 = 6$; $9 \div 1 = 9$. Finally, if you divide 1

Useful Numbers

by a counting number, the result is a fraction that is already in simplest form: $1 \div 2 = \frac{1}{2}$; $1 \div 8 = \frac{1}{8}$. All of this is extremely useful in many operations, and the rules are easily learned. In fact, the rules for adding 1 and subtracting 1 are among the earliest topics taught in grade 1 and are useful in developing the other basic addition facts using the counting-on model.

Two

The number 2 is very easy to use. No one knows why, but the ability to double numbers comes very easily to most people. As a result, doubling numbers is an important aid in learning addition and subtraction and in mental computation with multiplication and division. Perhaps the ability to double numbers is common because the basic multiplication facts of 2s are the first ones people learn.

But there is good reason to suspect that doubling ability is more basic. For one thing, children are good doublers for a couple of years before they learn the multiplication facts (although they may have learned the 2s in disguised form through counting by 2s). The most likely explanation is that children teach themselves to double at a very early age, possibly by arranging toys in pairs.

In any case, the chances are good that you can instantly add $6 + 6$ or $8 + 8$, but that you may have to think a second to add $6 + 7$ or $8 + 7$. (Try a few such doubles and near-doubles to see the difference.) Therefore, a good way to solve a problem quickly in your head is to think of a double that is near it. If you know $5 + 5$ is 10, then $4 + 5$ will be 1 less, or 9, and $5 + 6$ will be 1 more, or 11.

This pattern carries over to subtraction as well, although it usually takes a little more thought. If you want to subtract 9 from 17, it is quick to think of the next highest even number, which is 18. You probably remember $9 + 9 = 18$ and $18 - 9 = 9$ very easily. Since you added 1 to 17 to get 18, you need to subtract 1 from 9 to find the answer to $17 - 9$, which is 8.

In fact, people who are good at doing math in their heads are usually familiar with the doubles of at least all the counting numbers to 50—and sometimes far beyond. Confronted with a problem such as $37 + 39$, such people do not begin by thinking "$7 + 9 = 16$ and carry the 1." Rather, they think "37 + 37 = 74, and add 2 more." Or they think, "39 − 1 = 38; 37 + 1 = 38; and 38 + 38 = 76." While all three thought patterns if carried out correctly will produce the right result, 76, the doubling methods are more direct and lead to quicker results with fewer errors. Memorizing the doubles of numbers less than 50 is not hard to do and is well worth the effort. If you can memorize even more doubles, so much the better.

Of course, since doubles are also the products of counting numbers and 2, an added benefit of learning doubles is that you extend your knowledge of multiplication beyond the basic 100 facts. Similarly, since doubling is the inverse operation of halving, you also know how to instantly solve a wide range of division problems.

Because doubling is so easy, it can be used to solve problems that do not show a 2 at all. For example, it is easy to solve 13 × 4 by doubling twice. The first doubling is 26 and the second 52. As a result of the ease of doubling twice, 4 is also a useful number.

Going one step further, doubling three times can be used to solve multiplication problems that have 8 as a factor. For small counting numbers, doubling three times is often faster and more accurate than multiplying the long way. For example, to multiply 13 by 8, the additional doubling from 52 to 104 is easy even if you have not memorized doubles above 50.

In fact, doubling repeatedly makes it easy to use any number where 2 can be used as the only factor. Many people find this process so easy that they have memorized the first 10 such numbers. These numbers, which are called *powers* of 2, are often handy in other ways as well. For example, computers work in powers of 2, so there are computers that are based on 4, 8, 16, and 32. The sizes of computer memories are expressed in terms of 1024 times some other number, which is often 16, 128, 256, or 512. Displays on commonly used computer programs may involve 256 rows or 256 columns. All of the numbers in the last sentence are powers of 2. On the next page are listed the first 10 powers of 2. Note the small numerals written to the right and just above the main body of each 2. These numerals are called *exponents*. They indicate the power, or the number of times, 2 is multiplied by itself.

$$\text{first power of 2} \quad = 2^1 \quad = 2$$
$$\text{second power of 2} \quad = 2^2 \quad = 4$$
$$\text{third power of 2} \quad = 2^3 \quad = 8$$
$$\text{fourth power of 2} \quad = 2^4 \quad = 16$$
$$\text{fifth power of 2} \quad = 2^5 \quad = 32$$
$$\text{sixth power of 2} \quad = 2^6 \quad = 64$$
$$\text{seventh power of 2} = 2^7 \quad = 128$$
$$\text{eighth power of 2} \quad = 2^8 \quad = 256$$
$$\text{ninth power of 2} \quad = 2^9 \quad = 512$$
$$\text{tenth power of 2} \quad = 2^{10} = 1{,}024$$

Ten—the most useful number

For multiplication, ten is useful because any number times 10 is almost like the original number. The product is just the multiplicand with a 0 written after it. Thus, $10 \times 17 = 170$, $10 \times 932 = 9320$, and $10 \times 1{,}234{,}567{,}890 = 12{,}345{,}678{,}900$.

Furthermore, for division, the same rule works in reverse. If a number ends in 0, dividing it by 10 produces a quotient that is just like the dividend, but with the 0 taken off.

The way that 10 behaves in multiplication and division makes 5 a useful number too. The number 10 is the product of 5 and 2. Therefore, you can use the properties of both 10 and 2 to get answers in which 5 is a factor or divisor. For example, to solve 48×5 in your head, you can begin by multiplying 48 by 10 and getting 480. This is twice the desired answer because you multiplied by twice 5 instead of by 5. So you use doubles to find half of 480. Therefore, $5 \times 48 = 240$.

The same idea also works for division—but reversed, of course. If you need to divide 330 by 5, you can begin by dividing by 10. The answer, 33, will be half the size of the answer you get when you divide by 5, since 10 is twice 5. Therefore, the solution to $330 \div 5$ is 66.

The number 10 is also easy to add and subtract. Adding a number from 0 through 9 to 10 is almost automatic; for example, the word *eighteen* is easily perceived as $8 + 10$. *-Teen* means "ten." Similarly, learning to recognize two numbers whose sum is 10, such as 3 and 7 or 6 and 4, is very easy. This ease in working with 10 provides another important strategy for learning the basic addition and subtraction facts. For example, someone who has learned such facts as $8 + 2$ or $10 - 2$ can use these facts as a bridge to facts such as

8 + 5 or 13 − 5. The person can think "I know 5 =
2 + 3, and I know 2 + 8 = 10, so 8 + 5 is the same
as 8 + 2 + 3; 8 + 5 = 13."

Similarly, subtraction facts can often be related to
10. To find 13 − 5, the same thought pattern is used in
reverse: "I know 5 = 2 + 3. And 13 − 3 leaves me
with 10, so the answer is 10 − 2, or 8."

One advantage of learning strategies such as these
is that the basic facts can be relearned quickly if tem-
porarily forgotten, such as during a test. But taking a
problem apart into simple pieces that can be done
quickly, and then reassembling the pieces into the original problem, is the essence of mental arithmetic. Mas-
tering these strategies gives you an advantage no
matter what the situation.

The number ten can be used as a touchstone in addition problems of any complexity. When adding columns of numbers, they can be grouped to form 10s as
you go along. For example, if you need to add

$$
\begin{array}{r}
25 \\
37 \\
15 \\
53 \\
+\,46 \\
\hline
\end{array}
$$

the best way to begin is to look for the 10s. From the
first and third numbers, you find 5 + 5 and from the
second and fourth numbers, you find 7 + 3. The only
unmatched number in the second column is 6. Therefore, the sum of the first column is 10 + 10 + 6, or
26. This is much easier than thinking "5 + 7 = 12;
12 + 5 = 17; 17 + 3 = 20; and 20 + 6 = 26." Similarly, in the first column, you now have 2 (from the
26), 2, 3, 1, 5, and 4. You can begin either by noting
that 2 + 3 + 5 = 10 or that 1 + 4 + 5 = 10. In the
first case, the remaining sum is 2 + 1 + 4 = 7, so the
total in the first column is 10 + 7 = 17 (tens, since
you are working in the tens column). If you begin with
1 + 4 + 5, the remaining numbers are 2, 2, and 3,
which are also easily summed to 17 (tens). In either
case, the answer will be easier to find than thinking
"2 + 2 = 4; 4 + 3 = 7; 7 + 1 = 8; 8 + 5 = 13; and
13 + 4 = 17 (tens)." The sum of the addends in the
problem is 176 (17 tens and 6 ones).

The powers of 10 are also easy to use, just as the
powers of 2 are. What is more, you do not have to
memorize the powers of 10, since each is found simply

by writing 1 followed by the same number of zeros as the number of the power. For example,

the first power of 10   = 10^1 = 10
the second power of 10 = 10^2 = 100
the third power of 10   = 10^3 = 1000
the fourth power of 10 = 10^4 = 10,000
the fifth power of 10   = 10^5 = 100,000
the sixth power of 10   = 10^6 = 1,000,000

Multiplying or dividing by a power of 10 is quite similar to multiplying or dividing by 10. To multiply, you merely need to add on the appropriate number of zeros—which is the same number as the exponent of the power. For example, to find 1000 × 349, you write 349 followed by three zeros, so the answer is 349,000. If a number ends in several zeros, you can use the same method in reverse to divide. The quotient of 83,000,000 divided by 100 is just 83,000,000 with the last two zeros removed, or 830,000. The hardest part is keeping track of where to put the commas.

Other small numbers

So far you have looked at 1, 2, 4, 5, 8, and 10, all of which are easy to use in mental computation. Now look at some other small numbers that are useful in varying degrees.

On the surface, the number 0 seems to be nearly as easy to use as 1. After all, what could be easier than adding or subtracting 0, since any number plus or minus 0 is unchanged?

For addition, 0 really is quite easy, but many people have trouble with the other operations. In fact, the concept of 0 poses much difficulty. A symbol for 0 was not invented until long after people had become familiar with counting numbers and fractions.

It is generally believed that the first clear notions about 0 date from about A.D. 500, and that these ideas were worked out in India. In the Western Hemisphere, the Mayan mathematicians of Central America independently worked out the notion of 0. But 0 as a separate number—meaning something more than just "nothing"—was apparently unknown to the great Greek mathematicians, people who produced enduring works of mathematical beauty for over a thousand years, from the sixth century B.C. until the fifth century A.D.

For many people, it is not easy to solve a subtraction problem like

500,000
− 49,928

The difficulty arises from all the zeros in the top number. People become lost when they have to "carry over" numbers to complete the computation. (If you have trouble with this sort of computation, there is a quick solution. Subtract 50,000 from the top number and you get 450,000—a number easily arrived at mentally. Then, find 50,000 − 49,928. The answer is 72, which you can also arrive at mentally. Add this to 450,000 and you get 450,072. You have the correct answer. And you've done all the work in your head.)

Multiplication by 0 is not very hard in theory, either. Yet many students have problems with 0 in multiplication, especially if it appears as part of another number. In a problem such as 509 × 34, students are apt to forget that the 0 is there, which produces errors. (The correct answer here is 17,306.) Similarly, students have trouble recalling that 0 divided by any number is 0, but that it is impossible to divide any number by 0.

All in all, 0 is not so easy as it might appear at first glance. In mental computation, the main use of 0 is with powers of 10, which have already been discussed.

The number 3, on the other hand, is easier than it might seem at first glance. Because 3 is such a low number, addition problems with 3s can be solved by counting on, for example.

Multiplication by 3 can often be done in your head by first doubling, then adding the original number. For example, to multiply 37 by 3, you can think "2 × 37 is 74; and 74 + 37 is _____ ." Here it is good to remember how useful 10s can be. You should complete the mental computation by thinking "and 74 + 37 is (70 + 30) + (4 + 7), or 100 + 11 = 111."

This technique can be carried over to make 6 easier than it might otherwise be. Since 6 is the double of 3, you can first use the method for multiplying by 3 and then double the result. For example, to find 6 × 24 in your head, you can think "2 × 24 is 48, and 48 + 24 is 72, so 6 × 24 is the same as 2 × 72, or 144." Sometimes, it turns out to be easier to double first, and then use the method for 3. Had the problem been 6 × 25, for instance, most people would find it easier to think "2 × 25 is 50, 2 × 50 is 100, and 100 + 50 is 150."

When you work in this order, it is important to remember that the number to be added at the end is not the original number, but the result of the first doubling. You need to make a mental note such as "(doubling) $2 \times 25 = 50$; (tripling) $2 \times 50 = 100$; $100 + 50 = 150$." Otherwise, you may wind up with the wrong answer.

The method for 3 can be used twice to compute mentally with 9. For example, if you know that 3×15 is 45, to find 9×15 you may want to think "To triple 45, I double it to get 90 and add 45 to get 135." In that circumstance, tripling twice is an efficient method for multiplying by 9 in your head.

Another way of working with the number 9 is based on its closeness to 10. If you are adding 9 to a number, it is sometimes easier to add 10 and subtract 1. For example, you can find $37 + 9$ by thinking "37 + 10 is 47, and $47 - 1$ is 46." Especially when you have several 9s in a row, as in $3984 + 999$, going to the nearby power of 10 is definitely easier than working the problem out the long way. Think: "3984 + 1000 is 4984, and $4984 - 1$ is 4983." In fact, the same method can be used for numbers that are not quite so near a power of 10. If you are adding 3984 to 996, for example, you merely need to subtract 4 at the end, instead of subtracting 1.

One number has been overlooked in this survey of the whole numbers from 0 through ten—the number 7. The sad truth is that 7 is not very easy to work with. The best thing to do with problems involving 7 is to look for other numbers in the problem that are more useful and rely on them to get you through.

Clues from Division

Although many people have trouble with division, it provides a set of helpful clues to mental computation. As usual, some numbers are easier to work with than others. If you memorize the division clues, you will find easy ways both to compute in your head and to check computations you do with paper and pencil or a calculator.

First, here is some necessary vocabulary. A counting number *divides* a whole number if the resulting quotient is also a whole number—that is, if the remainder is 0. The property of dividing a number is called *divisibility*. Thus, you can talk about a *divisibility test* of a given whole number with respect to a given counting number. For example, the divisibility test for 3 tells whether a given whole number can be divided by 3 with a zero remainder. The number 9 passes the divisibility test for 3 because $9 \div 3 = 3$. The number 10 does not pass the divisibility test for 3 because $10 \div 3 = 3R1$. You should memorize the divisibility tests for the single-digit counting numbers because they have many uses in mental arithmetic and checking computations.

Every number is divisible by 1, and no number is divisible by 0. After that, the tests become progressively more complicated. The next easiest test is for 10. You probably know it already because it is an easy consequence of the rule for multiplying by 10. If a whole number ends in 0, the number is divisible by 10.

Other numbers follow the same pattern. To test for divisibility, you look at the last digit or digits of a number. You should be familiar with the rule for divisibility by 5, since it was referred to earlier. If a number ends in 0 or 5, it is divisible by 5. The first part of that rule, pertaining to 0, is a consequence of the rule for 10. If a number is divisible by 10, because $10 = 5 \times 2$, it also must be divisible by 5. The second part of the rule is also a result of the fact that $10 = 5 \times 2$, for it means that 5 is just halfway between 0 and 10. Since each multiple of 5 is 5 greater than the multiple preceding it, the end digits go from 0 to 0 (10 greater) in *exactly* two steps. Thus, every other multiple of 5 must end with 5.

A number that ends in 0 is also divisible by 2, since $10 = 5 \times 2$. Furthermore, for the same reasons that numbers ending in 5 must be divisible by 5, numbers ending in 2, 4, 6, or 8 must be divisible by 2. The fact that 2 divides 10 means that there is a cycle of numbers that repeat themselves each *decade*. (A decade in this sense consists of the numbers from one number that ends in 1 to the next number that ends in 0, just as a decade of years is defined.)

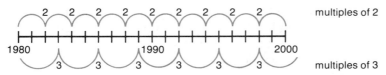

multiples of 2

multiples of 3

The principle involved here is a general one that can be used to explore divisibility in other ways. If one number divides another, the multiples of the divisor will repeat in a cycle that is exactly equal to the dividend. If the dividend is a power of 10, for instance, the cycle will be the same between each two powers of 10 and show in the last few digits of the number.

For example, the second power of 10 is 100 [(5 × 2) × (5 × 2)]. The numbers that divide 100, then, are 2, 5, 2 × 2 = 4, 2 × 5 = 10, 5 × 5 = 25, and 5 × 5 × 2 = 50. You already know divisibility tests for 2, 5, and 10. But the general rule suggests that the last two digits of any number can be used to determine whether that number is divisible by 4, 25, or 50. This discussion will demonstrate the rules for 4.

Clearly, if the last two digits of a number are divisible by 4, then the number must be divisible by 4. You know that this is true of the first one hundred whole numbers; that is, the numbers 0 through 99. Since the cycle repeats every one hundred numbers, the same will hold true from 100 through 199, from 200 through 299, and so forth. Suppose you want to know if 398,882 is divisible by 4. The last two digits are 82. It is easy to check that 82 is *not* divisible by 4; nor is 398,882. On the other hand, you can also see that 398,872 *is* divisible by 4, because 72 = 4 × 18. The rule will work no matter how large the number is.

The third power of 10 is 1000, which equals 10 × 10 × 10 and can be factored into primes as 5 × 2 × 5 × 2 × 5 × 2. Since three factors of 2 are involved, one number that has a cycle of 1000 for divisibility is 8 because 8 = 2 × 2 × 2. By the same line of reasoning that was used in the last paragraph, if the last three digits of a number are divisible by 8, the number must also be divisible by 8. As a result, you can reduce a problem such as determining whether 123,456,972 is divisible by 8 to the simpler problem of whether 972 is divisible by 8.

You can quickly rule out any number that does not end in 0, 2, 4, 6, or 8 as being divisible by 4 or 8. For a number to be divisible by 4 or 8, it must also be divisible by 2. (But the reverse does not hold; numbers divisible by 2 are not necessarily divisible by 4 or 8.) Thus, if a number is odd, you know immediately that it is not divisible by 4 or 8. Only if the number is even can you use the specific test for divisibility.

Mathematics is the study of patterns. If you see the way this pattern has been developed, you should also be able to see that the following statement is always true: For any number, if the last n digits are divisible by 2^n, the number is also divisible by 2^n. Notice how easy it can be in mathematics to go from a few specific examples to a far-ranging rule for all numbers.

Since 3 is not a factor of 10, its divisibility test is not based on the last digits of the dividend. Instead, if the sum of the digits of a number is divisible by 3, the number itself is divisible by 3. Thus, for example, 298,341 *is* divisible by 3 because 2 + 9 + 8 + 3 + 4 + 1 = 27. But 392,521 is *not* divisible by 3 because 3 + 9 + 2 + 5 + 2 + 1 = 22.

In practice, you do not have to add the numbers. Instead, you can look for sums of two or more digits that are divisible by 3 and "cast them out," working with only the ones that are left over. For example, the efficient way to determine whether 298,341 is divisible by 3 is to cast out the 9 and the 3, which are divisible by 3, leaving 2, 8, 4, and 1. You can cast out the 8 and 1, because they sum to 9, and also the 2 and 4, because they add to 6. Since all the digits were cast out, the number is divisible by 3. On the other hand, with the number 392,521, when you cast out the 3, 9, and 2 + 5 + 2 = 9, you are left with 1. Since the 1 cannot be cast out, the number is not divisible by 3.

The same rule that works for 3 also works for 9, only this time the digits cast out must sum to 9. To find whether 293,837 is divisible by 9, cast out 9s. Because 2 + 7 = 9, they can be cast out, as can be the digit 9. You are then left with 3, 8, and 3. You can cast out one more 9 by adding 3 + 8 = 11 and subtracting 9. That leaves 2 and 3. Since 2 + 3 = 5, there are no more 9s to cast out. Therefore, 293,837 is *not* divisible by 9. If a number is divisible by 9, the result when all the 9s have been cast out will be 0.

Now you have divisibility tests for 0, 1, 2, 3, 4, 5, 8, and 9. The only remaining single-digit numbers are 6 and 7.

The number 6 is easy to work with. Since 6 = 2 × 3, if a number is divisible by both 2 and 3, it must also be divisible by 6. Therefore, to determine whether 205,384 is divisible by 6, you note that it is even (and therefore divisible by 2) and proceed to cast out 3s. You are left with a remainder of 1, so 205,384 is *not* divisible by 6. Also, 205,383, which is divisible by 3, is not divisible by 6 because it is odd. But 205,386 is divisible by both 3 and 2, so it *is* divisible by 6.

A number of divisibility tests have been developed for 7, but all are very complicated. Here is one that is somewhat easier than the others. Given a number, remove its last digit and subtract twice that digit from the number you obtained by removing the digit. Repeat this until you get a single digit. If the last digit is 0 or 7, the original number is divisible by 7. Unless the single digit is either 0 or 7, the original number was not divisible by 7. Here is an example.

$$
\begin{array}{r}
493,826 \\
-12 \\
\hline
493\ 70 \\
-0 \\
\hline
493\,7 \\
-14 \\
\hline
479 \\
-18 \\
\hline
29 \\
-18 \\
\hline
-16 \\
-12 \\
\hline
-13 \\
-6 \\
\hline
-7
\end{array}
$$

The last digit you get may be positive or negative. But to apply the rule, you must end up with 0 or 7 (-7 does not count). The number in the example is *not* divisible by 7.

While this divisibility rule is interesting, you can see that it takes a lot of work. For most practical purposes, it is easier to divide the number by 7 to see if there is a remainder than it is to apply the rule. (Now for more practice in divisibility, *see* Pt. III, Sec. 2, "Divisibility rules" subsection.)

Fractions, Decimals, and Percents

The discussion so far has been limited to whole numbers. But mental computations can also be done with fractions, decimals, and percents as long as you memorize certain relationships.

Unlike the basic addition, subtraction, multiplication, and division facts, the basic facts about fractions, decimals, and percents are not drilled over and over in school (although there is usually a lesson or two in which some of the most important ones are discussed). As a result, most people have a good command of the basic facts of whole numbers, but few have a good command of the basic facts of fractions, decimals, and percents. Because understanding the relationships among fractions, decimals, and percents can be extremely helpful, you should seriously try to learn them.

Fractions and whole numbers

Much of what you have learned about the small whole numbers is immediately useful with fractions. In multiplying a whole number by a fraction that has a *numerator* (top number) of 1, the result is the same as dividing the whole number by the *denominator* (bottom number) of the fraction. Thus, to find $\frac{1}{2}$ of 52, you can divide 52 by 2. The divisibility tests become helpful as a result. For example, to find $\frac{1}{51}$ of 192, you can begin by noting that both 51 (5 + 1 = 6) and 192 (1 + 9 + 2 = 12) are divisible by 3. Dividing each by 3 changes the problem to $\frac{1}{17}$ of 64. Since 17 and 64 have no common divisors, the only operation left is to divide 64 by 17, which gives 3 with a remainder of 13. In stating the answer to a fraction problem, however, you should use fractions instead of remainders. The fraction form is found by writing the remainder over the divisor, so the final form of the answer to $\frac{1}{51}$ of 192 is $3\frac{13}{17}$. Working this way, you can do most problems involving whole numbers and fractions in your head if the numbers involved are fairly small.

There are other methods you can memorize for specific fractions. One group of rules applies to $\frac{1}{2}$ and $\frac{1}{5}$. Sometimes it is easier to multiply a number by 5 than it is to find $\frac{1}{2}$ of it, for example. The product will then be 10 times the answer you really want, so you must divide by 10. For example, to find $\frac{1}{2}$ of 25, you might find it easier to think "5 × 25 = 125, and 125 ÷ 10 = $12\frac{5}{10}$, or $12\frac{1}{2}$." Similarly, to find $\frac{1}{5}$ of a number, you can multiply by 2 and divide the result by 10. Suppose that you want to find $\frac{1}{5}$ of 193. The answer is 2 × 193 = 386, and 386 ÷ 10 = $38\frac{6}{10}$, or $38\frac{3}{5}$. While the same result can be obtained by dividing 193 by 5, in this case it is easier to multiply by 2 and divide by 10 than it is to divide by 5.

You can use the same ideas in reverse as well. To multiply by 5, you can take $\frac{1}{2}$ of a number and multiply by 10. This is a convenient way to find 5 × 58, for example. The result is 290. Also, to multiply by 2, you *could* take $\frac{1}{5}$ of the number and multiply by 10, but that method is usually less convenient than doubling.

Since 4 and 25 are related to 100, a similar set of relationships holds for $\frac{1}{4}$ and $\frac{1}{25}$. To find $\frac{1}{4}$ of a number, you can multiply by 25 and divide by 100. This can be convenient for a few numbers. For example, $\frac{1}{4}$ of 1000 is $1000 \times 25 = 25{,}000$, and $25{,}000 \div 100 = 250$. Similarly, to find $\frac{1}{25}$ of a number, multiply by 4 and divide by 100. Thus, $\frac{1}{25}$ of 87 is $87 \times 4 = 348$, and $348 \div 100 = 3\frac{48}{100}$, or $3\frac{12}{25}$.

Using fractions with decimals and percents

If you have learned the fraction-decimal-percent equivalents, you can often convert a difficult problem with decimals or percents into an easy problem with fractions.

Decimals are just another way to write a fraction whose denominator is a power of 10. For example, 0.3 is the decimal form of $\frac{3}{10}$. Each decimal place is the next power of 10, so 0.003 is 3 over the third power of 10, or $\frac{3}{1000}$. The basic way to convert a decimal to a fraction is to write a whole number over the appropriate power of 10 and simplify. For example, the decimal 0.25 is $\frac{25}{100}$, which simplifies to $\frac{1}{4}$. Similarly, the decimal 0.375 is $\frac{375}{1000}$, which simplifies to $\frac{3}{8}$.

Recall that the rule for dividing a whole number by 10 or by a power of 10 worked only if the whole number ended in 0 or a number of 0s. When working with decimals you can convert the rule to apply to any number. All you need to do is to move the decimal point as many places to the left as there are zeros in the power of 10. For example, $511 \div 100 = 5.11$.

It is often hard to change a fraction into a decimal in your head. So the best solution is to memorize the most common fractional forms of decimals. Some of the most useful are in the table on the following page. In the table, you may recognize that the relationships between 0.25 and $\frac{1}{4}$ and between 0.5 and $\frac{1}{2}$ form the basis of the shortcuts for using fractions with whole numbers. The same ideas can be used even more easily with decimal problems. For example, if you need to find 0.25×488, it is much easier to solve as $\frac{1}{4} \times 488 = 122$. The same applies to the other relationships. For example, to solve any multiplication or division problem using 0.875, you can first consider whether it would be easier to use $\frac{7}{8}$. In some cases, such as

1600×0.875, it is much easier to use $\frac{7}{8}$, because
$1600 \div 8 = 200$, and $200 \times 7 = 1400$.

0.05	$= \dfrac{1}{20}$	0.375	$= \dfrac{3}{8}$	0.75	$= \dfrac{3}{4}$
0.1	$= \dfrac{1}{10}$	0.4	$= \dfrac{2}{5}$	0.8	$= \dfrac{4}{5}$
0.125	$= \dfrac{1}{8}$	0.5	$= \dfrac{1}{2}$	0.875	$= \dfrac{7}{8}$
0.2	$= \dfrac{1}{5}$	0.6	$= \dfrac{3}{5}$	0.9	$= \dfrac{9}{10}$
0.25	$= \dfrac{1}{4}$	0.625	$= \dfrac{5}{8}$		
0.3	$= \dfrac{3}{10}$	0.7	$= \dfrac{7}{10}$		

Sometimes you must be very alert to spot a situation in which a fraction equivalent will simplify the problem. For example, $140 \div 0.875$ can be solved using fraction equivalents, although the solution may not be immediately obvious. You must recall that division by a fraction is accomplished by inverting the divisor and multiplying. Thus, the fraction form of $140 \div 0.875$, which is $140 \div \frac{7}{8}$, is solved by finding $140 \times \frac{8}{7}$. Since 7 divides 140, you can complete the solution in your head: $140 \div 7 = 20$, and $20 \times 8 = 160$.

Percents are easily converted to decimals. Therefore, the same fraction equivalents you learned for decimals can be used with percents. To convert a percent to a decimal, divide the percent by 100. In practice, this means that you place the decimal point (which is not shown for whole-number percents) two places to the left, writing or dropping 0s as needed. For example, 20% is the same as 0.20, or 0.2; $37\frac{1}{2}$ is the same as 0.375 (note that $\frac{1}{2}$% is 0.005); and 115% is 1.15.

Decimals are not usually written with fractions, but as the example of $37\frac{1}{2}$% illustrates, percents often do include fractions. Therefore, you need to learn some of the percents in fraction form and their corresponding decimal forms. Furthermore, many percents that correspond to fractions have decimal forms with an infinite number of digits that repeat a particular pattern. For example, $33\frac{1}{3}$% is equivalent to the decimal 0.3333 . . . , where the pattern of 3s repeats forever. On the following page is a list of percents that use fractions and have easy fraction equivalents.

$$12\frac{1}{2}\% = \frac{1}{8} \qquad 33\frac{1}{3}\% = \frac{1}{3} \qquad 66\frac{2}{3}\% = \frac{2}{3}$$

$$14\frac{2}{7}\% = \frac{1}{7} \qquad 37\frac{1}{2}\% = \frac{3}{8} \qquad 83\frac{1}{3}\% = \frac{5}{6}$$

$$16\frac{2}{3}\% = \frac{1}{6} \qquad 62\frac{1}{2}\% = \frac{5}{8} \qquad 87\frac{1}{2}\% = \frac{7}{8}$$

It is often easier to use the fraction equivalent of a percent than the decimal equivalent. For example, to find $66\frac{2}{3}\%$ of 99, it is much easier to multiply 99 by $\frac{2}{3}$ than it is to use the decimal equivalent: $99 \div 3 = 33$, and $33 \times 2 = 66$.

On the other hand, you may find it easier in some cases to convert from a fraction problem to a decimal or percent problem. Once you have the common equivalents memorized, you can choose the easiest form to use in a given situation. For example, to find $\frac{2}{5}$ of 24, you can think "0.4×24 is twice 24, or 48, twice 48, or 96, divided by 10, or 9.6." Then, if the answer needs to be in fraction form, you think "0.6 is $\frac{3}{5}$, so $\frac{2}{5}$ of 24 is $9\frac{3}{5}$." While the same result can be found by thinking "Twice 24 is 48, and 48 divided by 5 is 9 with a remainder of 3, so the answer is $9\frac{3}{5}$," many people prefer not to divide in their heads.

The important skill is to be able to convert instantly from fractions to decimals or percents and vice versa. Once you have the equivalents firmly in your memory, you will have many opportunites to use them. In particular, you will find them useful in working with handheld calculators because most calculators use decimals, but not fractions. If you know the decimal equivalents for the commonly used fractions, you can more easily solve problems using a calculator.

Mnemonics

The mathematician Alexander Craig Aitken memorized to a thousand digits the number pi (π), which is the ratio of the circumference of a circle to its diameter and which also crops up in many math situations, often quite unexpectedly. Pi is a mathematical *constant*—that is, a number that has a constant value. When written as a decimal, pi has no pattern that repeats, as does, for example, the decimal representation of $\frac{1}{3}$. In fact, although pi is an infinite decimal like 0.3333 . . . , the calculation of the digits from various formulas is more trouble than it is worth. Therefore, people memorize as many of the digits of pi as they need. If you want, you can take pi to 3.1415926 and further. But, for most purposes, pi to hundredths, or 3.14, is sufficient. It is also often useful to know a close fractional approximation of pi. For most purposes, $3\frac{1}{7}$, or $\frac{22}{7}$, is sufficient.

People who want more accuracy, of course, need to know more decimal places. Modern computers have calculated pi to thousands, and even millions, of digits. But Aitken himself had no practical use for knowing a thousand digits of pi. He just memorized them to amuse himself.

One trick for memorizing digits in any situation is to use a *mnemonic*, or memory aid. A mnemonic is a device to help the memory—in this particular case, a sentence in which the order and number of letters in each word correspond to the order and value of the digits to be remembered. For example, to memorize 3.14 you could think "Now I know," or "See a word," or some similar phrase that has a three-letter word, then a one-letter word, and then a four-letter word. (Note that the decimal point is not taken into account.) For a more lengthy version of pi, someone coined the mnemonic, "May I have a large container of coffee?" This translates into 3.1415926, which is certainly precise enough for most purposes. The physicist Sir James Jeans went a little further, however, with "How I want a drink, alcoholic of course, after the heavy chapters involving quantum mechanics" (3.14159265358979— skip the punctuation).

Patterns as Shortcuts

There are many ways to convert a difficult problem into an easier one. Some involve patterns in arithmetic. In some cases, special methods of computing may be easier for mental calculation than the usual methods.

Although these methods are especially helpful for mental calculation, they can also be used when working with paper and pencil. It is a mistake to approach every problem in the same way. If you have many different weapons in your arsenal, you can choose the weapon that fits the situation. You can also use these methods to check answers that you've computed in other ways.

The fundamental rule of arithmetic

Almost every branch of mathematics has one rule that mathematicians have termed *fundamental*. For arithmetic, the fundamental, or basic, rule is that any counting number can be expressed as the product of *primes* in just one way. A prime is a counting number greater than 1 that has no factors other than 1 and itself. For example, 2 is prime because its only factors are 1 and 2. Based on this rule, 12 could only be expressed in primes as $2 \times 2 \times 3$. Although 12 is also 4×3 and 2×6, 4 and 6 are not primes. The only *prime factorization* of 12 is $2 \times 2 \times 3$. (The order of the factors is not considered important, so $2 \times 3 \times 2$ and $3 \times 2 \times 2$ are considered to be the same prime factorization.)

When two numbers are multiplied, the product is also the product of the two unique prime factorizations. Often, it is possible to rearrange the prime factors to find numbers that simplify the multiplication. For example, to find 12×35, you can begin by factoring each number, to obtain $(2 \times 2 \times 3) \times (5 \times 7)$. This product can be rearranged as $(2 \times 5) \times (2 \times 3 \times 7)$, or 10×42. Thus, the answer is 420. In general, to solve a multiplication problem this way, you begin by looking for pairs of 2 and 5, since each pair becomes a 10. For example, to multiply 425 by 44, factoring gives $(5 \times 5 \times 17) \times (2 \times 2 \times 11)$. There are two pairs of 2 and 5, so the answer is 100 times the product of 17 and 11. Since 11×17 is 187, the product of 425 and 44 is 18,700.

The fundamental rule of arithmetic is also useful in working division and fraction problems. You may recall that if a fraction contains the same factor in the numerator as it does in the denominator, that factor can be "cancelled." For example, $\frac{4}{6}$ contains a factor of 2 in both the numerator and denominator. If you write the fraction in prime-factored form, you can cancel the common 2s.

$$\frac{4}{6} = \frac{\cancel{2} \times 2}{\cancel{2} \times 3}$$

This means that $\frac{4}{6}$ and $\frac{2}{3}$ are the same number.

It is usually easiest to cancel common factors by using prime factorizations when the numbers are fairly large. For small numbers, you may recognize common factors without using primes. For example, to put $\frac{357}{924}$ in simplest form, you can begin by finding the prime factors of 357. Since 357 is a multiple of 3, mentally divide 357 by 3 to get 119. Since 119 is not a multiple of 2, 3, or 5, try 7: $7 \times 17 = 119$. Since 17 is prime, the factored form of 357 is $3 \times 7 \times 17$.

Now work on 924. Since 924 is even, 2 is a prime factor. Divide by 2, to obtain 462, another even number. Divide by 2 again, obtaining 231, a multiple of 3. Divide by 3; the result is 77, which is easily recognizable as 7×11. Now you have all the prime factors, so $924 = 2 \times 2 \times 3 \times 7 \times 11$. You can proceed to cancel.

$$\frac{357}{924} = \frac{\cancel{3} \times \cancel{7} \times 17}{2 \times 2 \times \cancel{3} \times \cancel{7} \times 11}$$

So $\frac{357}{924}$ is equal to $\frac{17}{44}$.

To find the prime factors of any number, you need only check for factors up to the square root of the number. After that, you will find that the same factors repeat in reverse order. For example, after 7, the next factor of 119 is 17, so you get 17×7—the same as 7×17. If you have memorized the squares of the counting numbers through 15, you can easily recognize that 119 is just a little less than 121, or 11 squared. Thus, 11 is too big to bother checking. The next prime less than 11 is 7, so 7 is the largest prime that needs to be checked.

If you can recognize the factors easily, the same method can be used for mentally computing division problems or for turning a difficult division problem into an easier one to solve with paper and pencil. Fractions can be viewed as just another way of writing division. Thus, a problem such as $969 \div 105$ can be quickly seen to have a common factor of 3 that can be eliminated, reducing the problem to $323 \div 35$. Since 7 and 5, the factors of 35, are not factors of 323, that is the best you can do; but it does simplify the problem somewhat: $323 \div 35 = 9.23$.

The distributive law

Another principle that helps you break a problem down into simpler parts is the *distributive law*. For counting numbers, the distributive law can be illustrated by dot diagrams. Consider 6×5, for example:

The vertical line separates the diagram into two parts. The part on the left is the dot array for 6 × 2, while the part on the right is the dot array for 6 × 3. This diagram proves that 6 × 5 = (6 × 2) + (6 × 3).

Now suppose that you move the vertical line to another place in the diagram.

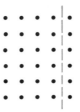

In this position, the diagram proves that 6 × 5 is equal to (6 × 4) + (6 × 1).

Such diagrams can be used for any product of counting numbers. In each case, the vertical line would separate the original factor into two parts whose sum is the original factor. In fact, if *a*, *b*, and *c* are any numbers (not just counting numbers), it is true that

$$a \times (b + c) = (a \times b) + (a \times c)$$

This is the general statement of the distributive law.

The distributive law is useful because it enables you to separate a multiplication problem into two problems. Furthermore, you can always choose at least one of the numbers so that it will be easy to work with. In fact, the most common use for the distributive law occurs when the factor to be separated is close to a power or multiple of the easiest of all numbers, 10.

For example, both 11 and 12 are close to 10. Therefore, one way to multiply 17 × 11 is to use the distributive law to change the problem to (17 × 10) + (17 × 1), or 170 + 17 = 187. Similarly, in multiplying by 12, you can change 12 × 341 to (10 × 341) + (2 × 341). The result is 3410 plus twice 341, or 3410 + 682 = 4092.

Notice that the rule suggests a mechanical way of multiplying by 11. You can always multiply by 11 by writing the original number twice, with the second version under the first, but moved 1 place to the left. Then you add as in the regular multiplication procedure. So to multiply 4937 by 11, merely write

```
 4937
 4937
54307
```

The same procedure can be used for numbers that are near multiples of 10. For example, to multiply 21 × 84, you can think "20 times 84 is 1680, and 1680 + 84 is 1764."

The distributive law also applies to subtraction. That is, for any numbers *a, b,* and *c* it is true that

$$a \times (b - c) = (a \times b) - (a \times c)$$

This version of the distributive law makes 9 a very useful number. Since 9 = 10 − 1, you can solve multiplication problems involving 9 using the distributive law. To find 78 × 9, think "10 × 78 is 780, and 780 − 78 is 702."

Also, you can use the subtraction version of the distributive law with factors that are near to multiples of 10 or powers of 10. So to solve 56 × 998, you would change the problem to (56 × 1000) − (56 × 2) = 56,000 − 112 = 55,888.

Estimating

There is an old saying that "Close only counts in horseshoes," which refers to the scoring system of the game of tossing horseshoes at a post. If one of the horseshoes that you toss lands within a certain distance of the post, you receive points, although not so many as when the shoe touches or circles the post. Similarly, in mathematics, you can receive "points" for being close, although perhaps not so many as you would receive for the exact answer. In fact, for many purposes, close is good enough in mathematics—an estimate will do.

For example, a bright young student announced to her teacher that the last Ice Age ended 11,005 years ago. When asked for an explanation, the student reported that her textbook said that the Ice Age ended 11,000 years ago, but that the copyright indicated that the book was five years old.

In this case, close is not merely good enough. It is really *better* than the student's more exact estimate. The textbook statement is intended to express a not-very-certain date. It implies that the Ice Age ended 11,000 years ago *plus or minus* 500 years. That is, the textbook statement was expressed "to the nearest thousand." Had the textbook been over 500 years old, the student would have been right to correct the date, but not to 11,505. Rather, the corrected date should be 12,000 years ago.

This example illustrates an important point. Mathematical statements must be reasonable. This especially applies to the solutions of word problems. There are a number of shortcuts to determining whether an answer is reasonable.

Reasonable answers

In solving any math problem, the first question you should ask about an answer is "Does this answer make sense? Is it reasonable or 'way out of the ballpark'?" For practical problems, such a test merely means comparing the answers to reality. In using algebra to solve some geometry problems, for example, you often end up with two answers. If the problem is about the dimensions of a rectangle, and one of the answers is 0 or less than 0, that answer must be discarded as unreasonable. (Such an answer may be acceptable in another context, but it cannot describe a rectangle.)

Some tests for reasonableness do not depend on physical reality. They are purely mathematical. People who are good at math apply such tests almost without thinking. This is a habit that you should develop. Automatically checking the reasonableness of your answers is one of the best ways to avoid making "dumb" mistakes.

The first test to apply in checking your work is to look at the relationship between the size of the proposed answer and the size of the numbers in the problem. The following relationships hold true for the four basic operations with counting numbers:

> *Addition:* The answer will be larger than the largest number in the problem.
> *Subtraction:* The answer will be smaller than the largest number in the problem.
> *Multiplication:* The answer will be larger than the largest number in the problem.
> *Division:* The answer will be smaller than the largest number in the problem.

In a problem of only counting numbers, if you obtain an answer that does not meet these four rules, your answer cannot possibly be right. Furthermore, you can use the rules in reverse to help you solve problems. For example, suppose that you are given this word problem: "Jack is 5 years older than his sister. Jack is 23. How old is his sister?" A good first step is to think "The largest number in the problem is 23. Clearly, the answer must be smaller than 23, so the solution cannot be found by addition or multiplication." This reduces your choices to subtraction and division, from which it is easy to choose subtraction as the correct method.

Some people may think that following such a procedure for problems involving counting numbers isn't necessary because these problems are so simple. But when a problem involves fractions, decimals, or percents, the story is quite different. People often make mistakes in working with these that could be avoided if the people first determined what a reasonable answer would be.

The situation is complicated by the fact that the rules for multiplying and dividing that apply here are different from those for counting numbers. Since many people learn the rules for counting numbers early in life, they make mistakes because they unconsciously apply a counting-number rule to a fraction, decimal, or percent situation.

For example, consider the problem "How many quarters are there in 8 dollars?" One temptation is to multiply $\frac{1}{4}$ times 8, producing the product 2. If you think about the four basic rules beforehand, however, you will realize that the answer must be greater than 8. Then you would know that $4 \times 8 = 32$ is the more likely solution. Similarly, some people might be misled by the word *divided* in the problem "24 apples are divided so that each person gets $\frac{1}{4}$ of the apples. How many does each person get?" They may think that $24 \div \frac{1}{4}$ should be the answer. Since $24 \div \frac{1}{4}$ is 96, however, it is unreasonable. The answer must be smaller than 24, the largest number in the problem, so the correct solution is $24 \div 4 = 6$ apples.

You should become familiar with the rules for numbers that are not counting numbers. The rules for counting numbers continue to apply for all numbers *larger* than 1. For numbers *between* 0 and 1, however, the rules for both multiplication and division are different. The rules for addition and subtraction, however, remain the same. Here is a summary of all the rules:

> *Addition:* Answers are larger than the largest number for all numbers greater than 0.
> *Subtraction:* Answers are less than the largest number for all numbers greater than 0.

Multiplication: Answers are larger than the largest number for all numbers greater than 1. Answers are less than the largest number for all numbers between 0 and 1.

Division: Answers are less than the largest number for all divisors greater than 1. Answers are larger than the largest number for all divisors between 0 and 1.

Notice that in division, it matters whether the numbers are dividends or divisors. While $24 \div \frac{1}{4}$ is greater than 24, $\frac{1}{4} \div 24$ is less than 24.

Getting closer

Merely knowing whether an answer should be larger or smaller than the largest number in a problem does not get you very close to the actual answer, of course. In many situations, you want an answer that is much more precise than that. For example, you may want to use an estimate to check a problem that you have already solved. There are various ways to make estimates that are good enough for such purposes.

Probably the most common way of estimating relies on rounding numbers. Numbers can be rounded according to three different rules, however. The most common rule is the one that is generally taught in arithmetic. If you want to round to a particular place, look at the digit just to the right of that place. If it is less than 5, change all the digits following the place to which you are rounding to 0s. But if the digit to the right is 5 or greater, increase the digit in the place you are rounding to by 1 and change succeeding digits to 0. Following this rule,

> 543,056 rounds to hundreds as 543,100
> 124,497 rounds to thousands as 124,000
> 1,923,846 rounds to millions as 2,000,000

The second method of rounding is used by stores in dealing with money. Any part of a cent rounds up to the next higher cent. This rule, which is important in dealing with purchasing problems, also has a place in estimating, as you will see. Refer to it as the *commercial method.* Using the commercial method

> $1.3333 rounds to $1.34
> $10.575 rounds to $10.58
> $6.999 rounds to $7.00

The third method of rounding is sometimes called *statistical rounding*. It depends on whether the place to which you are rounding is odd or even. When the digit to the right of the place to which you are rounding is not a 5, the statistical method is just like the method taught in arithmetic. If the digit to the right is 5, however, you round up (that is, increase the place to which you are rounding by 1) if the place is odd; if the place is even, you round down (that is, do not change the digit in the place to which you are rounding). This technique is based on the laws of probability. Using statistical rounding

> **64,643 rounded to tens is 64,640**
> **289,662 rounded to hundreds is 289,700**
> **796,551 rounded to hundreds is 796,600**
> **796,551 rounded to thousands is 796,000**

In adding long columns of numbers or in long operations of any kind, you get a better estimate using statistical rounding. In short problems, it is not essential.

Rounding with addition and subtraction

The smallest number that is longer than one digit should be rounded to its first digit. All other numbers should be rounded to the same place.

2394	rounds to	2400
598		600
9508		9500
+ 4		+ 0
		12500

The actual answer is 12,504, so the estimate is close enough for many purposes. If you had rounded to thousands instead of hundreds, the estimate would have been 13,000. If you had rounded to tens instead of hundreds, the estimate would have been 12,500, the same estimate.

Similarly, for subtraction

83748	rounds to	83700
− 451		− 500
		83200

The actual answer is 83,297. While the estimate is close enough for checking a calculator computation, it would be closer if you ignored the rule and rounded to the nearest 50, making the problem 83750 − 450, which gives 83300. Good estimators will take the second way, but people just learning to estimate may be better off following the rule.

Rounding with multiplication and division

The rounding methods that work fairly well for addition and subtraction do not work for multiplication and division because they produce problems that are almost as hard to do mentally as the original problems. Therefore, another rule is used: Round each number to its first place. For example,

$$
\begin{array}{r}
5937 \\
\times \;\; 64
\end{array}
\qquad \text{rounds to} \qquad
\begin{array}{r}
6000 \\
\times \;\; 60 \\
\hline
360000
\end{array}
$$

The actual answer is 379,968, so this estimate should be close enough. Multiplication estimates are seldom as precise as addition and subtraction estimates.

In division, the same rule works.

$$
48\overline{)392864} \qquad \text{rounds to} \qquad \overset{8000}{50\overline{)400000}}
$$

The actual answer is 8184 R 32.

If you are in a hurry, a fourth kind of rounding can be used for any of the four operations. It is similar to the method used for multiplication and division, but one step easier. Instead of rounding to a particular place, you drop all places beyond the first and work with the leading digit only. Here's how the previous examples would work out using the *leading-digits* method of rounding:

$$
\begin{array}{r}
2394 \\
598 \\
9508 \\
+ \;\; 4
\end{array}
\qquad \text{becomes} \qquad
\begin{array}{r}
2000 \\
500 \\
9000 \\
+ \;\; 4 \\
\hline
11504
\end{array}
$$

$$
\begin{array}{r}
83748 \\
- \;\; 451
\end{array}
\qquad \text{becomes} \qquad
\begin{array}{r}
80000 \\
- \;\; 400 \\
\hline
79600
\end{array}
$$

$$
\begin{array}{r}
5937 \\
\times \;\; 64
\end{array}
\qquad \text{becomes} \qquad
\begin{array}{r}
5000 \\
\times \;\; 60 \\
\hline
300000
\end{array}
$$

$$
48\overline{)392,864} \qquad \text{becomes} \qquad \overset{7500}{40\overline{)300000}}
$$

Compare these estimates with the previous estimates and the actual answers:

Addition: Previous estimate, 12,500; actual answer, 12,504

Subtraction: Previous estimate, 83,200; actual answer, 83,297

Multiplication: Previous estimate, 360,000; actual answer, 379,968

Division: Previous estimate, 8000; actual answer, 8184 R 32

As you can see, the standard rounding method tends to give more precise estimates than the leading-digits method. Since you are "throwing away" part of each number, leading-digits will always give you an answer that is too low for both addition and multiplication. Still, the leading-digits method is good enough if you need only a rough estimate.

All of these, and other methods of estimating, should be part of everyone's math skills. In many cases, an accurate answer is not essential. People who have studied the use of mathematics in everyday life have found that estimates are often as useful as exact computations. And in some cases, estimates are even more useful.

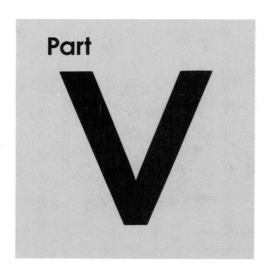

Part

V

Putting Math to Work

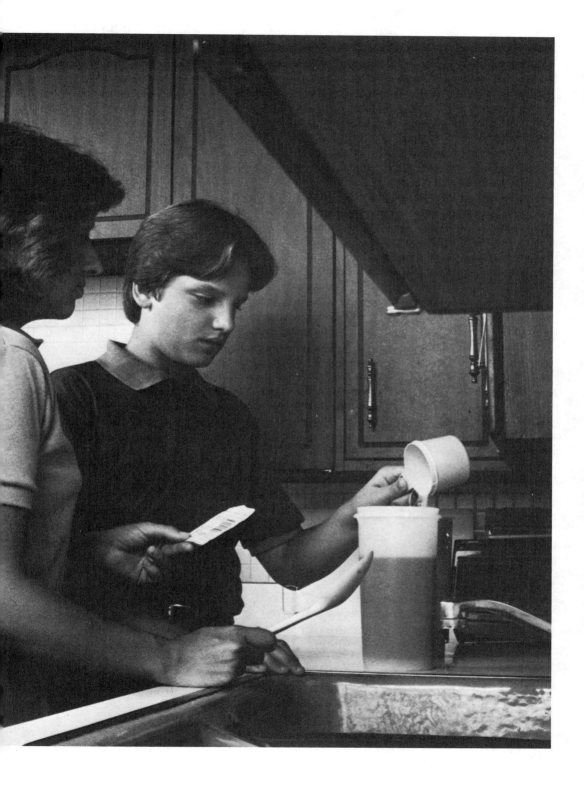

Part V introduces mathematics as a how-to science, a friend and ally, a way of solving problems of daily life. Math becomes a useful, practical tool as well as a means of dealing with numbers and concepts. You are entering the everyday world of math power.

Using ideas and methods developed in earlier sections, Part V will show you how to recognize problems that may call for math solutions, how to apply lessons and principles already presented, and how to work out answers.

The problems are all around us. Your home and its various components provide many examples. So does your yard. When you go on vacation, you can count on finding a whole new set of problems that you can solve easily with math. Three sections of Part V deal with typical home, kitchen, and travel situations.

A home is money as well as love and security; in a sense your home is a business. Just as in a business, money keeps the home "working," putting food on the table, providing light and warmth, paying for repairs and improvements. Two sections in Part V deal with money problems at home and in the typical business.

Keep two things in mind as you become familiar with Part V. First, it would be impossible to give examples of every kind of math problem that you might encounter in your daily life. The problems number in the thousands. For that reason, typical problems and situations have been selected for discussion here.

A second point is that many problems can be solved in more than one way. Where that is the case, Part V tries to show you the simplest way. The method used may have fewer steps than other methods. It may be the easiest to understand.

A special discussion in each section of Part V hints at yet another approach to practical problem solving: the handheld calculator. The calculator hints and information given in Part II, Section 4 should take on new meaning as you learn about calculator shortcuts. You may want to refer back to this earlier part of *Math Power* in Volume 1.

The following sections should also aid you as you try to sharpen other kinds of math-related skills. For example, you may find out how to draw better figures. You will learn to use your eyes and mind to visualize a math problem and plan a solution at the same time. ∎

(Preceding photo) Math power belongs in the kitchen as well as in the classroom.

How-to Math

In this section you will learn how to apply math in various kinds of do-it-yourself projects around your home. The section makes broad use of the types of math—mainly algebra and geometry—that deal with the shapes, sizes, and purposes of objects around the home. Most household projects involve simple geometric shapes: the walls of most rooms, for example, are simple four-sided figures.

You Need to Have a Plan

Drawing accurately and to scale enables you to work with pictures of objects or structures in your home. The object then "lives" for you; you do not have to see it. You can design or redesign almost any simple object or structure: a model toy, the furniture layout in a bedroom, the wall or floor covering, or some part of an electrical or plumbing system.

Various skills come into play when you draw. All of them can help with practical mathematical problems. One skill is being able to read and draw to scale. Another is to draw particular geometric shapes. A third is to use drawing to solve a geometric problem of size. Do you want to practice them?

On a grand scale

When you draw a picture or design, it is usually smaller than the object that it represents. An obvious example is the plan for a house. But in some cases, the drawing may be the same size as the object. This would be the case if you were planning to carve an animal from a piece of wood the size of your fist. Then, every line or curve on the drawing would represent an actual line or curve in the carving.

When the object differs in size from the drawing, each line or curve in the drawing must be *proportional* to the same feature in the object. To have proportion, you have to keep the same relative size, or *scale,* in all parts of your drawing.

In drawing to scale, you can work in metric or customary (English) units, in meters and millimeters, for example, or in yards and feet. On finishing (or while doing) your calculations, you can, if you desire, trans-

Drawing to scale.

late your figures into the other system of measurement. (For metric conversions, *see* Pt. VI, "Math Tables.")

As an example, suppose you hear from a math teacher that the school building will undergo remodeling. You are shown a draft plan for the remodeling work. You notice that the plan, or *design,* is drawn to a scale of 10 millimeters to 1 meter. You also find out that the design has these dimensions: 116 millimeters by 225 millimeters. You can now calculate the size of the actual building, the length and width in meters and the floor area in square meters.

Consider length and width first. Using millimeters, you want to obtain measurements in meters. You do so by applying the scale conversion formula 1 meter equals 10 millimeters. Multiplying each dimension according to this formula, you find that the width of the building is 116 millimeters times 1 meter per 10 millimeters.

The units are multiplied and divided as if they were plain numbers. The millimeters in the numerator are canceled out by the millimeters in the denominator

$$\frac{116 \text{ millimeters}}{10 \text{ millimeters/meter}} = 11.6 \text{ meters}$$

Figuring in the same way, you find that the length of the building is 22.5 meters. From these dimensions, the area of any floor of the building can be calculated.

11.6 meters × 22.5 meters
= 261 square meters (261 m²)

Could you calculate the area of any floor in a single operation? Yes, by using the following formula.

$$\left(116 \text{ mm}\right)\left(\frac{1 \text{ m}}{10 \text{ mm}}\right)\left(225 \text{ mm}\right)\left(\frac{1 \text{ m}}{10 \text{ mm}}\right)$$

$$= \frac{116 \,(225) \text{ square meters}}{100 \text{ millimeters}}$$

$$= \frac{26,100 \text{ square meters}}{100 \text{ millimeters}}$$

$$= 261 \text{ square meters}$$

You can repeat this entire process using customary measures. Your answer will be 313.2 square yards (m² × 1.2 = sq. yd.).

A square deal

It's easy to draw to scale when you have squared paper, called *graph paper*. This paper has lines that cross vertically and horizontally at equal intervals. Those intervals are generally ½ centimeter, or 5 millimeters, long and wide.

Say you are drawing the 11.6-meter by 22.5-meter school building. Using the scale of 1 meter to 10 millimeters, you find that every two squares on your paper represent 1 meter.

The length of the scale drawing is 225 millimeters, and you want to calculate the number of squares to use. The simplest way is to mark the number off with a metric ruler, which uses centimeters. Since 225 millimeters equals 22.5 centimeters, you want to mark off the distance from 0 on the ruler to halfway between 22 and 23 centimeters. The width is also marked off at 0 and at the 6-millimeter mark between 11 and 12 centimeters.

As another benefit, graph paper has horizontal and vertical lines that run at perfect right angles. You can draw a right angle anytime you need one, which is often in scale drawings.

On graph paper, finally, the area of each of the squares is the same. That means that you can find the area simply by counting squares.

This is highly irregular

Graph paper has other fascinating uses. Say you want to estimate the area covered by your lawn, which has irregular edges. Knowing the area, you can estimate more accurately how much fertilizer your family would need to cover the lawn lightly.

As noted, the area of a figure can be obtained by counting the squares in a scale drawing. You need only to pace off the major dimensions of your lawn and do a scale drawing according to your measurements in yards or meters. Then you count all the squares that fall entirely within the drawing, and finally you count those squares on the edges of your figure that have one-half or more of their space within the design. Omit all the other squares. You will have a reasonable estimate.

There's another method of computing the area of
an irregular figure. On cardboard, cut out a scale drawing of the figure and weigh it on a precision scale.
Then take a whole piece of identical cardboard the size
of a complete sheet of graph paper and weigh that.
Find the ratio of the two weights, since the figure will
weigh less in proportion to its smaller area.

$$\text{Ratio} = \frac{\textbf{Weight of Figure}}{\textbf{Weight of Whole Cardboard}}$$

Now say the figure weighs 1 ounce, and a whole
sheet of cardboard weighs 4 ounces. The ratio would
be 1 to 4, or .25.

In the next step, multiply the ratio by the area represented by a complete sheet. The sheet may, for example, have 43 by 56 squares, or 2,408 in all. If each
square is 10 feet by 10 feet, or 100 square feet, a whole
sheet would be 2,408 times that area: 240,800 square
feet. Multiplying by the ratio of .25, you find an area
for the figure of 60,200 square feet.

Are you getting cost and expense conscious? You can
use math to save money spent on electricity for your
home. You can also save money spent on your home's
electrical appliances and on keeping those appliances
operating. Further, math can help you to use electricity
safely in the home.

You Might Get a Charge Out of This

The starting point

You can make a start toward understanding the ways
in which electrical power can be saved by noting some
basic facts. The most basic may be the relationships
among the electrical units.

Power = Voltage × Current

Here, power represents the work that electricity does,
whether that work is lighting a room or operating a refrigerator. Power is measured in *watts*. Your local utility charges your family for the power your home uses.
The company calls this power *wattage*.

Some obvious rules apply. For example, the higher
the voltage, the higher the wattage. *Voltage* is the
strength of the electrical force. *Current* refers

to the number of electrons, or "juice," that pass through a circuit. Current is measured in amperes, *amps* for short.

Most household electrical circuits fall into one of two categories: 15 amps and 20 amps. The 15-amp circuit is used for most electrical outlets. The 20-amp circuit is used for refrigerators and for some air conditioners. You can certainly plug appliances designed for a 15-amp circuit into a 20-amp circuit.

Caution: don't plug that high-amp appliance into a 15-amp circuit. You'll blow a fuse or cause the circuit breaker to shut off, if you have one. Like voltage, the more amps you use, the more watts you consume.

Let's revise the previous equation to read

Watts = Volts × Amps

It should now be clear that, of the four kinds of common circuits, a 220-volt, 20-amp line is designed to deliver the most power.

220 volts × 20 amps = 4,400 watts
220 volts × 15 amps = 3,300 watts
110 volts × 20 amps = 2,200 watts
110 volts × 15 amps = 1,650 watts

Are your circuits adequate?

Most homes have standard circuits. Some are special circuits, including those for the electric kitchen-range. This circuit would have 220 or 240 volts and a capacity of 50 amps, providing 12,000 watts of power, more than enough for an average range.

Are you overloading a circuit? Let's say you have a 1,000-watt toaster and a 1,000-watt fryer operating on the same circuit. Simple addition shows that the total is 2,000 watts. A normal 15-amp circuit of 110 volts supplies only 1,650 watts, as you have seen.

The solution is either to put the two appliances on different circuits or to operate one appliance at a time. Now check the wattage information on all your key appliances per circuit and total the results.

Reading an electric meter

This brings us to the "business end" of electricity. The electric company has to figure out some way to charge your family for the power you use. Wattage comes closest to being the most useful unit for that purpose. It serves as a measure of total energy. If you conserve energy, you save money. Simple?

Watts would be a good unit of measure, except for one problem: watts don't measure the power used over a period of time. So someone invented the *watt-hour* (wh), or the use of 1 watt of electricity over a period of 1 hour. With the wh, you can measure the power consumed over longer periods of time, like a month. But the problem is that the watt-hour is too small a unit. So we have the *kilowatt-hour* (kwh), or 1,000 watt-hour.

Now think about electric meters, which tell both you and the electric company how much power your home is using—or wasting. The meter has four dials: from right to left, a ones, a tens, a hundreds, and a thousands dial. The ones and the hundreds dials move in a clockwise direction, the tens and the thousands dials in a counterclockwise direction. The meter in the illustration reads 1,276 kwh.

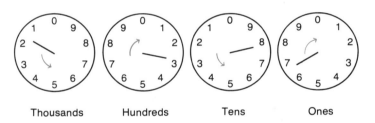

Thousands   Hundreds   Tens   Ones

The dials on an electric meter.

To read the meter, start with the ones dial. Always read off the last figure that the pointer has passed. The ones dial shows the pointer going about three-fourths of the way between the 6 and the 7. The tens dial is practically on the 8, indicating almost 80 kwh. This is consistent with the hundreds dial, which has gone eight-tenths (four-fifths) of the way between 2 and 3.

How much electricity are you using?

Knowing how to read a meter, you can find out how much electricity your family uses. You can determine how much you use in a day, a week, or a month. Simply take two readings a month apart and subtract the earlier meter reading from the later one.

How much power are you using to operate a particular appliance? Use the table "Electrical consumption

Electrical consumption of household appliances

Appliance and typical wattage	Average use	Average monthly kilowatt-hour use		Your average cost per kilowatt-hour		Estimated monthly cost
blender 385 watts	6 times per week	.1	kwh	× _____	=	_____
can opener 100 watts	3 uses per day	.03	kwh	× _____	=	_____
clothes dryer 4900 watts	6 loads per week	83	kwh	× _____	=	_____
clothes washer (automatic) 512 watts	6 loads per week	9	kwh	× _____	=	_____
coffee maker 600 watts	once a day	5	kwh	× _____	=	_____
dishwasher 1200 watts	25 loads	30	kwh	× _____	=	_____

freezer (15 cu. ft.)
  manual defrost
  341 watts
	every day	100	kwh	× _____	=	_____

frost-free 440 watts	every day	147	kwh	× _____	=	_____

hair dryer
  hand held
  600 watts
	5 times per week	2	kwh	× _____	=	_____

microwave oven 1450 watts	20 minutes	16	kwh	× _____	=	_____
radio 25 watts	2 hours every day	2	kwh	× _____	=	_____
range 12,200 watts	for a family of 3	100	kwh	× _____	=	_____
self-cleaning process	twice a month	9	kwh	× _____	=	_____

refrigerator/freezer
(14 cu. ft.)
  manual defrost
  326 watts
	every day	95	kwh	× _____	=	_____

frost-free 615 watts	every day	152	kwh	× _____	=	_____
slow cooker 200 watts	twice a month	3	kwh	× _____	=	_____
stereo/hi-fi 109 watts	2 hours per day	9	kwh	× _____	=	_____

television
  black & white
  solid state
  55 watts
	6 hours per day	10	kwh	× _____	=	_____

color solid state 200 watts	6 hours per day	37	kwh	× _____	=	_____
toaster 1400 watts	twice a day	4	kwh	× _____	=	_____

of household appliances'' to find the average kwh consumed per month and year by a variety of appliances.

Here are some examples. If you have a solid-state color TV and use it an average of 6 hours a day, you might use a hypothetical 37 kwh a month. What if you watch 10 hours a day instead? First, compute how many kwh you would consume in watching TV 1 hour a day for a month. Divide 37 kwh per month by 6 hours per day. Your answer is 6.17 kwh per month. Then, to find the consumption for 10 hours a day, you multiply 6.17 by 10. Your answer is 61.7 kwh.

Simple math can show what you can save by figuring the dollars-and-cents factors. Your family's electric bill will tell you the local cost of power. That cost can vary from 4 cents per kwh to 12 cents per kwh or more. Let's say it's 4 cents in your area. If you watch TV for 6 hours a day, you would spend 37 kwh × $.04/kwh = $1.48 per month for TV (the kwh cancel out). If you watch 10 hours a day, you would spend 61.7 kwh × $.04/kwh = $2.47. That makes a difference of $.99. If your local rate is 8 cents per kwh, the difference is twice as great.

Saving when you buy appliances

The federal government has required that all major appliances carry a special *energy label*. This label tells how much your family can expect to spend on power over a year while operating that model.

If your family is shopping for an appliance that does not have this convenient label, you can still figure which model is the most economical to operate. The power usage of TV sets can be compared according to the amps or watts used. If only the amps are shown, multiply these by 110 volts to find the watts.

What lighting do you need?

Do you want to make sure your room has enough light? You read and work in it; you want to protect your sight.

Figuring how much lighting you need can be complex. There are many factors that affect need: the purpose of a light, the size of the room, the distance from the lighting source, the colors of the walls and ceilings (which affect light reflection), and the kinds of fixtures used. You also might have to consider other factors.

Light is measured in two kinds of units. The most basic, the *lumen,* is usually used to measure the total output of a light source. A 25-watt incandescent bulb, for example, gives off an average of 235 lumens; a 75-watt bulb gives off an average of 1,175 lumens (bulbs of the same size vary a little by brand). The smaller bulb gives off only 9.4 lumens per watt, while the larger bulb gives off 15.7 lumens per watt.

Generally, the larger the bulb, the more "efficient" it is. Fluorescents are even more efficient: a 20-amp source gives off 65.0 lumens per watt.

An important consideration is the purpose of the light source. You will have to consider both light concentration and intensity, using the *foot-candle* as a unit of measurement. The foot-candle represents 1 lumen per square foot. Some tasks require 100 foot-candles or more. Most commercial uses require 20 to 50. Familiar activities, including recreational ones, call for 10 to 20. Passageways with light traffic need less than 5 foot-candles of illumination.

Let's say your bedroom measures 8 feet by 10 feet. To estimate how many foot-candles of light you need for reading and studying, according to lighting experts, you would apply a relatively high standard. You would need a minimum of 50 foot-candles of light.

Average watts, lumens, and lumens/watts

Lighting wattage	Lumens	Lumens/watts
Incandescent		
25	235	9.4
40	455	11.4
60	890	14.8
75	1175	15.7
100	1750	17.5
150	2800	18.7
30/ 70/100	275/1050/1325	9.2/15.0/13.3
50/100/150	550/1500/2050	11.0/15.0/13.7
100/200/300	1300/3600/4900	13.0/18.0/16.3
Fluorescent		
20 cool white	1300	65.0
40 cool white	3150	78.8
40 daylight	2600	65.0
75 cool white	6300	84.0

Knowing how many foot-candles you need, you can determine the total lumens needed. You do so by multiplying the area concerned by the required number of foot-candles.

$$\textbf{Square Feet} \times \left(\frac{\textbf{Lumens}}{\textbf{Square Feet}} \right) = \textbf{Lumens}$$

Remember that lumens per square feet are foot-candles. Once you know the lumens, you can choose a bulb adequate for the task.

But there are other factors to think about. If the walls are dark colors, less light will be reflected. You may need either a larger bulb or lighter paint. How about the distance from the light to the user? As the distance increases, the foot-candles decrease in intensity in proportion to the square of the distance. If the distance doubles, the intensity dwindles to one-fourth of what it was.

Do you want to add a little color to your life? Read on; the following discussion should shed some light on the many ways your family can improve the inside of your home—if you can apply what you know about math.

Painting and Decorating

Room planning

Try using your scale-drawing skills to plan a room. Your materials should include graph paper, either 5 millimeter or $\frac{1}{4}$-inch gauge; sharp pencils, pens, or fine markers; ruler, compass, and scissors; and a bunch of catalogs from department stores or mail-order houses.

Now draw to scale the room you want to redecorate. Let's suppose you have an extra bedroom you want to turn into a recreation room or den. Don't forget the doors and windows. If a door opens into the room, use your compass to draw an arc. The radius should be equal to the width of the door because you don't want anything to block the door when you open it. If a door normally stays open against a wall, mark the width of the door along the wall. The door, obviously, takes up a certain amount of floor and wall space.

Maybe you are dissatisfied with the present arrangement of furniture. You like some of the furnishings, but you wish they were in different places. In this case make a scale drawing of each piece on graph paper, then cut out the drawings. Now you can move furniture around "on paper" to your heart's content until you come up with the right combination.

Suppose you come up with more than one plan that you like. You will want to be able to refer back and forth between plans without constantly rearranging the pieces. The simplest strategy is to make a copy of the plans you like so that you have permanent drawings. For the best method of doing this, let's backtrack a little. When you are making your scale drawing of the room, make a few copies of that drawing by using tracing paper. When you have worked out a floor plan you want to preserve, simply trace the outline of each piece on the drawing.

Give your creativity a workout. Design an ideal recreation room. Consider everything that you want to do in that room: read, play games, study, watch TV, or listen to music. Think about the furniture that would allow you to do those things. Make the room match the furniture, rather than the other way around.

Estimating materials

The family must decide whether to do the rec room walls over with paint or wallpaper. You may want to put in a new tile or wood floor. If you like a cushiony feeling, you may decide on carpeting. This section touches on all of these choices.

The first thing to look at is the size. Your rec room has the following dimensions: 12 feet 8 inches by 10 feet 9 inches, with a height of 8 feet. You now have all the information you need to estimate materials for floor, walls, or ceiling.

Floor plan of recreation room with furniture.

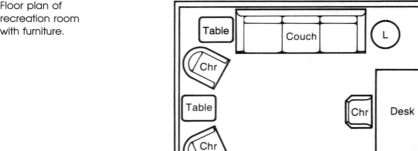

The areas of the floor and the ceiling can be computed readily.

12 feet 8 inches $\times$ 10 feet 9 inches = 12.67 feet $\times$ 10.75 feet
= 136.2 square feet

Length times width in feet gives you 136.2 square feet. The area of the walls is the product of the *perimeter* (the distance around all four walls) and the height, as follows.

(12.67 feet + 12.67 feet + 10.75 feet + 10.75 feet) $\times$ 8 feet
= 46.84 feet $\times$ 8 feet
= 374.72 square feet

Wood flooring

Let's start at the bottom. Floors can be made of different materials. Hardwood floors can be made from strips, planks, or blocks. Strips come in widths from $1\frac{1}{2}$ inches to $2\frac{1}{4}$ inches, and in thicknesses from $\frac{3}{8}$ inch to $\frac{35}{32}$ inches. The wider and thicker strips are the most typical. The strips fit and lock together by means of tongues and grooves on the sides and ends. Planking comes in 3- to 8-inch-wide planks, with the same range of thickness as strips.

Parquet flooring comes in square blocks that are 9 inches by 9 inches or 12 inches by 12 inches. Since the floor area of the bedroom was 136.2 square feet, for simplicity you can drop the decimal while figuring the number of parquet squares needed. Rounded estimates are good enough.

Clearly, one block of 12 by 12 inch parquet covers 1 square foot. Equally clearly, you need at least 136 parquet blocks, and probably more than that. Why? For one thing, you can expect some waste. For another, the dimensions of your floor may not conform neatly to the dimensions of the tiles when laid out. You will have to cut or split some tiles to make them fit at the edges of the room.

You should allow 5 percent for waste. That comes to an additional 7 tiles (5% of 136 is 6.8). But since you can't buy fractions of tiles, you will need 7 extra tiles, for a total of 143 tiles.

But what about the 9 by 9 inch tiles? How many of them would you need? Figure this by calculating the area of 1 tile. Since 9 inches = $\frac{3}{4}$ foot, or .75 foot, the area of 1 such tile would be .75 $\times$ .75 = .56 square foot. Divide the total area of the floor by the area of 1 tile and you get the number of tiles.

$$\frac{136}{.56} = 242.86 = 243 \text{ tiles}$$

As a check on this computation, include the units, dividing total area by area per tile.

$$\frac{\textbf{Square Feet}}{\textbf{Square Feet per Tile}} = \textbf{Number of Tiles}$$

It can be seen that the area units in the numerator and the denominator cancel out, while the unit—tiles—goes into the numerator to give the answer. Adding 5 percent for waste gives 12 extra tiles. So 243 plus 12 equals 255 total parquet tiles 9 inches by 9 inches.

Other kinds of tile

You would calculate your needs for other tiles just as you did for parquet tiles. Resilient floor tiles—asphalt, cork, and vinyl—come primarily in 12 by 12 inch and 9 by 9 inch sizes. Ceramic tiles come in 8 by 8 inch and 4 by 4 inch squares, or even as hexagonals, octagonals, or odd-shaped curved pieces. You can also buy carpeting in tile form.

Whatever tiles you buy, math will help you place them. Usually, you have to lay the tiles according to the *center lines* of the floor. Mark off the midpoint of each edge of the floor. Use a chalk line to connect the midpoints of the opposite sides. A chalk line is simply a length of twine covered with powdered chalk of some color. (You can make your own chalk line by putting a piece of heavy string and some ground chalk in a coffee can.)

The center lines are used to align the whole formation of tiles. A widespread method is to start by laying tiles in the angles made by the lines and working out in

Center-line method

A pattern for laying floor tiles. Notice that the extra space around the edges of the floor will have to be covered by split tiles.

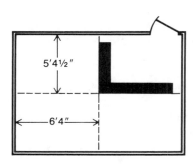

a pyramid shape. This method involves two quadrants at a time. Each successive line of tiles becomes shorter. Finally, the remaining tiles are filled in.

An alternate method presents a mathematical problem. This method would give you a tile square in the middle of your room. You start by laying a line of tiles precisely over one center line, so that half of each tile rests on one side of the line and half rests on the other.

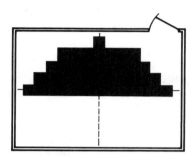

Centered-tile method

It can be seen that the tiles, when laid out, will not neatly touch each edge of the floor. If you look at the laid-out tiles along the lengthwise center line, you will see that each side of that center line stretches 6 feet 4 inches. That represents half the 12 feet 8 inch length of room.

Let's say you are using 12 by 12 inch tiles. First subtract 6 inches from 6 feet 4 inches, giving 5 feet 10 inches. Why? Because each tile laid across the center of the room takes up 6 inches on each side of the center chalk line. Then, how many whole tiles can go into the length of 5 feet 10 inches? The answer is 5. The complete length of this center line will therefore require 11 tiles, 5 on each side and 1 in the center.

You can figure the same way for the other center line. Half of 10 feet 9 inches is 5 feet 4½ inches. Subtracting the center tile leaves 4 feet 10½ inches. This means 4 complete tiles can be laid out on this side. The total for the entire center line is therefore 4 + 4 + 1, or 9 complete tiles.

How many whole tiles will you need? The formula is 11 × 9 = 99. But you know already that about 136 tiles would cover the entire floor. The remaining tiles, numbering 136 − 99, or 37 tiles, would be split to cover the edges of the floor.

In effect, your floor has been divided into four quadrants separated by what look like four spokes on a wheel. You can now lay the remaining tiles by filling in one quadrant at a time. In each case you should start at the center line and move out.

Strip linoleum

In calculating the amount of strip linoleum you will need, allow 10 to 20 percent extra for trimming. If you have 136 square feet to cover, allow 14 to 27 square feet extra. This gives a total of 150 to 164 square feet, the amount of linoleum you want.

Carpeting

Carpeting is available in 12 by 12 inch tiles as well as larger sizes. To compute how many of these tiles are needed, use the same math formulas that you used for other kinds of tiles.

Carpeting is more typically sold in rolls. These come in 6-, 9-, 12-, and 15-foot widths. What do all of these have in common? They are divisible by 3. The reason is that carpeting is sold by the square yard. If you bought 15 feet of the 15-foot wide roll, you would have 25 square yards because 15 feet = 5 yards, so $5 \times 5 = 25$.

If you decide to carpet this recreation room, how much carpeting will you need? Since the floor covers about 136 square feet, you can easily figure the area in square yards. It takes 9 square feet to make 1 square yard, so you divide 136 by 9 to get 15.11 square yards. Allow 10 to 20 percent extra for waste. For 15 square yards, 20 percent is 3 square yards, giving a total of 18 square yards.

Math is saving you time and money. But remember that rolls of carpeting come in certain widths. You may have to purchase more than you figured on.

Look at your floor plan again. You could end up buying as much as 20 square yards of carpeting. If you decide you need 15 feet of the 12-foot width, that's 5 yards times 4 yards, or 20 square yards. This figure may be more than you need and should be considered as the absolute maximum you should purchase.

Wallpaper

Estimating for wallpaper should give you no problems. Remember that the area of the walls was figured as the product of the perimeter and the height. That came to about 375 square feet. (You can round off this figure.)

The actual area to be papered will be less than 375 square feet. You will want to subtract doors from your wall area as well as windows. Don't forget to subtract the fireplace, if there is one.

Let's assume the room has a window measuring 3 feet by 5 feet for an area of 15 square feet. If you have a door measuring 7 feet by 3 feet, you have another area of 21 square feet that doesn't need papering. Thus the total area to be papered is 375 − 15 − 21 = 339 square feet.

Wallpaper comes in various widths, from 18 inches to 48 inches. The 18-inch paper comes in 24-foot lengths, the 22-inch paper in 21-foot lengths, and the 30-inch paper in 15-foot lengths. The 18-inch and 30-inch widths are the most frequently used. Whatever the width, the area of a roll is about 37 square feet. This is clear from the above dimensions: the wider the roll, the shorter it is.

You want to find how many rolls you need. Figure on the amount of *useful* area on a roll to be 30 square feet. This is because you have to allow for trimming and matching. Compute the number of rolls by dividing the area to be papered by the useful area on a roll. In this example, that figures out to be

$$\frac{\textbf{339 square feet}}{\textbf{30 square feet/roll}} = \textbf{11.3} = \textbf{12 rolls}$$

To allow for mistakes, add 1 more roll. This makes a total of 13 rolls.

Wallpaper comes in single, double, and triple rolls. These calculations assumed that you were using single rolls. But often single rolls are less convenient. In our example, 6 double rolls or 4 triple rolls should be sufficient to get the job done, plus 1 single roll to allow for mistakes. On the next page there is a table to help you estimate the wallpaper you need in single rolls.

When you know the distance around your room, 2 × (length + width), use the table to determine how many rolls of wall covering you will need. Deduct 1 single roll for every 2 ordinary-size doors or windows or every 30 square feet of opening. A roll of wall covering contains 37 square feet.

Estimating amount of wall covering required

Distance in feet	No. single rolls		
	8 ft.*	9 ft.*	10 ft.*
28	8	8	10
32	8	8	10
36	8	10	10
40	10	10	12
44	10	12	14
48	12	12	14
52	12	14	16
56	14	14	16
60	14	16	18
64	16	18	20
68	16	18	20
72	18	20	20
76	18	20	22
80	20	20	24
84	20	22	24
88	20	22	36

*Height of ceiling.

Painting

Does your family want to redecorate with paint? Most paint is purchased by the gallon. A gallon of paint will cover from 400 to 500 square feet. A room with dimensions of 12 feet by 15 feet with an 8-foot ceiling, for a total of 432 square feet, would fall within this range.

Paints vary with regard to the area they cover; the can or container should give you an indication. You may need more than one coat if the surface is porous or rough textured, or if you will be covering many defects.

For the rec room project, 1 gallon would be adequate to cover 339 square feet. If your walls need two coats, you should figure on covering 678 square feet. If 1 gallon of the paint you are using covers 400 square feet, you may as well buy two 1-gallon cans rather than 1 gallon and 3 quarts. One reason is that paint is cheaper by the gallon. Another is that you may be cutting it close in your estimates. Some walls seem to "drink" paint. A coat of primer, which is relatively inexpensive, may save your family a substantial amount of money. Purchase primer, if needed, when you buy the paint—and be sure to ask your salesperson which primer is the correct one for the job.

You can figure the ceiling area as you did the floor. For your rec room, that is 136.2 square feet, or 136 rounded off. If you want to paint the woodwork, figure on 20 to 30 percent as much paint as is required for the walls. For every 1 gallon of wall paint, plan on getting 1 additional quart of paint of the appropriate color for the trim.

How long will it take?

How much time will be involved in your family's decorating job? Where you can count tiles or square feet, you will want to do some calculating. Let's say you're painting the recreation room. If you painted one of the widthwise walls of that room, without doors or windows, in 1 hour, you painted 86 square feet. You have painted nearly 25 percent of the wall area. If you needed 1 hour to paint $\frac{1}{4}$ of the wall surface, it should take approximately 4 hours to complete the job.

Will your family work together? What if two of you paint the room? At the end of 1 hour, one may have painted $\frac{1}{4}$ of the room while the other has painted $\frac{1}{3}$. How long will it take to finish the job? That's easy. The combined rate for both of you is $\frac{1}{4} + \frac{1}{3} = \frac{7}{12}$ of the room per hour. As in our earlier rate problem, the job can be divided by the rate achieved during part of the time to obtain the answer in total time. This makes sense if you realize how the units are handled.

$$\frac{\text{Total Square Feet}}{\text{Square Feet/Hour}} = \text{Total Hours}$$

The area terms cancel out, with the time going into the numerator. In your case the total estimated time for the painting will be 1 hour divided by $\frac{7}{12}$, or $\frac{12}{7} = 1\frac{5}{7}$ hours.

Calculator Shortcuts

You can use a calculator to simplify or speed up many kinds of home improvement calculations. In general, the fewer steps you have to make in calculating, the smaller the chance of error.

Keep in mind as you practice the following technique that calculators differ in the way they operate. If the shortcut here doesn't work for you, consult the user's manual that came with your calculator. Then adapt this technique to the instructions for your machine.

In computing wall areas for painting or papering, you learned that multiplying the perimeter by the height would give the answer. You actually added the widths of the four sides of the room, then multiplied that sum by the height.

Consider the calculator alternative. Find the area of each wall separately and then total these areas. For one wall these would be the operations involved.

1	2	3	4		5
8	×	12.67	=	101.36	CLEAR

Each box represents a press of a key. So there are 5 steps, or 5 chances for error, not to mention that you must remember to write down the answer, unless your calculator has a print-out feature.

These 5 steps are then repeated for the other three sides of the room, for a total of 20 steps. Then the areas for the four sides are summed. How many steps is that? If you answered 8, you were correct. That makes a total of 28 steps, excluding writing down the intermediate answers.

You can, of course, simplify this approach, since you have two pairs of equal sides. You can calculate the area for a pair of walls.

1	2	3	4	5	6		7
2	×	8	×	12.67	=	202.72	CLEAR

This sequence would be repeated for the other pair of walls, for a total of 14 steps. But you're not through. You still have to sum the two intermediate answers, for an additional 4 steps. This reduces the number of steps from 28 to 18.

The number can be reduced further by doing all summing first, followed by whatever multiplication is necessary. This eliminates intermediate answers and the need to write them down or clear the calculator.

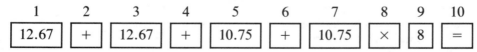

1	2	3	4	5	6	7	8	9	10
12.67	+	12.67	+	10.75	+	10.75	×	8	=

You have the answer, 374.72, in just 10 steps. One thing to note is that in step 8, it is not necessary to press ⌷=⌷. That's because the calculator is automatically summing the previous figures. That sum will read out on your display when you press ⊠ , so you can go right to your final answer. This *chain calculation* has reduced your work by almost two-thirds.

Plumbing

Your family can save money on your home plumbing system. You may save tubs of money.

Maybe you can't do all the things a plumber can do, but you can certainly do some things—and calculate others. You can use a plunger on a stopped-up drain. Just as easily, you can use simple math to work out some plumbing problems.

Some "for-instances" are useful. With a little measuring you can determine the hardness of your water. (You want to know that for a variety of reasons.) With a little more measuring, you can figure out how much water that leaky faucet is wasting over a period of time.

Hard water: an easy problem

The term *hard water* refers to water that contains certain chemicals naturally found in some areas. Most hard water has absorbed minerals while in contact with the ground. The term has practical meaning because hard water can be hard on things it comes in contact with. It's more difficult for a soap or detergent to form suds in hard water and therefore more difficult to wash things thoroughly. If you wash clothes in hard water, they don't last as long. Finally, hard water can wear out your plumbing system faster.

There's a quick and inexpensive test you can perform that will tell you how hard your water is. All you need is some tincture of green soap, which you can buy for a low cost at the drugstore. You'll also need a small bottle.

Here's what you do. Add 1 drop of green soap to $\frac{1}{2}$ ounce of water in the bottle, and shake vigorously. Repeat—add a drop and shake—until a thick layer of suds appears.

When that happens, you have determined the hardness of the water you are using. If the number of drops needed to form suds is this:

1	2	3	4	5	6

then the hardness of your water is this:

0	$2\frac{1}{2}$	4	$7\frac{1}{2}$	10	$12\frac{1}{2}$

If the hardness level exceeds 4, your family should consider doing something about it. Otherwise, your soap, clothing, and plumbing bills could climb, if they haven't already. Water softeners added to the laundry will solve the problem there. But softeners won't prevent damage to your plumbing. For that you should consider a water-softening system.

Are you in hot water?

A leaky faucet means money down the drain, in two ways. It means a higher water bill. It means, too, that your water heater is working harder than it needs to. A few drops each minute from a leaky faucet means millions of drops over a year. Put another way, the water system in your home can lose hundreds of gallons of cold or hot—and expensive—water.

How much money can your family lose in a year? That depends on how much it costs to heat the water. And that depends on the type of water heater. With an oil water heater, the cost of 1 gallon of oil might range from 45 to 75 cents. In that situation, heating 100 gallons of water would range from 31 to 51 cents. For a gas water heater, the price of 100 cubic feet of gas may range from 20 to 50 cents. The corresponding cost for heating 100 gallons of water would range from 19 to 47 cents. An electric water heater might cost from 2 to 6 cents per kilowatt-hour (kwh), so 100 gallons of hot water would cost correspondingly from 39 cents to $1.17.

How to measure? Take a measuring cup and put it under the leaky faucet. Let the cup sit for 1 hour. If the leak is really serious, use a pint-sized measuring cup. A leak of 1 cup per hour means a loss of 550 gallons per year. If you have an electric water heater that costs $1.17 for 100 gallons, that means $\frac{550}{100} \times \$1.17 = 5.5 \times \$1.17 = \$6.44$ a year.

Not much, you say? But how long has it been going on? And maybe that faucet is not the only one that leaks.

Remodeling and Home Improvement

You say you want to paint those living room walls? Well, wait. Before your family decides on anything that will make the room look better, you really should consider some remodeling, in the form of insulation.

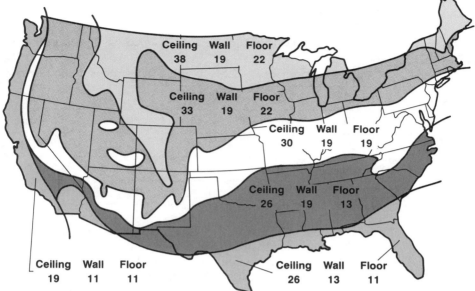

Ceiling Wall Floor
  38   19   22

Ceiling Wall Floor
  33   19   22

Ceiling Wall Floor
  30   19   19

Ceiling Wall Floor
  26   19   13

Ceiling Wall Floor
  19   11   11

Ceiling Wall Floor
  26   13   11

Insulation

Insulation does more to cut heat loss in the winter and prevent heat from entering in the summer than almost anything you can do. The ability of a material to resist such heat transfer (loss) is called its *R-value*. Homes have different R-value requirements for floors, walls, and ceilings. These requirements vary according to the type of construction and the geographic location. The map shows how insulation needs vary by region.

These R-values are recommended for achieving highest net savings on heating and cooling costs. As fuel costs rise, so will the optimum R-values.

Once you know the R-values for your area, you can determine how much insulation you need. The amount depends on the material you are considering. Materials include: *batts* (or *blankets*) of fiberglass or rock wool; *loose fill* (poured in) of fiberglass, rock wool, or cellulosic fiber; and *rigid plastic foams* of urethane or styrene.

How much insulation would you need for your frame house? The map above shows in which zone you are located. The insulation thickness table on the next page tells you how much insulation of four types you would have to install to give your home a specific R-value. Put the two together and you have your estimate.

How about an example? Your family wants to make sure that next winter the walls of your home have an R-value of 19. You know you can pour fiber-

Insulation thickness

	Batts or blankets		Loose fill (poured in)	
	Fiberglass	Rock wool	Fiberglass	Rock wool
R–22	$3\frac{1}{2}''$–$4''$	$3''$–$3\frac{1}{2}''$	$3\frac{3}{4}''$–$5''$	$3\frac{1}{4}''$–$4''$
R–19	$6''$–$6\frac{1}{2}''$	$5\frac{1}{4}''$–$6''$	$6\frac{1}{2}''$–$8\frac{3}{4}''$	$5\frac{3}{4}''$–$6\frac{3}{4}''$
R–22	$6\frac{1}{2}''$–$7\frac{1}{2}''$	$6''$–$6\frac{1}{2}''$	$7\frac{1}{2}''$–$10''$	$6\frac{1}{2}''$–$7\frac{3}{4}''$
R–30	$9''$–$10''$	$8\frac{1}{4}''$	$10\frac{1}{2}''$–$13\frac{3}{4}''$	$9''$–$10\frac{1}{2}''$
R–38	$12''$–$13''$	$10\frac{1}{2}''$	$13''$–$17\frac{1}{2}''$	$11\frac{1}{2}''$–$13\frac{1}{2}''$

glass loose fill into your walls, so you check the table to find out what thickness brings you close to R-19.

The answer clarifies but doesn't solve the problem. The exterior walls have $5\frac{3}{4}$-inch spaces from outside covering to inside wood. You would need $6\frac{1}{2}$ to $8\frac{3}{4}$ inches of fiberglass loose fill to have an R-19 defense against the chill of winter. Obviously, you can't put a $6\frac{1}{2}$- to $8\frac{3}{4}$-inch thickness of fiberglass into a $5\frac{3}{4}$-inch space.

What to do? Why not consider rock wool loose fill, which would bring you exactly to the R-19 target? Installation can be a job for a professional, but you would get the job done.

Generally, the different kinds of insulation have specific uses. Blankets go in unfinished walls or ceilings; loose fills work best in walls. Foams also serve to insulate walls, but their use is controversial due to health hazards they are said to provoke.

Batts in the attic?

Your family has made "winterizing" a high-priority item. You found that the attic needed insulation just as much as the walls. Let's assume that the attic is unfinished—it has no flooring—so you can measure the floor joists. They are 6 inches deep and 16 inches apart. You decide on fiberglass blankets because they are easy to install.

Estimating needs

How many blankets will you need? You decide on a total R-value of 36. Since fiberglass has an R of about

3.1 for each inch of thickness, you calculate the inches of thickness you want as follows.

$$\frac{36}{3.1/\text{inch}} = 11.61 \text{ inches}$$

Blankets come commonly in 6-inch thicknesses, so two layers will be just about adequate. One layer will fit between the floor joists; the other layer will go crosswise on top of that. The first layer should have a vapor barrier, typically metal foil, on one side to keep moisture in the interior of the attic from neutralizing the insulator. Remember, you are actually insulating the rooms below the attic.

How many blankets should you buy? The attic measures 30 feet by 60 feet, a total area of 1,800 square feet. The joists are 16 inches apart; with that spacing they take up about 10 percent of the floor area. If they were 23 inches apart, they would take up about 6 percent of the floor area. Now you calculate how much you need for the first layer.

90 percent $\times$ **1,800 square feet = 1,620 square feet**

How many rolls for the first layer? Each roll, an advertisement tells you, covers 30 square feet. Some simple division follows.

$$\frac{\textbf{1,620 square feet}}{\textbf{30 square feet/roll}} = \textbf{54 rolls}$$

The rolls are 15 inches wide. That means that because of the space taken up by the joists, the rolls just fill the open area to be insulated.

Installation

Installing the blankets may be the easiest part of all. The first layer, with each blanket strip 24 feet long, involves laying a whole row of complete rolls. You then go back and cut 6-foot lengths to fill the remaining spaces. You are working across the width of the attic.

The second layer will have to cover the entire 1,800 square feet. The batts are installed across the first layer, along the 60-foot length of the attic. This time you are using unbacked rolls, without vapor barriers. You know that each roll covers 48.96 square feet and is 1.25 feet wide. To find out how many of these rolls you will need, perform this calculation.

$$\frac{1,800 \text{ square feet}}{48.96 \text{ square feet/roll}} = 36.76 \text{ rolls}$$

You will need 37 full rolls, since you can't buy parts of rolls. To find the length of each roll, perform this calculation.

$$\frac{48.96 \text{ square feet}}{1.25 \text{ feet}} = 39.17 \text{ feet}$$

Now you know you can lay down entire rolls for this layer as well, then cut lengths to fit the remaining lengthwise spaces.

Heating and Air Conditioning

Insulation has simplified the jobs of your family's heating plant and air conditioning system. That means your family will save money during the seasons when these appliances are operating.

Heating

Many factors help to determine what kind of furnace a home needs or how well a heating plant works. Some of the factors include the total area of the rooms in the home; the climate, including the average outdoor temperatures; and the number of windows in the home and the directions in which they face.

You can't measure exactly how much heat is lost from your home as a result of leaks or structural factors. But a rule of thumb will give you a standard. The average house without insulation or other retrofit (fuel-efficiency) protection loses 70,000 British thermal units (Btu) or more per hour. The greater the heat loss, the larger the furnace or boiler you need.

Does your family need a new furnace? Go window-shopping, remembering to bring pencil and paper.

In the furnace department of a large heating/air conditioning equipment store you will see energy labels like those on other appliances. But the furnaces also have *Energy Efficiency Ratios* (EER) expressed as percentages. An EER of 65.2 means that a furnace will deliver as useful heat 65.2 percent of the energy consumed.

What about efficiency? Boilers are usually about 70 percent efficient. Gas or oil furnaces have EER ranging from 75 to 80. Electric heating is 100 percent efficient, but electricity costs more, generally, than oil or gas.

Try some figuring. Let's say that you have checked and found that the rate for natural gas in your area is 50 cents per *therm,* which is equal to 100,000 Btu. Assume that the energy loss in your home would be an average 50,000 Btu an hour. The point of intersection on the chart required on the energy label for 50 cents per therm and 50,000 Btu appears as $626 in heating costs per year.

Now you decide to compare the costs of operating an oil furnace and the gas furnace already described. The oil furnace has an EER of 78.1.

You've brought some other facts with you. Heating oil costs a relatively inexpensive 94 cents per gallon in your area. On the label, reading across the row for 94 cents to the column for 50,000 Btu, you find the figure $714, which is the cost per year. The oil furnace costs $88 more per year to operate than the gas furnace; $714 − $626 = $88.

Since furnaces have an expected lifespan of 20 years, you can now calculate the difference in the operating costs of the two heating plants over two decades.

20 years × **$88/year** = **$1,760**

For ease of estimating, you are assuming that the costs of different fuels will remain the same over the next 20 years. That is, of course, unlikely.

The more help you can give your furnace, the more dollars and cents you can save. One way is to caulk around the outside of your home. To find out how much caulking you need for your caulking gun, note some rules. A window takes about ½ cartridge, a door about the same, a chimney about 2 cartridges, and the foundation sill about 4 more.

Air conditioning

A word on air conditioning puts some more basic math in perspective. A unit's cooling capacity is measured in short tons and Btu; 1 ton equals 12,000 Btu. Central air conditioners typically have capacities ranging from 2.5 to 5 short tons, meaning they have 30,000 to 60,000 Btu capacities.

To calculate cooling capacity, your family should figure 12,000 Btu for every 500 square feet of floor space. If your enclosed porch has an area of 250 square feet, you would need a 6,000-Btu room unit. Other factors raise or lower that estimate. For example, large window areas and southern exposures indicate more required capacity.

Your next concern, efficiency, is actually the amount of cooling capacity for a given amount of electric power used. This is the Energy Efficiency Ratio (EER) again, which is expressed as

$$EER = \frac{Btu/hour}{Watts} = \frac{Btu}{Watt\ Hour}$$

The higher the Btu and the lower the watts, the higher the efficiency; and the higher the EER, the better.

An air conditioner with an EER of 12, just twice as efficient as one with an EER of 6, will use half as much power. Units of 10,000 Btu with these EER can be compared with regard to operating costs. If the units are run for 800 hours, and the cost is 6 cents per kwh, the more efficient model will cost $400 to operate and the less efficient model, $800.

Air conditioners have energy labels. You can, as before, estimate the lifetime operating costs, figuring an average life span of 12 to 15 years.

Outdoor Home Care

Outdoor home care can involve the use of math as much as any other handiwork around the home. You encounter, particularly, problems of space calculation and material cost estimating. Reasonable estimates can be made for this purpose. Math can offer some surprising solutions to outdoor problems.

Shadow measurement

How do you measure something without actually measuring it? You measure it indirectly, using geometry.

Suppose you want to know the height of your home. You want a fairly precise figure because you are going to borrow or buy a ladder to work on the roof. Measuring can be a tall order unless you measure indirectly. The sun provides a solution. The crest of the roof casts a shadow at a given time of day. You can measure that. The sun casts many other shadows. Stand a ruler (you know its length) on end in the sun. It will cast a shadow that you can measure.

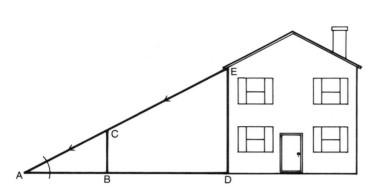

Using the "shadow" method of measurement.

You now have two similar triangles: ABC and ADE. Bring them together. The angle of elevation is the same for both, an acute angle. Geometry tells us that in such triangles, the two corresponding sides in each will have the same proportion as the other two corresponding sides. Thus:

$$\frac{\overline{AB}}{\overline{AD}} = \frac{\overline{BC}}{\overline{DE}}$$

You have calculated every term in this equation except $\overline{DE}$. You can, however, solve for $\overline{DE}$ this way.

$$\overline{DE} = \frac{(\overline{AD})\,(\overline{BC})}{\overline{AB}}$$

If your ruler, line BC, is 1 foot long and its shadow, line AB, is 1.5 feet long, while the shadow of the roof, line AD, is 25 feet long, how high is the roof?

$$\overline{DE} = \frac{(25)\,(1)}{1.5} = \textbf{16.66 feet}$$

Shingles

The roof needs new shingles. How many will you buy? Wooden shingles are sold in bundles of random width, but on the average a bundle holds 250 shingles 4 inches wide. They come in lengths of 16, 18, and 24 inches with varying thicknesses in the butt end. A 16-inch shingle may have 4 inches, 4.5 inches, or 5 inches exposed to the weather. A 24-inch shingle may have 7.5 or 10 inches exposed. This vertical exposure multiplied by the average width of 4 inches gives the exposure area for one shingle.

A roof segment 10 feet by 10 feet in area is called a *square*. You can estimate the number of bundles needed to cover a square according to the exposure:

Exposure	4	4.5	5	6	7.5	10 (in inches)
Bundles per square	4	3.6	3.2	2.7	2.1	1.6

For your roof, which is 500 square feet in area, 5 squares will be covered. With a 10-inch exposure, the number of bundles required would be

$$(1.6) (5) = 8 \text{ bundles}$$

Concrete

Concrete has a number of ingredients—and purposes. The mixture can vary depending on the purpose.

Mix calculator

This mix calculator shows some of the different types of cement mix you might need for your yard.

Kind of mix	Bag weights	Coverage area
Mortar mix For joints between brick, stone, cinder and concrete blocks	20, 45, 80 pounds	80-pound bag provides for laying approximately 40 to 50 bricks or 15 to 20 blocks
Sand mix For filling cracks in cement walks, steps, stucco walls, foundations	11, 20, 40, 45, 80 pounds	80-pound bag will cover 8 square feet with 1-inch topping
Concrete mix For post collars, building steps, and walks	45, 90 pounds	90-pound bag will make $1\frac{2}{3}$ cubic feet or enough to cover 12 inch by 12 inch by 9 inch area
Waterproof mix For topcoat surfaces around pools, on walks and steps	45, 80 pounds	80-pound bag will cover 16 square feet with $1\frac{1}{2}$-inch topping

This mix makes about 4 cubic feet of concrete:

Cement	1 bag, or 1 cu. ft. (94 lb.)
Water	5.5 gal. (46 lb.)
Sand	2 cu. ft. (200 lb.)
Coarse aggregate	3 cu. ft. (260 lb.)

Coarse aggregate is made up of particles graded $\frac{1}{4}$ to $\frac{3}{4}$ inch in size.

Concrete is a great aid to the home repairperson. It is fireproof, watertight, and relatively inexpensive and easy to make. Your family shouldn't hesitate to make home improvements by using concrete for walkways, driveways, and other conveniences (and necessities). All you need is the desire, the right information, and a little math power.

Section

Kitchen Math

Need some food for thought? Learn some ways to use math in and around the kitchen, the subject of this section.

Kitchen math has practical advantages. Your family can cut food bills without sacrificing nourishment. Inexpensive food is not necessarily inferior food. Simple math can actually make your family's meals more nourishing. You can learn to figure calories, compute costs per unit (a key to savings on all kinds of foods), and even impress your family with your consumer know-how.

Sometimes no figuring is necessary. In food matters, a great deal of figuring has already been done for you, in tables, for example. Some important tables appear in this section, providing much useful information in limited space. You can even learn to make more tables yourself.

The first subsection shows you how to use math in shopping for food. You'll learn how to compare the prices of food, avoiding confusion and getting to the "bottom line" by applying the price-per-unit principle. With this approach, you can make a variety of comparisons: among brands, among sizes, among stores. You also find out how math can help you to buy good meat and minimize what you don't need—fat—or don't use—bone. This subsection further includes some tips on saving time and minimizing mistakes when using your handheld calculator to solve food problems.

A second subsection shows how math gives guidance in the storage and preparation of foods. The measures used and the methods of conversion from one standard of measurement to another become important. Math also helps you figure cooking times for different foods prepared under different conditions. That basic ingredient of many meals, the recipe, turns out to be our old mathematical friend, the ratio. It's easy to adjust recipes to suit different needs.

A final subsection applies math to nutrition. You can find the figures you need to keep your figure in shape. The same simple math used to count calories helps you find out whether you're getting enough basic nutrients.

Food Shopping as an Adventure

You are going on a supermarket expedition. You are concerned about your family's nutrition; everyone seems to be talking about saving money.

Observing and listening, you've learned things. You know that not every grocery "special" offers a real bargain and that you can save money by comparison shopping. Brand-name products usually cost more. Ready-to-use items are more expensive than do-it-yourself products. Buying in quantity can also save money.

You want to apply your basic math. You want to know *how much* of *what*. You want to stress economy and nutrition, the twin goals of most everyday food shopping.

Shopping by the unit

You can use math in economical food shopping in different ways. A basic one is to make accurate cost comparisons of food. For example, you want to know whether a particular size of food container is more economical than another size. The math underlying this kind of comparison can be extended to other comparisons, such as comparing brands or comparing stores. The math referred to here is the *cost-per-unit* approach.

For example, you want to buy a can of tomatoes. On the grocery shelf, you find an 8-ounce can selling for 40 cents. A 1-pound (16-oz.) can of the same brand

The shopping tour challenges your math, but it may be only the first step toward real savings on food.

costs 72 cents. Which is more economical? If you bought two 8-ounce cans you'd pay 80 cents. So you buy the larger can.

Comparison shopping can be difficult or easy. You can make it easier by following a few hints.

It's harder to shop economically for food when you are hungry. Experts say you're more likely to buy on impulse when your stomach is rumbling. So don't go into the supermarket when you are hungry.

Another hint is to decide ahead of time what you want to buy. Look for sales in the newspaper, especially during the middle of the week, when sales ebb and stores are trying to lure customers in. Most important, always make up a list of the things you plan to buy, with their cost. But stick to the list—no more, no less.

A sample shopping list shows what yours could look like. You know exactly how much you can expect to spend when you use the list, including the tax, if food is taxed in your area. (Sales tax rates and application vary from state to state. A common rate is 5%.)

Look at what is on the shopping list and how it is arranged. First, you know what you will buy. Second, you know exactly how much of each item you will buy. Third, you know how much is charged for one of each item. Fourth, you know how much you will pay for that item according to the quantity purchased. If you're shopping during a sale, you may want to note the sale and regular prices. Now you can add up your bill.

In drawing up your shopping list, you've done two kinds of calculations. First, you used multiplication or division to arrive at total cost for an item of food. Which type of calculation is used depends on how the item is sold. Green beans are priced at 2 cans for $1.00; but since you are buying only 1 can, you divide $1.00 by 2 (you could allow for a possibly higher single-unit price of 55¢ or more). The potatoes are sold by the pound, so you multiply the per-pound cost by the number of pounds. The apples are sold in 3-pound bags, so you pay by the bag. The second step (*see* far-right column in the illustration) is simple addition of costs for each food item.

A short grocery-shopping list.

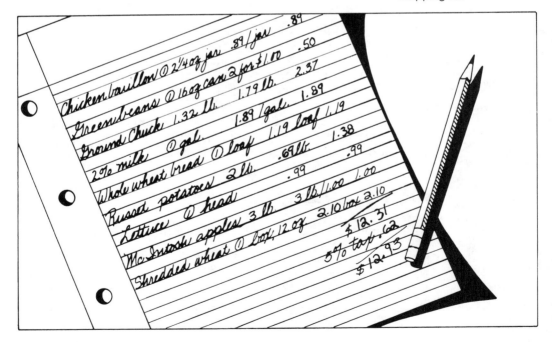

Units help you save

In making up your shopping list, you've taken a big step toward economy. But you may be in for some surprises once you arrive at the supermarket. You may want to adjust your list to reflect unexpected bargains.

In the earlier example, all you had to do was double (8 oz. × 2) to find out which can of tomatoes was the best buy on the shelf. But suppose you see a 15-ounce can of peaches of Brand A selling for 75¢. Then you see a 20-ounce can of Brand B for 90¢. The arithmetic is trickier. You divide the cost by the number of ounces. The 15-ounce can costs

$$\frac{75¢}{15 \text{ oz.}} = 5¢/oz.$$

Figuring the same way, you find the 20-ounce can costs

$$\frac{90¢}{20 \text{ oz.}} = 4.5¢/oz.$$

Clearly, the 20-ounce can is the better buy because you are receiving more for your money. You are paying more, for more.

Using units systematically

Many supermarkets today show the cost per unit already calculated (by law in most states). That saves you some math work. Whether you have to calculate them or not, you can use the per-unit information to discover some additional facts about foods on the shelf.

Why compare only two brands and two sizes of containers, as was done here? You can easily prepare a table listing an array of different sizes and brands all at once.

Brand of tomato juice	Size			
	5½ ounces	12 ounces	18 ounces	46 ounces
A	$1.15/qt.	$1.12/qt.	80.1¢/qt.	68.9¢/qt.
B	$1.12/qt.	$1.15/qt.	81.9¢/qt.	68.9¢/qt.
C	$1.33/qt.	$1.26/qt.	87.1¢/qt.	74.4¢/qt.

What kinds of information could you learn from such a table? First, the larger the container, the lower the per-unit cost, whatever the brand. Also, throughout the size range, one particular brand has a higher per-unit cost than the other brands. Finally, one brand has a lower per-unit cost in one size, while a second brand leads in another.

After compiling such a table, you simply scan it until you have found the lowest figure. But you can take your figuring one step further, by compiling a table for each store or chain. Then you find the cheapest combination of brand and size at each store. From this list, you can pick the one cheapest combination of brand, size, and store.

Usually, *generics,* products with no brand shown, have the lowest per-unit costs, followed by store brands. National brands generally cost more. But don't forget quality and preference. Even if one brand is less expensive, you may not like it. The taste may not be what you want, or the brand may contain too much of some ingredient you don't care for (more on finding out about ingredients later in this section). You needn't buy that item.

Beefing up your larder

Math works quite well when you're shopping for meats. To save dollars and cents most simply, you can calculate per-unit costs by minimizing unwanted waste ingredients.

You love hamburgers. But did you know that ground beef contains much fat? You want, wisely, to avoid fat. You're also paying more for fatty ground beef than you need to. With leaner meat you can enjoy a cheaper, better burger.

Commercially ground beef has a fat content that may range from 20 to 30 percent. In the supermarket meat department, you may see ground beef marked as 70 percent lean (30% fat), 75 percent lean (25% fat), or 80 percent lean (20% fat). You are paying for fat every time you buy ground beef. Even lean supermarket-ground beef (80% lean) has much fat.

Let's say you've been buying 80 percent lean ground beef at $1.55 per pound. You chose the leaner (but more expensive) meat because you want to cut down on fat in your diet.

Now consider this. Every time you cook yourself a hamburger made of 80 percent lean ground beef, most of the 20 percent fat runs off. For every pound of raw hamburger meat that you put in the skillet, a little more than 80 percent, or .8 pound, remains as cooked meat. If that pound of raw meat costs $1.55, the portion that remains as cooked meat is about

$$80\% \times \$1.55 = \$1.24$$

So you have lost about 31¢ ($1.55 − 1.24 = $.31) of your investment, or about 20 percent.

Now you want to know how much you are actually paying for one pound of *cooked* ground beef derived from 80 percent lean beef. This "yield" is found by using proportions.

1. You know that 80 percent of every pound is lean meat, giving you .8 pound. You want to figure 100 percent cooked meat in each pound, or 1.0 pound.

    So you have the ratio $\frac{.8}{1.0}$.

2. Similarly, you spend $1.55 for each pound of 80 percent ground beef, giving $1.55. You want to find the cost, *x*, for a pound of 100 percent cooked beef.

    So you have the ratio $\frac{\$1.55}{x}$.

3. These two ratios can be set into a new proportion:

    $$\frac{.8}{1} = \frac{\$1.55}{x}$$

4. Now solve the proportion:

    $.8x = \$1.55$; so $x = \$1.94$

    for a pound of cooked beef. So you're actually spending 39¢ more a pound ($1.94 − $1.55 = $.39) than you thought for lean beef. That comes to 25.1 percent extra. (Divide the excess cost, 39¢, by the base cost, $1.55, to get 25.1%.)

Notwithstanding these figures, ground beef with more fat is usually still a better bargain in dollars and cents, though not in terms of your waistline and health. Work the problem through in the way just shown, using the prices of two grades of ground beef from your own store to see which is a better bargain for you. Sales or specials may change the relationships at different times.

The Coupon Saver

A veteran (13-year-old) coupon saver has confessed that she saved 10 or 15 to 50 percent of her family's monthly grocery bill. How did she do it? "I used simple math and some common sense," she noted. "I took on the job of coupon keeper for the family. Now they collect coupons for me." Some of her secrets follow.

—Clip and collect all coupons, even those you don't plan to use. You can probably trade those with friends or "coupon club" members for other, more useful ones.

—Keep a simple file for all coupons, organized by grocery category, and all mail-in forms or combination mail-in and cents-off coupons. Keep a master list by the month in which the coupons expire.

—Subscribe to several coupon-carrying magazines, usually those dealing with home and family life. The coupons more than pay for the subscriptions; you can subscribe to some through discount services.

—Set up a cardboard carton file, by category again, for proofs of purchase (POPs), including labels, code numbers, hang tags, and cash register receipts, so that you have them and can produce them when needed. Don't forget to keep (and mail) mail-in refund blanks, organized by month.

—While checking food ads, pull out of your file the coupons you will want to take to the store. Attach these coupons to the grocery list.

—Once organized for the shopping junket, get your tools together, at least a working pen or pencil and a pad of paper, in addition to coupons.

—Check, using addition and subtraction, to make certain you got full value from your coupons at the checkout.

There are cheap and tasty alternatives to buying ground beef. But you need to know how much you are wasting, and how to save. Here's one alternative. Buy a roast, take the bone out, and grind the meat yourself (or have the butcher do so).

Let's say you buy a chuck roast on sale at $1.10 a pound. If $\frac{1}{4}$ of this is bone and fat that are trimmed away, the actual cost per pound is figured by ratios as above, $\frac{.75}{1} = \frac{\$1.1}{x}$, so that $x = \$1.47$ per pound. That's still 47¢ a pound less than the actual cost for store-ground beef. But more than that, it tastes better.

One caution you should keep in mind if you're grinding your own meat is that fat adds texture and flavor. If you buy a round steak and trim away all the fat, the remaining meat when ground and cooked may be dry and flat tasting. Chuck roast, which is more marbled with fat, will do better when cooked with all excess fat trimmed, but it will be higher in calories per ounce.

Do you need a breakdown of the fat content of various meats? A table can help in both cost cutting and ensuring healthful eating.

Beef, raw	Veal, raw	Lamb, raw	Pork, raw
Round, 12%	Chuck, 13%	Leg, 21%	Loin, 28%
Chuck, 20%	Loin, 11%	Loin chops, 32%	Ham, 29%
Sirloin, 27%	Round, 9%		Spareribs, 33%
Rib roast, 43%			Sausage, 51% average
Porterhouse, 36%			Bacon, 55–70%
Hamburger, 20–30%			

Calculator Shortcuts

Your calculator has a decimal point key. You can use it to mark off dollars from cents. But in adding figures, as you would when totaling your shopping list prices, it should be clear where the point goes without actually entering the point. That eliminates one operation in each entry.

Adding a column of, say, nine figures, you can eliminate nine operations right away. If you are adding up for the shopping list on page 673, your entries would be 89, 50, 237, 189, 119, 138, 99, 100, and 210. These total 1231. Then comes the tax, 62, and the grand total of 1293 ($12.93).

Incidentally, you can figure a 5 percent sales tax quickly in your head because 5 percent is half of 10 percent. You quickly get 10 percent of 1231 by showing the decimal point: 123.1. For dollars and cents, round up to the whole penny: $1.24. To get 5 percent, divide that by 2 to get 62¢. So 62 is added to 1231 for the total.

Where a few cents are involved, you can simplify the addition still more, ending with an estimate rather than an exact total. But see how close it is. You round each cents entry to the nearest 10. So 33¢ becomes 30¢, and $2.37 becomes $2.40, or, rather, 240. You have nothing but zeroes in the ones column. You don't have to add a bunch of zeroes, so eliminate them. Now you have a maximum of two digits to add for each entry. Try it. What total do you get before the tax?

You should have gotten a total of 106. If you add a zero, you have 1060, or $10.60—a very close estimate. The tax still comes out to 53¢, for a total estimate of $11.13.

The preparation and storage of food add up to a timely and weighty topic. It's timely because cooking times lead into the kinds of math figuring that are essential to proper preparation. The topic is "weighty" because you can't go very far in the kitchen without knowing the various measures of weight and volume or ways of converting from one measure to another.

Weights and measures require some study. Only a few have been touched on so far. That's partly because fewer measures are used in the packaging of foods than in their preparation. The basic ideas of the subsection on shopping apply here as well, however.

Talking the language of weights and measures, you can deal with almost any problem in the kitchen. It's especially important in nutrition, where the units are typically metric.

Food Preparation and Storage

Kitchen weights and measures

Food involves small numbers. One reason is that with food, your family is usually dealing with daily needs. You don't, for instance, talk about thousands of pounds of food needed over a period of several years. You're concerned with a few pounds of steak for that family barbecue next Sunday. Even in preserving foods, you are generally talking about a few quarts or gallons in a batch.

Kitchen numbers are small, too, because the units used make it so. If you want a quart of something, you measure it as a quart and not in teaspoons. You could figure the number of teaspoons of liquid in a quart, but why bother?

Measuring volume

Volume represents the kind of measurement most often used in the kitchen. The various units of volume range in size from the grain to the gallon. You can go from one measure to another. Here are some of the ways.

This is (are) equal to	this
a few grains	less than $\frac{1}{8}$ teaspoon (tsp.)
3 teaspoons (tsp.)	1 tablespoon (tbs.)
4 tablespoons (tbs.)	$\frac{1}{4}$ cup (c.)
5 tbs. plus 1 tsp.	$\frac{1}{3}$ cup
8 ounces (oz.) (liquid)	1 cup
1 cup	$\frac{1}{2}$ pint (pt.)
4 cups	1 quart (qt.)
2 pints	1 quart
4 quarts	1 gallon

These equivalents come in handy. Let's say you want to try a recipe that normally serves 12 persons, but you want to make only enough for your family of 3. That means you need only $\frac{1}{4}$ as much as the recipe calls for: you need only $\frac{1}{4}$ as much of each ingredient.

Your recipe calls for $\frac{1}{4}$ cup of vegetable oil. To adjust it to your needs, you calculate that you need $\frac{1}{4}$ of that amount, or $\frac{1}{4} \times \frac{1}{4} = \frac{1}{16}$ cup. But looking at your measuring cup, you notice that it is marked off in $\frac{1}{4}$-cup and 1-ounce intervals. You could try to guess with the naked eye, but you decide that you want to be precise.

What accurate measure will give you the equivalent of $\frac{1}{16}$ cup? You see that 4 tablespoons equal $\frac{1}{4}$ cup, so 1 tablespoon will give you what you need in order to adjust the recipe to 3 servings.

Suppose you are giving an ice-cream party for 9 friends. If you estimate that $\frac{1}{2}$ pint will feed each person, and you have a total of 10 persons including yourself, how much ice cream will you need? You can find the answer in pints for starters: 10 persons $\times \frac{1}{2}$ pint = 5 pints. You know that 2 pints equal 1 quart, so you'll need $2\frac{1}{2}$ quarts. You use a conversion factor to get from pints to quarts: 1 quart/2 pints. Multiplying 5 pints by this factor gives $2\frac{1}{2}$ quarts. You decide to get 3 quarts, each a different flavor, to be safe.

Measuring weight

When measuring weight, all you need to know is that 16 ounces equal 1 pound. Only remember that the ounce used to measure weight is not the same as the ounce used to measure volume.

You've already encountered ounces in the supermarket. If you buy a box of hot wheat cereal weighing 1 pound 12 ounces and costing $1.57, what is the cost per ounce? Since 1 pound equals 16 ounces, you have a total of $12 + 16 = 28$ ounces. So the cost per ounce is

$$\frac{1.57}{28 \text{ ounces}} = 5.6 \text{ cents per ounce } (\text{¢/oz.})$$

Kitchen metric

If you're using metric units of measurement, computations are still simple. Metric works in 10s or multiples of 10. A deciliter is $\frac{1}{10}$ liter, a milliliter is $\frac{1}{1000}$ liter. A milligram is $\frac{1}{1000}$ gram.

Using metric measures for cooking seems harder at first only because you are unfamiliar with them. You have a sense of how large a quart of milk is, but how about a liter of milk? (A liter is a little more than a quart.) As you use metric measurements in the kitchen and get acquainted with their conversions, you will learn the metric sizes of familiar items.

For a recipe, do you need to convert to (or from) familiar measures from (or to) metric? The following *conversion factors* should simplify that task. (For more conversions, *also see* Pt. VI, "Math Tables.")

To convert	multiply	by
ounces to grams	the ounces	28
grams to ounces	the grams	0.035
liters to quarts	the liters	1.06
quarts to liters	the quarts	0.95
inches to centimeters	the inches	2.5
centimeters to inches	the centimeters	0.4

To round off the conversions between customary and metric measures, you can use the table of equivalencies of cups and deciliters on the next page.

Cups	Deciliters	Cups	Deciliters
$\frac{1}{4}$	0.59	$1\frac{1}{4}$	2.96
$\frac{1}{3}$	0.79	$1\frac{1}{3}$	3.15
$\frac{1}{2}$	1.18	$1\frac{1}{2}$	3.55
$\frac{2}{3}$	1.58	$1\frac{2}{3}$	3.94
$\frac{3}{4}$	1.78	$1\frac{3}{4}$	4.14
1	2.37	2	4.73

Now you can make any kitchen conversions you need. Say you are using the recipe that you earlier adjusted to a group of 3. Recall that you needed $\frac{1}{16}$ cup of oil. How much is $\frac{1}{16}$ cup in metric? From this table you learn that $\frac{1}{4}$ cup is .59 deciliters. You need $\frac{1}{4}$ of that amount, so $\frac{1}{4} \times .59 = .15$ deciliter. This is easily converted to milliliters. If a deciliter is $\frac{1}{10}$ liter and a milliliter is $\frac{1}{1000}$ liter, a milliliter is $\frac{1}{100}$ deciliter. So if you're using a unit $\frac{1}{100}$ the size, you should be using 100 times as many of those units.

100 milliliters/deciliter $\times$ .15 deciliter
= 15 milliliters

Freezing and canning

Math can help you take some "measures" to help keep your food safe to eat while maintaining its nutritive value. Very few foods can be stored for long periods without losing their quality. Onions, potatoes, sweet potatoes, and some squash are examples of the kinds of vegetables that can be stored successfully for months in a cool room. Most other vegetables deteriorate after only a few days in the refrigerator. Meats and dairy products are also highly perishable.

Various methods of *preservation* are available. With some of them, math can be your guide. For example, when canning you can calculate how much preserved food you can obtain from your raw supplies. Temperature calculation is also an important factor in ensuring safe canning results. Freezing is a good method of food preservation. By knowing the storage times for different frozen foods, you can organize your freezer for maximum efficiency.

Can you can it?

Canning has to be done at a specified high temperature. Very high temperatures destroy bacteria. That is why most foods, when canned properly, can be kept for relatively long periods.

If you decide to can, you will need to know how much canned food will result from a given quantity of fresh food. The table that follows shows how to convert from fresh food quantities to canned food quantities.

Canning has special advantages. One is that large quantities of a particular food can be processed, then stored at room temperature. Suppose you don't want to can a large amount of food, but you've decided to experiment. You bought only a 3-pound bag of McIntosh apples and you want to preserve them. What quantity of canned apples will you obtain?

Conversions, fresh to canned foods

Food	Fresh	Canned
Fruit		
Apples	1 bu. (48 lb.)	16 to 20 qt.
Apricots	1 bu. (50 lb.)	20 to 24 qt.
Berries, except strawberries	24-qt. crate	12 to 18 qt.
Cherries, as picked	1 bu. (56 lb.)	22 to 32 qt.
Peaches	1 bu. (48 lb.)	18 to 24 qt.
Pears	1 bu. (50 lb.)	20 to 25 qt.
Plums	1 bu. (56 lb.)	24 to 30 qt.
Strawberries	24-qt. crate	12 to 16 qt.
Vegetables		
Asparagus	1 bu. (45 lb.)	11 qt.
Beans, lima, in pods	1 bu. (32 lb.)	6 to 8 qt.
Beans, snap	1 bu. (30 lb.)	15 to 20 qt.
Beets, without tops	1 bu. (52 lb.)	17 to 20 qt.
Carrots, without tops	1 bu. (50 lb.)	16 to 20 qt.
Corn, sweet, in husks	1 bu. (35 lb.)	8 to 9 qt.
Okra	1 bu. (26 lb.)	17 qt.
Peas, green, in pods	1 bu. (30 lb.)	12 to 15 qt.
Pumpkin	50 lb.	15 qt.
Spinach	1 bu. (18 lb.)	6 to 9 qt.
Squash, summer	1 bu. (40 lb.)	16 to 20 qt.
Sweet Potatoes	1 bu. (55 lb.)	18 to 22 qt.
Tomatoes	1 bu. (53 lb.)	15 to 20 qt.

You note on the chart that 48 pounds of apples will yield 16 to 20 quarts of the canned fruit. You are using

3 pounds of apples. That is a fraction of the 48 pounds in the table. To be precise, that is

$$\frac{3 \text{ pounds}}{48 \text{ pounds}} = \frac{1}{16}$$

as much. Multiplying that fraction by the quantity in the table gives you the answer. The minimum quantity you will have is

$$\frac{1}{16} \times 16 = 1 \text{ quart}$$

The maximum is

$$\frac{1}{16} \times 20 = 1\frac{1}{4} \text{ quarts}$$

Frozen foods

You can preserve meat, of course, by freezing. Other ways include dehydration through exposure to heat or cold. If a separate freezer or the freezer compartment of your refrigerator is the only one of these methods available to you, it's important to know how long different meats will keep. Chicken and turkey will last up to 12 months. Beef and lamb roasts will keep for 8 to 12 months, pork and veal roasts for 4 to 8 months. Chops and organ meats last 3 to 4 months, ground and stew meats 2 to 3 months. Cooked poultry lasts up to 6 months, while cooked meat dishes last 2 to 3 months.

Periodically, make sure you check the temperature of your freezer (and refrigerator, for short-term storage). A good freezer temperature is 0°F (−18°C). (For refrigerators, 30° to 40°F. [−1°C to 4°C] is a good average.) There are special, inexpensive thermometers for sale at hardware and grocery stores that are designed for refrigerators/freezers. But other thermometers can also be adapted to this use.

If the temperature starts to climb, you are risking food spoilage. Fixing the appliance may prove less expensive than losing your frozen foods (at worst) or decreasing the amount of time you can count on them to remain preserved (which you can only guess, at best). When you freeze meat, carefully wrap it so that it is as airtight as possible, then mark what it is and the date on which it was frozen. One more bit of information belongs on the package, the date beyond which the

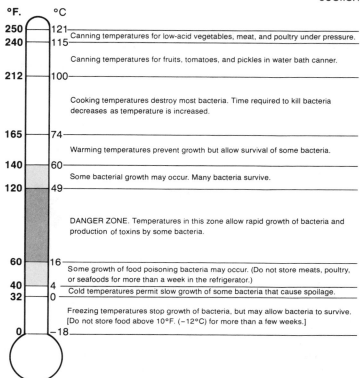

The effects of different temperatures on bacteria.

°F.   °C

250 — 121
240 — 115 Canning temperatures for low-acid vegetables, meat, and poultry under pressure.

Canning temperatures for fruits, tomatoes, and pickles in water bath canner.

212 — 100

Cooking temperatures destroy most bacteria. Time required to kill bacteria decreases as temperature is increased.

165 — 74

Warming temperatures prevent growth but allow survival of some bacteria.

140 — 60

Some bacterial growth may occur. Many bacteria survive.

120 — 49

DANGER ZONE. Temperatures in this zone allow rapid growth of bacteria and production of toxins by some bacteria.

60 — 16
Some growth of food poisoning bacteria may occur. (Do not store meats, poultry, or seafoods for more than a week in the refrigerator.)

40 — 4
32 — 0 Cold temperatures permit slow growth of some bacteria that cause spoilage.

Freezing temperatures stop growth of bacteria, but may allow bacteria to survive. [Do not store food above 10°F. (−12°C) for more than a few weeks.]

0 — −18

meat may begin to spoil. Meats should be arranged according to this date. Meats about to end their "keeping" period should be at the top of the freezer or at the front of the freezing compartment so they will be seen and eaten.

Here's a math insight on how to freeze the ground beef that you've just learned how to buy on a yield basis. Did you ever notice how a frozen package of ground beef thaws from the outside in? The core always thaws last. That portion may take a long time to thaw, depending on how thick the package of meat is. How do you speed up the process? Suppose you want to thaw the hamburger meat as quickly as possible. Then the best shape to freeze it in is that of a donut. Many meat shops or departments sell prepackaged ground beef in a donut shape.

Math gives you two reasons for using this shape. First, the amount of surface area exposed to the air is greater in a donut shape than in a solid. The hole in the center creates some added area, with warmer room air striking the meat on both the "outside" and the "inside." The second reason is that the distance from the outside surface to the core is shorter.

Meat storage periods

Product	Refrigerator 30°–40°F.* days	Freezer 0°F.** months
Fresh meats		
Chops (lamb and pork)	3–5	3–4
Ground and stew meats	1–2	2–3
Roasts (beef and lamb)	3–5	8–12
Roasts (pork and veal)	3–5	4–8
Sausage (pork)	1–2	1–2
Steaks (beef)	3–5	8–12
Variety meats	1–2	3–4
Processed meats		
Frankfurters	7	1–2
Ham (half)	3–5	1–2
Ham (slices)	3	1–2
Ham (whole)	7	1–2
Luncheon meats	3–5	Freezing
Sausage (dry)	14–21	not
Sausage (smoked)	7	recommended
Cooked meats		
Cooked meats and meat dishes	1–2	2–3
Gravy and meat broth	1–2	2–3
Fresh poultry		
Chicken and turkey	1–2	12
Duck and goose	1–2	6
Giblets	1–2	3
Cooked poultry		
Cooked poultry dishes	1–2	6
Fried chicken	1–2	4
Pieces (covered with broth)	1–2	6
Pieces (not covered)	1–2	1

* –1°C to 4°C
** –18°C

Ground beef in a donut shape thaws faster. Notice how the donut shape shortens the distance to the core *(R)*.

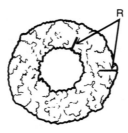 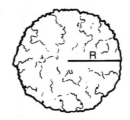

Can you think of some other shapes that might help to thaw meat and other frozen foods efficiently? How about arranging vegetables such as beans in single layers between sheets of wax paper, rather than freezing the beans in a lump? This is the quickest way to freeze many fruits, too, preserving texture and flavor. Once frozen, store in convenient bags or boxes.

Cooking by the numbers

Time and *temperature* are two measures that figure both in preserving foods and in cooking. Common sense tells you that the higher the cooking temperature, the less time you have to spend in cooking something, whether it's a steak or a bowl of hot cereal.

Very often, either the time or temperature or both are fixed for a particular dish. Then other factors come into play, notably the sizes of portions. In some cases, for example, meats, the portion size affects cooking time. In cooking cereals, however, you can ignore portion size. All you have to worry about is making sure you have the right proportions.

Roasting and broiling meats

You're grilling a hamburger. You know that the thicker the burger is, the longer you have to grill it. If you take that thick burger and flatten it out, what happens? It takes less time to cook. You have plenty of heat throughout the skillet surface to cook the whole hamburger. Each square inch of meat receives the same amount of heat, regardless of the burger's diameter.

Thickness, then, affects cooking time in meats. Heat must penetrate the surface of the meat before reaching the core. In cooking vegetables, you don't usually have a weight/time problem. That's because most vegetables are not a solid slab like meat but come in smaller units or pieces. A larger pot of water takes more time to heat up than a smaller pot, obviously, but the actual cooking time should be the same with any size of pot or pan.

Microwave cooking is faster for both meats and vegetables. Microwaves can penetrate $\frac{3}{4}$ inch instantly. You will learn more about microwave cooking in the next subsection.

Generally, the heavier the piece of meat, the thicker it is. That means more cooking time. In any reliable, general cookbook, you can find thorough timetables for cooking beef. Use these tables to calculate how long your favorite cuts will take to cook. The partial tables here demonstrate how cooking times depend on the cut, the size, and the way you prepare the beef.

Timetable for roasting beef

Cut	Weight (lb.)	Oven temperature	Time*
Standing rib	4–6	325°F.**	23–35
Rolled rib	5–7	325°F.**	32–48
Delmonico	4–6	350°F.†	18–24
Tenderloin, whole	4–6	425°F.‡	45–60
Tenderloin, half	2–3	425°F.‡	45–50
Rolled rump	4–6	325°F.**	25–30
Sirloin tip	3.5–4	325°F.**	35–40
Standing rump	5–7	325°F.**	25–30

*Approximate, in minutes per pound.
**163°C
†177°C
‡218°C

Suppose you want to cook a standing rib roast weighing 5 pounds. How long will it take? The table shows a range of 4 to 6 pounds for standing rib. You will use an oven set at 325°F. (163°C). You like your meat quite rare, so your cooking time will be 23 minutes per pound. Since the meat weighs 5 pounds, the total cooking time is

$$\text{5 pounds} \times \text{23 minutes/pound} = \text{115 minutes}$$
$$= \text{1 hour and}$$
$$\text{55 minutes}$$

Remember that these cooking times are approximate. You should check your results by using a meat thermometer. That way you can tell when the meat is done the way you want it.

Now let's say you want to broil a steak. Better yet, you are broiling that steak for tonight's meal at the same time you are preparing a rib roast for tomorrow's picnic. Why is that better? Because, provided your type of range allows it, you're using the same energy to fix more food. The next table shows approximate cooking times for different kinds of steak. Note that

Timetable for broiling beef

Cut	Thickness (in.)	Weight (lb.)	Time*
Chuck steak	1.5	2–4	40–50
Club steak	1.5	1.5–2	25–35
Delmonico steak	2	1	35–55
Beef patties	1	.25	15–35
Porterhouse steak	1.5	2–3	30–40
Rib steak	1.5	1.5–2	25–35
Sirloin steak	2	3–5	40–50
T-bone steak	1.5	2–3	18–25

Editor's Note: The times are estimated at 350°F. (177°C) in a preheated broiler. Thicker steaks need 25–50% more broiling time than shown on chart.
*Approximate, in minutes, rare to well-done

the broiler can be set at a moderate 350°F. (177°C) rather than at the "Broil" setting. You'll need more time, but that's okay. The temperature is almost the same as for cooking the roast.

If you want to fix a Delmonico steak that is 2 inches thick, how long will it take? Remember you like it rare, so it should take 35 minutes at 350°. If you are cooking the steak and the roast at the same time, you will use a setting of 325°. The roast takes priority because it has a longer cooking time, and you don't want to overcook it.

The table doesn't give an exact way to adjust for the lower oven setting. So, allow an extra 10 minutes (a total of 45 minutes) for cooking if needed and make a test cut.

If you want to serve dinner at 7 P.M., at what times should you start cooking the roast and the steak? The roast takes 1 hour and 55 minutes. Now subtract that amount from 7 P.M. The answer is 5:05. And the steak? For 45 minutes of cooking time, you can pop it into the broiler around 6:15 P.M.

What about microwave?

Microwave ovens offer a cheaper way to cook. With this kind of oven, you are cooking food not by heat but by the use of special radio waves that make the food molecules vibrate. What does this mean? You can forget the rules for roasting and broiling times above. Microwaving is wholly different.

If it's not temperature that affects microwave cooking times, then what does? It's the amount of power behind the radio waves. You can make a rough translation from percentages of power to the more familiar settings on conventional ranges.

Percentage of power	Conventional settings
100	High
70	Medium High, or Roast
50	Medium, or Simmer
30	Medium Low, Low, or Defrost
10	Low, or Warm

A good microwave recipe should include the power setting just as an ordinary recipe should specify the temperature. Another unconventional aspect of microwaves is cooking time. An amount of food that is twice the volume of another batch of the same food will take twice as long to cook. It doesn't matter what kind of food it is. Two potatoes take twice as long to bake as one, a 3-pound steak twice as long as a 1½-pound steak. Note that the food molecules become so excited that food continues to cook for a while after being taken out of the oven. So it's better to undercook than to overcook.

Math's Role in Nutrition

You are what you eat, and math can help your family eat more wisely. Math not only helps you determine whether you are getting the proper nutrition, it can help ensure that you stay well nourished or help your family correct flaws in your diet. Once again, tables are useful for basic, valuable information.

Providing the proper nutrition involves math in two basic ways. First, you use math to determine what your individual needs are. No two people are alike. Each person differs from every other because of age, sex, height, weight, and other characteristics. Some factors affect nutritional needs more than others. For instance, protein requirements change with a person's age, and certain mineral needs are determined by one's sex. Another way math helps is in determining the nutrition available from different foods and finding out how much of each food will meet your needs.

In all of these calculations, tables help. But the tables can't by themselves tell you what you need to know. *You* have to use math to combine the facts from different tables.

Nutrition needs fall under two main headings: (1) proteins, fats, and carbohydrates; and (2) vitamins and minerals. Usually, more food is needed to supply the first group than the second. Protein is the body's essential element, while fat appears in greater or smaller amounts in various parts of the body. Carbohydrates are a main supply of energy.

Vitamins and minerals perform important functions in the body. Not everyone agrees on how much of each of these substances is needed. Some believe that large amounts of some vitamins can cure certain illnesses. But it's also true that excess amounts of some can be harmful. You can avoid such issues by concentrating on the amounts documented to be the minimum needed for good health.

RDAs

The National Research Council periodically develops a list of *recommended dietary allowances,* or RDAs. The list has been revised eight times, reflecting additions to the understanding of what constitutes a balanced diet.

The allowances assume that the user is healthy and is not taking medications, which can affect how well the body is able to use essential nutrients. If you are taking medicine, you should consult your doctor to determine your special needs. This also applies if you have a chronic condition that could affect your body's efficient use of nutrients.

What are your RDAs?

Most persons can follow general RDA guidelines. The RDAs are adjusted for age and sex. The table on the following page shows RDAs for infants and children and for males and females of different ages.

Can you read the table? For example, a 14-year-old boy weighing about 99 pounds would need 2,700 calories, 45 grams of protein, 1,200 milligrams of calcium, 18 milligrams of iron, and so on across the table. A young man of 21 needs more calories (2,900), more protein (56 g), but less calcium (800 mg), and consider-

Recommended daily allowances of some chief food elements

	Age	Weight In lb.	In kg	Calories	Protein (g)	Calcium (mg)	Iron (mg)
Children	1–3	29	13	1,300	23	800	15
	4–6	44	20	1,700	30	800	10
	7–10	62	28	2,400	34	800	10
Males	11–14	99	45	2,700	45	1,200	18
	15–18	145	66	2,800	56	1,200	18
	19–22	154	70	2,900	56	800	10
	23–50	154	70	2,700	56	800	10
	51+	154	70	2,400	56	800	10
Females	11–14	101	46	2,200	46	1,200	18
	15–18	120	55	2,100	46	1,200	18
	19–22	120	55	2,100	44	800	18
	23–50	120	55	2,000	44	800	18
	51+	120	55	1,800	44	1,200	10

lb. = pounds;   kg = kilograms;   g = grams;   mg = milligrams;   mcg = micrograms;   R.E. = retinol equivalents;
N.E. = niacin equivalents
Above figures intended for normally active persons in a temperate climate.
Source: *Recommended Dietary Allowances*, Ninth Ed., 1980. Food and Nutrition Board, National Academy of Sciences.

ably less iron (10 mg). The vitamin and mineral requirements vary between ages 14 and 21.

On the other hand, a 14-year-old girl needs fewer calories, though more protein, than a boy the same age. How do vitamin requirements compare between these two groups? A girl requires less vitamin A (800 mcg as opposed to 1,000 mcg), the same amounts of vitamins C and D, less thiamine (1.1 mg versus 1.4 mg), less riboflavin (1.3 mg as opposed to 1.6 mg), and less niacin (15 mg instead of 18 mg) than a boy the same age. Notice that some vitamin requirements are in trace amounts—micrograms rather than milligrams.

The "big" foods

Protein, fat, and carbohydrate elements have different patterns of composition. Yet the three share a common basis for measurement: *calories*. Anyone who has been on a calorie-reducing diet knows that unit of measurement well. You can keep track of the calories in your food as a total number. You can also specify how many protein calories, fat calories, and carbohydrate calories you are taking in.

Vitamins					
A (mcg R.E.)	**C (mg)**	**D (mcg)**	**Thiamine (mg)**	**Riboflavin (mg)**	**Niacin (mg N.E.)**
400	45	10.0	0.7	0.8	9
500	45	10.0	0.9	1.0	11
700	45	10.0	1.2	1.4	16
1,000	50	10.0	1.4	1.6	18
1,000	60	10.0	1.4	1.7	18
1,000	60	7.5	1.5	1.7	19
1,000	60	5.0	1.4	1.6	18
1,000	60	5.0	1.2	1.4	16
800	50	10.0	1.1	1.3	15
800	60	10.0	1.1	1.3	14
800	60	7.5	1.1	1.3	14
800	60	5.0	1.0	1.2	13
800	60	5.0	1.0	1.2	13

Opinions differ on what the proper proportions of these three food elements should be. Total calories, or the *calorie count,* however, remains a useful measure of the total amount of energy you take in each day.

How much energy do you need?

Your daily energy needs, just like your RDAs, change with age. They also differ according to your sex. These variations are shown in the table.

Let's say that you are a 14-year-old girl. Can you find your energy requirements? The table on the next page shows these in *kilocalories* (kcal), with a range for each grouping. That range is affected by weight, height, and amount of activity. The heavier and more active you are, the more energy you need in food form.

Assume that your weight is about the *mean* for your age group. Assume too that you are about as active as most young persons your age. That means that half are more active than you and half are less active. Your daily energy needs are about 2,200 kcal. This means that you need to take in 2,200 kcal daily to supply your energy needs.

You don't really need to take in anything in excess of 2,200 kcal. What happens if you do eat a little extra? It turns to fat. You can even tell how much fat it will turn to. The formula for converting energy into fat

Recommended energy intake

Category	Age (years)	Weight (lb.)	Height (in.)	Energy needs (kcal)	Range
Infants	0.0–0.5	13	24	690	570–870
	0.5–1.0	20	28	945	720–1,215
Children	1–3	29	35	1,300	900–1,800
	4–6	44	44	1,700	1,300–2,300
	7–10	62	52	2,400	1,650–3,300
Males	11–14	99	62	2,700	2,000–3,700
	15–18	145	69	2,800	2,100–3,900
	19–22	154	70	2,900	2,500–3,300
	23–50	154	70	2,700	2,300–3,100
	51–75	154	70	2,400	2,000–2,800
	76+	154	70	2,050	1,650–2,450
Females	11–14	101	62	2,200	1,500–3,000
	15–18	120	64	2,100	1,200–3,000
	19–22	120	64	2,100	1,700–2,500
	23–50	120	64	2,000	1,600–2,400
	51–75	120	64	1,800	1,400–2,200
	76+	120	64	1,600	1,200–2,000
Pregnancy				+300	
Lactation				+500	

is 3,500 kcal = 1 pound. That is, every time excess energy intake totals 3,500 kcal, that represents 1 pound gained.

You have a male friend your age who eats 3,000 kcal a day on the average. How long will it take for him to gain 10 pounds? Assuming his energy need is 2,700 kcal/day, his intake of 3,000 kcal/day means an excess of 300 kcal/day. You divide

$$\frac{3{,}500 \text{ kcal/lb.}}{300 \text{ kcal/day}} = 11.67 \text{ days/lb.}$$

It will take about $11\frac{2}{3}$ days to gain 1 pound. To gain 10 pounds, it will take 116.7 days, or about 3 months and 27 days. That weight gain sneaks up slowly. But weight losses can also be achieved gradually—and with minimum discomfort. That's better than a crash diet any time.

Your nutrition audit

Are you meeting your energy requirements? If you are typical, the chances are that the answer to that question is yes. If you're not sure you are fulfilling your requirements, you can conduct an energy audit on yourself as part of your nutrition audit. Using tables and nutrition labels from food packages, estimate the calories you've taken in on your sample day. Then total up the calories just as you totaled up the RDAs.

Caloric values

	Total calories	Carbohydrate calories	Protein calories	Fat calories
Banana	86	80	4	2
Butter	717	2	3	712
Fryer chicken, light				
meat without skin	102	0	88	14
Potato	78	69	8	1
Round steak,				
separable lean	135	0	92	42
Shrimp	91	6	77	7
Sugar	385	385	0	0
Wheat flour, all-				
purpose,				
enriched	364	301	40	8

Editor's note: Calories are based on a 3.5-ounce edible portion.

As you become conscious of the foods you eat, you can also note something besides the numbers of calories in them. That other item, *caloric density,* is the concentration of calories relative to the volume of food in which they are found. As an example, refined sugar has high caloric density. A piece of fruit has low caloric density because of the fruit sugar, abundance of water, and fiber. But fruit juice has higher caloric density than the fruit because the fiber, or pulp, has been removed. Can you think of other examples of high- and low-caloric density foods?

The lesson here is simple. Eat as many low-caloric density foods as possible. They will fill you up as well as high-density foods and they contain fewer calories. You may find an apple to be more satisfying than a piece of cake.

What are some other high-density foods? They include corn oil extracted from whole corn; pureed foods; foods fried in oil; animal products; nuts; dried fruits; and processed foods. Vegetables have the lowest density, followed by fruits and then by grains.

Were you surprised to find so much math in the kitchen? Now let's take it on the road in Section 3.

Road Math

Vacation time coming? Would you like to show your family how to travel more economically? More efficiently? More enjoyably? With less confusion? Then you have to master road math.

As you will see in this section, math can actually help your family get more out of traveling. Whether you are driving cross-town or flying cross-country, with math you can sharpen your abilities as a traveler. People have been using mathematics to help them travel for thousands of years. It's time you learned some old—and new—road math to make your traveling easier.

How so? For starters, map reading relies on math skills. Reading a map is like looking at a picture of the area where you want to travel. A sound knowledge of math can speed up your understanding of that picture. For example, this section will show you how math can help you find your destination on a map, then calculate how long you will take to get there. You will also learn how to estimate the time you will arrive.

Vacation planning is a cinch with good math skills, as you are about to learn. Math can show you how to get the most out of your trips with accurate scheduling. It can also show you how to economize, making vacations possible that you didn't think you could afford.

Finally, math can help your family get more out of your car. You not only save hard-earned money, you also save gas—a valuable resource. And, at the end of this section, you will learn about some calculator shortcuts you can use to make gas economy even easier.

Archaeologists believe that prehistoric peoples used the concepts of direction and distance to go from one place to another. But they had to locate themselves in nature's terms. A hunting ground might be "two suns" (two days) distant; a lake teeming with fish might lie forward from the family cave by "half a sun's march." Distance and direction, in short, were expressed as travel time from one point to another.

You have it easier. You can compute on the basis of coordinate systems and directions, which you learned about in Part III. Here is a simpler application.

Maps and Math

Coordinates and directions

Let's say you want to draw a map of your backyard on a piece of graph paper. Start at the lower left corner of the paper. Moving along the bottom margin, count to the 14th vertical line and make a mark where it intersects with the margin. Return to the left corner. Now move up the margin on the left and mark the 10th horizontal line. Move across this horizontal line until it intersects with the 14th vertical line; that is the point of intersection.

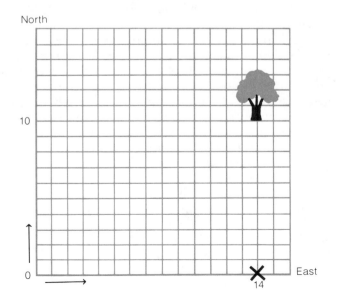

A simple map using graph paper.

That point has a location that can be identified. It is exactly 14 lines to the right and 10 lines up. These are the point's *coordinates,* 14 and 10. The first number refers to the *horizontal* aspect of the location, the second number to the *vertical* aspect. You have just drawn a map. Imagine that the graph paper represents your backyard and that the point with these coordinates (14,10) is the site of a tree. East is to the right and north is up. Now you can describe the tree's location as 14 units east and 10 units north.

Gridiron maps

On your map, you decided to place the *zero point,* or *point of origin,* in the lower left corner. That's one way to locate the zero point, and it's probably good enough for mapping your backyard. But suppose you want to map a much larger area, like your town. Every town and city has a center. If someone asks you for directions in your home town, you probably would have little trouble if you used the center as a point of origin. You would say, "Go to the center of town, then head 14 blocks east and 10 blocks north."

Since the numeration system would start at zero point, with all blocks named or numbered from that point, you might give the directions differently. Say the streets running parallel to the east-west axis are named alphabetically; the tenth street may be called Jonquil Street. The streets running parallel to north-south axis are numbered. The fourteenth street would be named, simply, 14th Street. Each block has a value of 100. The point you are looking for is at 1400 east and 1000 north. If the point is facing Jonquil Street, the number is 1400 East Jonquil Street. If the point is facing 14th Street, the number is 1000 North 14th Street. You can find and name any point in the town from the zero point. Since you use the designation north, south, east, and west, you have no need of negative numbers on this map. All points, which you would call *addresses,* are designated in positive numbers on the map.

Many towns are laid out in *gridiron,* or *grid,* patterns such as this. Seen from the air, they would look like graph paper. Each street represents a line; each intersection of streets, an intersection of lines. Is your town like this? Well-known American cities laid out like gridirons include Chicago, Detroit, Denver, Kansas City, and parts of New York.

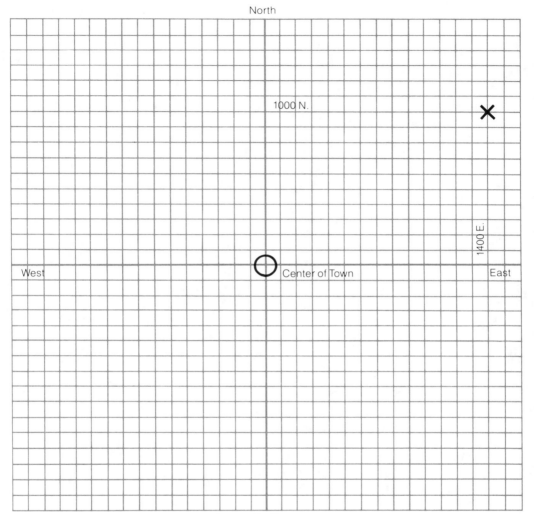

North

1000 N.

✗

1400 E.

West

◯ Center of Town

East

South

The four directions of a map, showing horizontal and vertical coordinates. Note the area you sent someone to: 14 blocks east, 10 blocks north.

Squared maps

As you work with maps, you will often find it more practical to use general areas rather than particular coordinates. Some maps have areas already marked off for you. For example, city maps may have the downtown area squared off.

But suppose you are taking a long car trip and are planning your schedule. Rather than finding a single location you would like to reach by nightfall, you could square off a general area in which you have estimated convenient locations would be. And, you could square

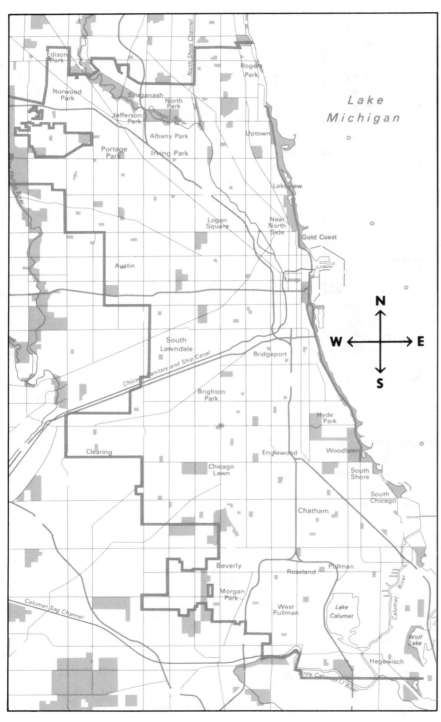

Chicago's grid from the air.

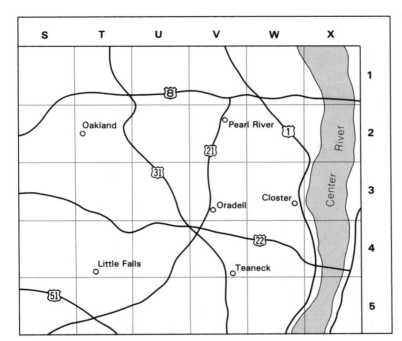

The alphanumeric system on a segment of a road map.

off areas for each night. If traveling from Washington, D.C., to Los Angeles, for example, you might square off an area approximately every 450 miles along your chosen route if planning a six-day road trip.

On world maps, you can partition off continents and nations, then sections of nations. On city maps, you can partition off sections of the city: southwest, northwest, southeast, or northeast sections.

Mapmakers "square off" many maps in a more formal, but easy-to-follow, way. The squares on the road map illustrated here are labeled. The vertical coordinates are simply numbered, with the lowest number at the top of the map. Letters of the alphabet identify the horizontal coordinates, running from left to right in order. This is the *alphanumeric* system used on many maps. The system's style may also be reversed, with numbers running horizontally and letters vertically. The lines of the squares are rarely actually drawn across the entire map, but are rather meant to be imagined. The illustration shows the lines so that you can clearly see where they would fall.

Making maps

You can have some fun—and learn—by using map skills in your immediate surroundings. Practice in reading maps can be a way to familiarize yourself with your environment. You can also profit from practice in making maps. In these activities you'll be learning the basics of road math.

Orienteering

Has your family ever tried *orienteering?* If not, read on. You can make a game of it.

Orienteering involves reading a map to find your way around. Suppose the children in your family are having a party. You have a backyard available. You designate a game organizer and have the organizer arrange various items in the yard. These can include tires, balance beams, bike racks, planters, or whatever is on hand. The organizer then draws a simple map of the yard with the locations of the objects sketched in. The sketch also includes permanent features of the lot such as trees, sidewalks, and fences.

Each participant has a copy of the map and a pencil or pen. Various objects on the map are numbered, from 1 up. Each player's goal is to proceed to each numbered item in the proper order. At each object, a

A sample orienteering map with 18 stops.

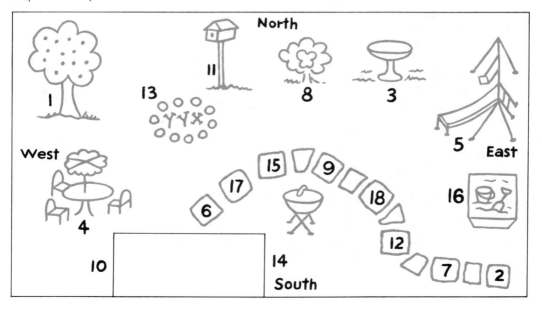

letter of the alphabet appears. It is painted on or other-wise attached to the object so that the letter can't be removed. The player writes down the letter and moves to the next location. The letters must be written down in the order in which they are found.

If the players have proceeded in the proper order, each should have spelled out a message. Those with the correct message receive a small prize. If you want to make the game more competitive, you can specify that the first player to complete the message receives an additional prize.

To make this game more difficult, the map can be made more complicated, more objects can be placed in bigger areas, and the messages can be longer and can appear in a code that must be cracked. Participants can play singly or in teams.

Neighborhood maps

Maps help you do the things you want to do. To prove it, make yourself a map. Not just any map will do. Make a map of the places you enjoy.

Children especially can find many favorite places in their neighborhoods. What are they? The movie the-ater? The ice-cream stand? The baseball stadium? The video arcade? The bowling alley? A special friend's house? The library?

To make a neighborhood map, start with a rough sketch on graph paper. Place home at the center. Us-ing the lines of the paper, sketch the neighborhood streets. Work outward in the directions of spots of in-terest, using the points of the compass (north, south, east, and west) as guides.

These early sketches need not be exact. Later revi-sions will make the map as precise in scale as you wish. In revising, mapmakers may wish to add new places. Town or city maps are especially helpful in re-fining maps you make.

Are you giving a party? Send a copy of a map you make yourself to all those attending. Consult a town map for the main routes that your guests would take to reach you. Mark the neighborhood streets that lead to your own. Place a star at the spot where your home is. Be sure to note your address on the map and your tele-phone number in case somebody needs to contact you.

Road maps

Road maps are useful tools that contain much information in a small space. For example, you can pinpoint a location on a road map and then calculate the distance there from the information on the map.

Pinpointing your destination

Locating towns and cities on a road map can be simplė. An index with towns and cities listed alphabetically indicates the alphanumeric coordinates of the square that contains each one. Folding maps generally have the index on the bottom or the back. If you have a road atlas with a map for each state, you will find the index at the back of the book.

Calculating distances with maps

It's easy to find the distances between main cities and towns. The routes on most highway maps are marked with little *mileage numbers*. These are not the route numbers, which are printed over each route, but the mileage numbers, which appear alongside the route.

Often you'll find several mileage numbers along a single highway or road line. Each number applies to a

A segment of a road map with mileage numbers, printed in color, and other information.

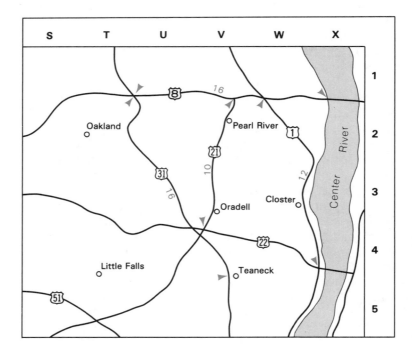

particular stretch. But how do you know which stretch? Look at any route; you'll see little markers, often shaped like arrowheads, pointing at the route. The markers may lie above or below the line. At route junctions, only one marker may be used for both intersecting routes. Then it is angled to indicate the portion of highway to which it refers. Within cities, the intersections themselves may serve as markers.

Road maps can also have two sets of mileage numbers. Numbers in black represent distance between each town or intersection. Numbers in color represent distance between major cities, which may be marked with a circled star. (Towns are usually marked by circles.)

If you need to find the distances between cities and towns on a road map, simply find the mileage numbers along the route and add them up. On a long trip, you would probably not have to add up a long column of figures. A road atlas would most likely include a *mileage map* that shows driving distances and average driving times between various points.

If you live in a small town in your state and need to go to a city to pick up a major highway, you would first use the mileage numbers on your road map to compute the distance to the city. Then, looking at the mileage map, you would find the distance from the city to your destination—provided that destination is also a city large enough to appear on the mileage map. If not, you would find the distance to the city nearest your destination and then use a road map again to compute the distance from that city to your destination.

Using mileage charts

You have a good alternative to the mileage map called a *mileage chart*. Here you'll find a number of cities listed alphabetically. The illustration on the next page shows a typical mileage chart. To find distances, you can use three devices—the road map, the mileage map, and the mileage chart—in combination.

Globes

The same ideas that you applied in making flat maps of your backyard and your hometown can be applied on a much larger scale, to the globe, if you want. Picture

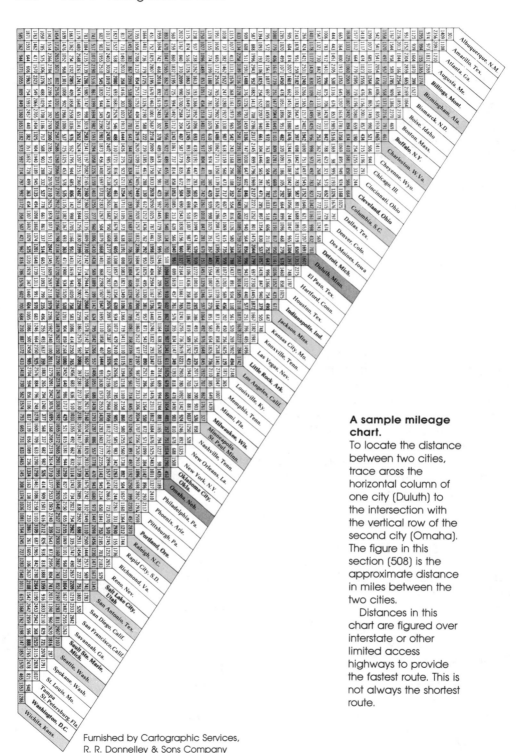

A sample mileage chart.

To locate the distance between two cities, trace across the horizontal column of one city (Duluth) to the intersection with the vertical row of the second city (Omaha). The figure in this section (508) is the approximate distance in miles between the two cities.

Distances in this chart are figured over interstate or other limited access highways to provide the fastest route. This is not always the shortest route.

Furnished by Cartographic Services, R. R. Donnelley & Sons Company

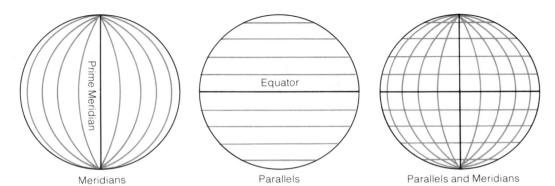

Meridians   Parallels   Parallels and Meridians

the globe covered with imaginary crisscrossing lines such as you'd find on graph paper. You can see squares in all directions. The east-west imaginary lines are called *parallels*. They stay the same distance apart. But, on the surface of the globe, the north-south lines, called *meridians,* run more closely together as they approach the poles, finally meeting there. So the "squares" are not really perfect squares on the globe.

Meridians of longitude and parallels of latitude on the globe. Note how meridians meet at the poles, but parallels keep the same distance from one another.

You still have four directions, as on flat maps. But where is the zero point?

On flat maps, the zero point lies at the intersection of the horizontal and vertical axes. But where are the axes on a globe? What line could be called the horizontal axis? That could be anywhere, but to mapmakers it seems natural to choose the equator, which runs around the middle of the earth. Then one can measure north and south from the equator to each pole. There are 90 degrees (90°) of curvature on either side of the equator to each pole.

The choice of a vertical axis is more arbitrary. No meridian seems a better choice than any other. So by international agreement, the meridian running through Greenwich, England, serves as the zero meridian. This meridian, sometimes called the *prime meridian* or the *Greenwich Meridian,* slices the globe into two hemispheres. Each hemisphere has 180° of curvature. Any point to the right is east of Greenwich; any point to the left is west of Greenwich. The zero point on the globe is where the prime meridian crosses the equator.

To measure the space between these imaginary lines, the terms latitude and longitude have been applied. *Latitude* is the number that measures how far north or south one is from the equator. *Longitude* is the number that measures how far east or west one is from the prime meridian.

On-the-Road Calculations

Sometimes you haven't any schedules to help you figure out how long it will take you to get to your destination. Perhaps you know how fast you will travel, however, and the distance you must travel. Basic algebra tells you that if you know any two of three factors—time, distance, and speed (rate)—you can calculate the third.

Simple equations express these relationships:

$$\text{Time} = \frac{\text{Distance}}{\text{Speed}}$$

$$\text{Speed} = \frac{\text{Distance}}{\text{Time}}$$

$$\text{Distance} = \text{Time} \times \text{Speed}$$

Time is usually expressed in hours; speed in miles per hour (mph or miles/hr.); distance in miles.

Speed

Look at a simple example. Let's say the family traveled a distance of 12 miles to your aunt's house, driving for 24 minutes. The speedometer was broken. You want to find out what your average speed was.

You noted your distance and time, so you divide miles by hours. First convert 24 minutes to .4 hours (24 min. ÷ 60 min./hr. = .4 hr.). Then divide 12 miles by .4 hours to get 30 mph.

$$\text{Speed} = \frac{12 \text{ mi.}}{.4 \text{ hr.}} = 30 \text{ mph}$$

Now try the other equations. You will find they also work.

How about a more complicated example? Suppose your family is taking a trip. You travel the whole day. At times, you are zipping down the interstate highway at 55 mph. You stop for gas. A little later you stop for lunch. At one point, you slow down to 20 mph because of road repairs. Later, you take a side trip into a national park.

With all these different speeds, including 0 mph, how can you figure out your average speed for the entire day's driving? It would be a major job to jot down the time spent in each phase and the distance from stop to stop. Fortunately, you have a mathematical way that automatically takes the changes of speed into account. The method is the same as for the simpler example you just read about.

Finding your total distance and total time takes some preplanning. Figure the distance by noting the miles registered on your car's odometer at the start of the trip. Then note the miles at the end. Subtract the first figure from the second, and you will have the miles traveled that day. The time traveled is just as easy: use your watch to record the time you leave and the time you stop. Then calculate the hours in between. (Don't forget to take time zones into account.) Now simply divide distance by time, as you did earlier. That gives you the average speed for the day. Say it was 35 mph.

Time and distance

How about tomorrow? Would you like to estimate the distance you will (or must) travel on the next leg of your journey? Are you going to try to get from point A to point B as rapidly as possible? Or are you interested in making all those stops between points A and B?

You already know speed equals distance divided by time. Now you will use algebra again to manipulate that equation. Yesterday, you calculated your average speed at 35 mph. Today you have to cover a 200-mile stretch. Can you make 200 miles in a single 8-hour day if you travel at 35 mph?

Remember that

$$\text{Time} = \frac{\text{Distance}}{\text{Speed}}$$

Using the figures above, you have this equation.

$$\text{Time} = \frac{200 \text{ mi.}}{35 \text{ mph}} = 5.7 \text{ hr.}$$

The answer becomes obvious. You can easily cover 200 miles in an 8-hour driving day at an average speed of 35 mph.

Now a discussion starts. Some family members would like to cover more ground today so you can spend more time in the national park you are visiting tomorrow. Others object; they have enjoyed the leisurely pace so far and don't want to rush.

Math won't decide the family argument for you, but it can help you find compromises by providing useful information. Your family decides not to speed up today or skip any stops. What about increasing the hours of driving instead? How much will that increase the distance traveled? You must manipulate the equation again.

Changing from 5.7 hours to 8 hours, at your average speed of 35 mph you will cover this distance.

Distance = 8 hr. × 35 mph = 280 mi.

The argument is settled. The extra 80 miles you will travel today will provide the family with plenty of leisure tomorrow to enjoy the national park.

Vacation Planning with Math

The skills that you have already acquired should qualify you to serve as the family's vacation planner No. 1. Knowing how to read maps, you can figure out distances from one place to another. Once you know distances, you can use math to estimate how long it will take to get there. Once you know how much time will be available, you can compute how fast you have to travel to arrive within the time frame.

Knowing distance, time, and speed, you have some basic tools that will help you to plan other aspects of your vacation. For instance, you can calculate vacation costs such as gas, lodging, and meals based on these factors. Math can produce solutions to other vacation-budget problems. For example, you can figure out how to spend a fixed amount of money more effectively and get more relaxation out of your vacation days.

Schedules

Suppose your family will have 10 days free for a traveling vacation this year. A decision is made to follow a route that will cover a total of 1,000 miles. Along that route are some resort areas and scenic sites where everyone would like to stop—either briefly or for a day or more. How should you plan the vacation?

The problem comes into sharper definition if you ask how much time should be spent driving and how much relaxing and sightseeing. Looking at a road map and examining your information, you figure that 700 miles will be straight highway driving and 300 miles more leisurely stop-and-go traveling.

You estimate that the average speeds will be 55 mph for straight driving and 35 mph for stop-and-go traveling. The time spent on the highway (distance divided by speed) is 700 miles ÷ 55 mph = 12.7 hours.

The time spent in leisurely driving is 300 miles ÷ 35 mph = 8.6 hours. Rounding off these figures and adding, you come up with 13 + 9 = 22 hours of driving.

Assume that 1 driving day equals 8 hours. That means 2 days and 6 hours, or almost 3 days, will be spent traveling. Then, 7 or more days are available for relaxing and sightseeing.

Costs

Taking a vacation can be either expensive or cheap. Your family may enjoy vacations that are inexpensive and informal, such as camping or hosteling. If you do, your costs will be relatively easy to keep down. But suppose you want to go to a resort hotel in Miami Beach, Florida. Costs of the same vacation plan can vary depending on several factors.

During the off-season, for example, Miami is enjoyable and definitely less expensive than going when the season's at its peak. You may find package deals that include bargain rates for plane tickets and rental cars; air and rail passes; and tour packages.

There are many tactics to bring costs down on any vacation. Some techniques are especially useful for certain types of situations. For example, would you like to go on a fishing trip on a faraway lake, but most of the family doesn't think the trip is worth it? Can you justify the cost of the trip if everyone isn't going along?

The answer to your problem may be ride sharing with friends who are also interested in the trip. If you know one person who will share the costs of driving, you can reduce your gas expenses by one-half. With two ride sharers, you can cut those expenses by two-thirds. If you are in a hurry, extra passengers can also mean more drivers. You may be able to eliminate a stopover.

Let's suppose that two of your family are planning a 2,000-mile drive round trip. Your car gets 15 miles per gallon (mpg) and gas costs $1.20 per gallon. What would your gas cost your family if you had no ride sharers? If you had one? Two?

To calculate the cost of the drive, you multiply as follows.

$$\frac{\text{Miles Traveled}}{\text{Miles/Gallon}} \times \text{Dollars/Gallon}$$

So you have this equation.

$$\frac{2,000 \text{ mi.}}{15 \text{ mpg}} \times \$1.20/\text{gal.} = \$160.00$$

If your family paid the full cost of gas for the trip, you would pay $160.00. Sharing gas costs with one other person, you would spend only $80.00. If two other persons came along, you would pay about $53.00. Add a fifth passenger, and your family's share would be only $40.00, a saving of $120.00. Further, with this many passengers, you would be able to drive straight through rather than stopping at a motel twice (once going and once returning). You would also save on meals, since you wouldn't be on the road so long. The total savings from all these budget measures may give you enough to pay for the rental on a fishing boat.

Fuel Economy

Gasoline costs rank as a major car expense for many American families. Recently, all U.S. motor vehicles were estimated at using 300 million gallons of gasoline and diesel fuel a day.

Fuel economy has international importance because oil, from which gasoline and diesel fuel are derived, is a nonreplenishable resource. In other words, oil will eventually run out. Merely observing speed limits, improving fuel economy, and using public transportation would greatly reduce the amount of gasoline used per day.

Figuring yearly gas costs

How much your family spends yearly on gasoline depends on three things: the price of gas, how many miles the car travels, and the rate of fuel consumption (mpg). Fuel economy is a ratio, as expressed in this equation.

$$\text{Fuel Economy} = \frac{\text{Distance}}{\text{Fuel Used}}$$

The longer the distance and the less fuel consumed, the greater the fuel economy. Distance is usually expressed in miles; fuel use, in gallons.

How about an example? Say your family car is driven 15,000 miles a year. Gas costs $1.30 per gallon in your area. Your yearly gas expenses could run as

low as (A) $390, if your car gets 50 mpg, and as high
as (B) $2,438, if your car gets 8 mpg.

A. $\dfrac{15,000}{50} \times \$1.30 = \$390$

B. $\dfrac{15,000}{8} \times \$1.30 = \$2,438$

You have no control over the price of gas, but you can
shop around to find the most economically priced service stations. And your family can cut costs by driving
only when necessary. A third way to cut costs is to improve the car's gas economy. Do all three, and your
family could save enough for a small vacation.

Do you want to calculate your family's real yearly
gasoline costs? If you know the number of miles
driven, the average mpg of your car, and the price of
gas, you can get the yearly costs in the same way you
figured your gas costs for the fishing trip in the previous discussion.

Fuel Cost/Year $= \dfrac{\textbf{Miles Traveled/Year}}{\textbf{Average Mpg}} \times \textbf{Dollars/Gallon}$

Say the car was driven 12,000 miles last year. The car
averaged 15 mpg and the gas cost $1.30 per gallon.
You divide and multiply.

$\dfrac{\textbf{12,000 mi.}}{\textbf{15 mpg}} \times \textbf{\$1.30/gal.} = \textbf{\$1,040}$

You can devise other ways of finding yearly gas
costs. For example, you can consult the car fuel expenses table on the following page. Because the table
assumes that miles traveled annually total 15,000 miles,
you would have to adjust for the difference. Here is
how you would find your cost.

1. Find the yearly cost for 15 mpg and $1.30 per gal-
   lon. This table has the cost for 14 mpg and 16 mpg
   but not 15 mpg. You find the average for these two
   figures:

   $\dfrac{\$1,219 + 1,393}{2} = \$1,306$

2. This figure gives you the total annual cost of gas
   for 15,000 miles. To get the figure for 12,000 miles,
   multiply $1,306 by $\frac{12,000}{15,000}$ or .8, to get $1,045.

Fuel expenses per year

Estimated MPG	Price per gallon								
	$1.50	$1.40	$1.30	$1.20	$1.10	$1.00	$.95	$.90	$.85
50	$ 450	$ 420	$ 390	$ 360	$ 330	$ 300	$ 285	$ 270	$ 255
48	469	438	406	375	344	313	297	281	266
46	489	457	424	391	359	326	310	294	277
44	511	477	443	409	375	341	324	307	290
42	536	500	464	429	393	357	339	321	304
40	563	525	488	450	413	375	356	338	319
38	592	553	513	474	434	395	375	355	336
36	625	583	542	500	458	417	396	375	354
34	662	618	574	529	485	441	419	397	375
32	703	656	609	563	516	469	445	422	398
30	750	700	650	600	550	500	475	450	425
28	804	750	696	643	589	536	509	482	455
26	865	808	750	692	635	577	548	519	490
24	938	875	813	750	688	625	594	563	531
22	1023	955	886	818	750	682	648	614	580
20	1125	1050	975	900	825	750	713	675	638
18	1250	1167	1083	1000	917	833	792	750	708
16	1406	1313	1219	1125	1031	938	891	844	797
14	1607	1500	1393	1286	1179	1071	1018	964	911
12	1875	1750	1625	1500	1375	1250	1188	1125	1063
10	2250	2100	1950	1800	1650	1500	1425	1350	1275
8	2813	2625	2438	2250	2063	1875	1781	1688	1594

Note: Figures are rounded to the nearest dollar and based on an average annual mileage of 15,000 miles.

How much could your family save? Are you buying the least expensive gas you can find that is suitable for your car? If not, you can achieve cost reductions just by buying a lower-priced gasoline. Can you cut down on the number of miles traveled per year? You can compute that saving. How about increasing mpg? Assume an increase of 3 mpg over your present rate—it can be done. You will find out how later.

Figure the savings from each of these measures separately and then together. Let's say you find gas at $1.25 a gallon, reduce your family's total driving to 9,000 miles a year, and improve the car's fuel economy to 18 mpg. The yearly cost is figured this way.

$$\frac{9,000 \text{ mi.}}{18 \text{ mpg}} \times \$1.25/\text{gal.} = \$625$$

You would have reduced your yearly gas cost from $1,040 to $625, a savings of $415, or 40 percent. Sound unrealistic? The figures don't lie.

Finding MPG

All this assumes you know what gas mileage the family car gets. But what if you don't know that? How do you find out?

There are two ways. One is to buy a vacuum gas gauge, preferably the kind with mpg figures, and attach it to your car's intake manifold according to the directions on the package. The gauge tells you the gas mileage you are getting from moment to moment.

You now have a good-bad situation. It's good because you receive instant feedback about how economically you are driving. That way you can eliminate wasteful driving habits. It's bad only because the gauge doesn't tell you the overall mpg of the car. You'd have to record a number of figures and calculate numerous averages over a long period of time to get that. A gauge is, however, still a good investment.

What is the second way of finding your mpg? Math and your odometer can do it again. Make some simple notations the next time you stop to fill the gas tank, and you'll have what you need. First, note the odometer reading to the nearest whole mile. At the first stop, it doesn't matter whether you record how much gas went in, as long as you fill the tank completely full.

Fuel economy varies widely due to a number of factors. Here are the ranges in fuel economy for eight different cars over three tankfuls.

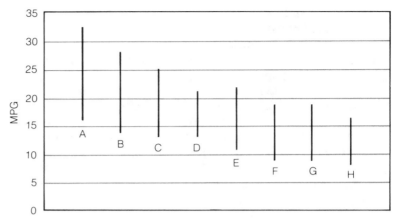

But the second time your family tanks up, you should record both the mileage and the number of gallons to the nearest tenth.

Now subtract the earlier odometer reading from the newer reading. The difference gives you the number of miles traveled on a tankful of gas. Divide the difference by the number of gallons put in the tank the second time. The resulting ratio is the miles-per-gallon figure.

Every driver in your family is cooperating. Each one is faithfully recording odometer mileage and gasoline purchased, taking the gallons figures from charge slips or the pump. Each driver is also doing the pumping, an option that saves money on every gallon.

Your initial odometer reading is 24,328. You record that figure. The next fill-up puts 17.8 gallons in the tank. You write the new odometer reading of 24,505 on the charge slip or on a piece of paper reserved for this purpose. You have traveled 177 miles on 17.8 gallons. You compute as follows.

$$\frac{177 \text{ mi.}}{17.8 \text{ gal.}} = 9.9 \text{ mpg}$$

There is definitely a need for better fuel economy for your family car.

Improving MPG

Your family is now talking about improving mpg. As the "expert," you state some facts:

Gas mileage is affected by many factors, from purchase of gas to driving itself. When at the gas pump, don't try to "top off" the tank. When the nozzle stops, stop pumping. Don't let the gas run in too fast as you approach the full mark; some fuel may slosh out. Don't buy gas at midday; heat makes gas expand, and at that time you actually get less gas for your money.

In terms of driving, jackrabbit starts gulp gas; so does stomping first on the gas, then on the brake. A "cold" engine burns more gas than a warmed-up engine. (An engine usually warms up completely after a few miles of driving.) If your car is out of tune, it will burn more gas; and your engine will work harder if there is any excess weight in or on the car. At higher rates of speed, wind resistance becomes an increasing obstacle to movement—and fuel economy.

Any driver can do something to reduce the opportunities for these factors to operate. For example, since high speeds reduce fuel economy, don't drive too fast. Can "your" drivers take advantage of the fact that a warmed-up engine is more efficient? Yes. When running a number of errands, manage them in one trip. This could also provide a good argument for car pooling. Fewer cars commuting mean fewer cars that need to be warmed up.

Calculator Shortcuts

If you're calculating mpg for one tankful of gas, you should of course divide the number of miles traveled by the number of gallons pumped into the tank. The operation isn't complicated. You can do a chain calculation, a subtraction followed by a division. If the earlier odometer reading is 12,324 and the present reading is 12,517, and 17.1 gallons were pumped in, this is your calculation.

| 12517 | − | 12324 | ÷ | 17.1 | = | 11.286549 |

Note that the first two digits of the two odometer readings are the same. It is unnecessary to punch in those digits. The difference will still come out the same. Here's the shortcut.

| 517 | − | 324 | ÷ | 17.1 | = | 11.286549 |

Calculating your gas mileage every time you tank up, you acquire a whole series of such calculations. But now it's the end of the year. You want to find your average yearly gas mileage. And you don't need any of these previous mpg calculations to do so. You do need three figures, however: the total gallons of gas you purchased, plus the odometer readings from the beginning and the end of the year.

To compute the average for the year, first subtract the odometer reading at the beginning of the year from the one at the end of the year. Then divide that difference by the sum of gallons of gas. You have your average yearly mpg.

You can use this yearly average to estimate gas costs for future years. If the price of gas goes up or down, you must adjust the annual cost, but the average mpg will go unchanged. (The estimation will be accurate depending on whether your driving habits are unchanged and your car's fuel efficiency remains roughly the same.)

Notwithstanding the shortcut shown above, recording odometer readings on each gas purchase is very important. The readings serve special purposes at the end of the year. They can be used to compare everyday mpg at home with mpg during highway driving on family vacations. Or you might want to compare winter mpg with summer mpg. A third possibility is seeing whether your mpg improved substantially after a tune-up or use of a gas additive.

Whatever mpg information you are seeking, keep your calculator—and the results of your calculations—handy. They can help you project and work toward a lifetime of fuel efficiency.

Money Math

So far you've found out how math can help your family in handling various kinds of everyday problems. Now for some talk about money.

The fact is that everyone uses math in handling money, whether aware of it or not. When you count your money, you are using basic math operations—counting and adding. When you check to see if your change on a purchase is correct, you are subtracting. When you share the costs of a purchase with someone else, you are dividing.

When it comes to money, math talks in two main ways: how to spend it and how to save (or invest) it. You can speak of *consumer math* as the kind used in guiding your spending. *Money management math* includes all the math tools that help you handle the money you decide to save.

You already know some applications of consumer math from previous sections in this part. For example, you learned how to figure what materials your family would need to do a home do-it-yourself job economically. You found tips on how to buy food more economically.

Consumer math has more general and very practical aspects that will be discussed in this section. Consumer math deals with comparison shopping and with discounts and rebates as selling devices. Once your family decides to buy something, you will need to know how to figure any sales tax and add it to the basic cost. You may want to look into bulk buying as one way to get the most for your money. Finally, remember that the decision whether to buy with cash or on credit affects the actual amount of money your family will spend on a purchase.

Money management math as discussed in this section can serve you well in many situations. Math will tell you about the money you put in the bank, into either a checking or savings account. You will learn how to figure your family's income tax under the latest tax laws and how to keep records that will help to hold your taxes down. You will learn how to compute the interest to be paid on money you are saving or borrowing.

Is your family considering buying a house or some other "big ticket" item such as an automobile? You'll need to know the costs of borrowing purchase money. How about insurance needs and coverage, the varieties of investments your family can select to "put money to work," and checking up on your financial health so that you can plan your financial future realistically? This section discusses all these possibilities.

More calculator hints also appear here. These have direct reference to examples in this section but can be applied to problems in other sections as well.

As you read, you will find many charts and tables of numbers. These tables are mathematical diagrams to help you understand the relationships of numbers in subjects such as inflation, interest on loans, income taxes, home mortgages, insurance, and stocks and bonds. You will learn how to solve sample problems in each of these fields using appropriate tables. Being able to use these math tables will help you get along with the money-related areas of everyday life.

Consumer Math

You and your family *consume*. You probably buy something every day, either goods, like pencils and paper, or services, like laundry and dry cleaning. As a consumer, you owe it to yourself to get the best price you can when you make a purchase. You can do so by shopping wisely, that is, comparing prices and merchandise before you buy. Look for sales and discounts offering lower prices. And think about buying in larger quantities to save even more money. Be aware that using a credit card costs more than using cash. Sales taxes add to the consumer cost of any purchase, so include them in your comparisons.

Inflation

While inflation does not directly affect how much your family can spend, it does determine how much your dollar is worth. Inflation adds to the price of everything you buy. With inflation, buying the same item usually costs more this year than last year.

Inflation can be measured. A 5-percent rate of inflation means that an item costing $1.00 last year typically costs $1.05 this year. If the same rate persists next year, that item will cost $1.10 (105% × $1.05 = $1.10¼). The year after that, it will cost $1.16. In the short run, a "low" rate of inflation such as 5 percent may seem harmless enough. But it has a way of sneaking up on you because of the way inflation compounds its effects over the years. If you examine a span of 45 years, the effect can be dramatic.

	Beginning level*	After 45 years
Grocery Items		
Bread (1 lb. loaf)	$ 1.34	$ 12.04
2% milk (1 gal.)	1.89	16.98
A-Large eggs (1 doz.)	1.39	12.49
Ground beef (1 lb.)	1.69	15.18
Chuck roast (1 lb.)	1.99	17.88
Whole fryer (1 lb.)	1.09	9.79
Round steak (1 lb.)	3.99	35.85
Cabbage (1 lb.)	0.29	2.61
Potatoes (1 lb.)	0.69	6.20
Canned tomatoes (16 oz.)	0.72	6.47
Peanut butter (28 oz.)	2.67	23.99
Butter (1 lb.)	2.11	18.96
Toilet paper (4 rolls)	1.25	11.23
Clothing		
Man's suit	299.00	2,686.52
Man's coat (all-weather)	95.00	853.58
Man's dress shoes	65.00	584.03
Woman's dress	40.00	359.40
Woman's coat (all-weather)	79.99	718.71
Woman's slacks	30.00	269.55
Woman's dress shoes	35.00	314.48
Housing		
Average house	75,130.00	675,043.64
1 bedroom apartment	400.00/month	3,594.00
Automotive		
ABC car	8,134.00	73,084.05
XYZ car	10,478.00	94,144.91
Unleaded gas (1 gal.)	1.29	11.67

Effects of a permanent 5-percent inflation rate.

*1990

As you can see from the table, it is possible to understand inflation concretely if you think in terms of how much you can buy with a dollar. The table projects forward for 45 years. It is highly unlikely that the inflation rate will remain at a steady 5-percent rate, of course. In recent years, the inflation rate has varied from about $3\frac{1}{2}$ percent to about 12 percent. But an example from the past will show that the inflation rate, variable or not, usually cuts drastically into your buying power in the long run unless your income increases at the same rate.

At one time, the price of a candy bar was 5¢; $1 bought 20 candy bars. When the price went to 10¢, $1 bought 10 bars. At 30¢ a bar, $1 can purchase only $3\frac{1}{3}$ candy bars. Assuming the size of the bar hasn't increased, that represents a dramatic drop in the buying power of a dollar from 20 to $3\frac{1}{3}$ candy bars.

The prices of individual items can vary at different rates. For convenience, you can indicate the value of a dollar with an overall index, an average of the prices of various items. Such an index, the *Consumer Price Index* (CPI), shows the value of a dollar in a particular period of time, such as a year.

Since the value of a dollar changes from year to year, everything is relative. When was a dollar *really* worth a dollar? The period 1982–1984 is the base for the CPI. In that period the CPI was set by agreement at 100. You can think of that as $1.00 or as 100 percent.

With inflation, the CPI rises. That means it takes more than $1 this year to purchase what $1 bought in the 1982–1984 period; it takes more than 100 percent of later money to reach 100 percent of 1982–1984 money. In 1988, the CPI was 118.

Do you want to find out how much a 1988 dollar would have bought in 1982–1984 terms? You want to solve for *x*, the amount of money in 1982–1984 dollars. To do so you will have to use a proportion.

$$\frac{\text{1982–1984 dollars}}{\text{1988 dollars}} = \frac{\text{100 (or 1982–1984 CPI)}}{\text{118 (or 1988 CPI)}}$$

This translates to $x/\$1 = 100/118$; so $x = \$1 \times 100/118 = 84.7$¢. That is, a 1988 dollar is worth 84.7 percent of a 1982–1984 dollar. The current dollar will buy only 84.7 percent as much. Thus $1,000 in 1988 dollars is only worth $847 in 1982–1984 dollars.

Note that the CPI went up 18 percent between the 1982–1984 period and 1988. The rate of increase is figured as follows.

$$\frac{\text{1988 CPI} - \text{1982–1984 CPI}}{\text{1982–1984 CPI}}$$

Suppose your family bought a house in 1985 for $84,000. How much is it worth in 1988 dollars if the 1985 CPI was 108? This is how to compute the rate of inflation.

$$\frac{118 - 108}{108} = 9.26\%$$

So the present value of the house would theoretically be 109.26 percent of the 1985 value, or $91,778. But remember that the CPI is an average of the costs of different kinds of items. Real estate property prices may go up more rapidly or more slowly than the average, and there are many other factors that affect the value of your home.

If your family has money in a bank checking account that pays no interest, because of inflation the money will be worth less as time passes. On the other hand, if you are borrowing money, you will be paying back in dollars that are worth less. Thus, borrowers profit from inflation while creditors lose from it. Keep this in mind later in this section when banking, loans, and credit come under discussion.

Suppose you borrow $100 for one year and are charged 7-percent interest. That means you are charged $7 for borrowing $100, and you will pay back $107. Right? Yes and no. You will be paying back $107, but in the dollars of the year in which you *repay* the loan, not in the dollars of the year in which you borrowed it.

Say the CPI was 108 when you borrowed the money and 110 when you paid back the loan and interest. How much is the $107 worth in the borrowing year? You use this proportion.

$$\frac{x}{\$107} = \frac{108}{110}$$

Solving for x, $x = \$107 \times 108/110 = \$105.05$. That means the loan cost only $5.05 in dollars of the borrowing year, contrasted with $7 in dollars of the payback year.

Inflation may seem a little bewildering because the buying power of a dollar shifts constantly. You may feel as if you're watching a motion picture when you want to look at a snapshot. There is little an individual consumer can do to change the effects of inflation. However, you need to know how inflation affects the time factor of your spending and saving.

Comparison shopping

Shopping wisely for specific items may call for the application of special "rules." Other rules apply equally to all or most items.

Do you want an example of a rule that applies to a great variety of items? The cost-per-unit comparison rule is one. Remember it? It appeared in Section 2 of this part, "Kitchen Math," in the discussion on shopping for food.

Can you think of other times when you could apply the cost-per-unit rule? Here is an example. Underwear is often sold in packages of two or more. One store sells a T-shirt for $2.50 while another store sells a package of three for $5.99. Rounding figures, you can see that the second store sells each T-shirt for about $2.00 apiece, a better buy.

In another example, your family patronizes two different gas stations. One sells regular unleaded gas for $1.26\frac{9}{10}$ per gallon. Another station has converted its pumps to metric and is selling the same grade of gas for 33¢ a liter. Which is cheaper? Since 1 gallon is 3.8 liters, 1 gallon costs

$$3.8 \times 33¢ = \$1.25 \frac{4}{10}$$

The metric station is cheaper by $1\frac{1}{2}$¢ a gallon. A fillup of 15 gallons, 57 liters, would mean a total saving of 22.5¢ at the metric pump.

Obviously the cost-per-unit approach is a mathematical way to help you make comparisons among products. The more expensive an item, the more you'll want to save money—and the more likely it is that a single item gives you the only unit of concern. Cost-per-unit represents the cost of the item. That simplifies matters in one way.

In another way, matters become more complicated. With a more expensive item, you may have a choice of a variety of features that can affect the price of the item greatly. Just think of your automobile. You first saw a basic car. Then came such special features as a larger engine, automatic transmission, power steering, power brakes, tinted windshield, special wheel covers, and so on, adding hundreds of dollars onto the sticker price. Combinations of features have ruled out standard units almost entirely.

Today the basic prices of cars plus extras, or options, run so high that "sticker shock" has become a common ailment. How can math help? Math can't drive down the sticker price, but with math you can determine how much below the sticker price the car can sell for.

Your family is looking at new cars. The most attractive model has a sticker price of $9,000. Call this the list price, or L. The dealer could sell the car below the list price, but not too far below; he has to make some profit. You want to figure approximately what the car cost the dealer; call that figure D. Part of the list price is shipping and dealer preparation, or S.

The dealer's cost, D, is obtained from a formula including L and S.

$$D = (0.80)(L - S) + S$$

If L = $9,000 and S = $150, then D is calculated to be $7,380.

$$D = (0.8)(9,000 - 150) + 150 = 7,080 + 150$$

This formula is a rule of thumb; the multiplier of 0.80 represents an average percentage. On a lower-priced car, you would use a multiplier of .85; on a higher-priced car, it would be .75. This means that on a lower-priced car, the dealer's cost is closer to the list price than it is on a higher-priced car.

Now that you have an estimate of D, what can you reasonably offer for that car? Try 10 percent over the dealer's cost, or 110 percent of D.

$$1.10 \times \$7,230 = \$7,953$$

That allows the dealer to make $723 and could save your family $1,047 off the list price ($9,000 − $7,953 = $1,047).

Your family has an old car to trade in on the new model. The oldie has a book value of $1,300. If the dealer offers you a trade-in value of $1,500, on condition that it be applied only to the full list price of $9,000, should your family take it? Remember that the old car is worth at least $1,300. If traded, that amount becomes part of the payment for the new car. Even a trade-in of $1,500 means that you are paying more than you should. Only $200 (over the cash value of the old car) has been taken off the list price, as opposed to the $1,047 that might be taken off the list price on a straight purchase.

Chances are that you will not save the full $1,047 if you trade the old car in. (The dealer probably won't agree to both deals.) As an alternative, sell the old car on your own if it's in good shape. Skyrocketing new-car prices mean that someone will probably be interested in a good used car. You might get more than the book value and save on the new-car price too.

With most goods, you can save by comparison shopping at certain times of the year. Automobiles, for example, sell for less during the late summer because dealers are trying to clear their showrooms to make room for next year's models. Your family is more likely to make a good deal at that time. On the other hand, buying fall fashions in the late summer may guarantee that you will have to pay top price. You would do better in mid-fall, when merchants are clearing the clothes racks to make way for winter styles.

Discounts

Traditionally, each kind of household product had a specific sale season. But in many stores now there are more small sales. *Discounts* are used by a variety of businesses to reduce the prices of articles for buyers. The discount may actually be the amount that your family will save. A business that sells both retail products (directly to the consumer) and wholesale products (to retail businesses to resell) may figure the lower price it charges its wholesale customers by discounting the retail price.

In math terms, discounts are percentages. You want to know by what percentage the discount reduces the regular price. A discount consists of four parts: the regular price, the discount percentage, the discounted price, and the amount saved. If you know any two of these four factors, you can calculate the other two. The relationship among these quantities is expressed by this equation.

$$\text{Discount Percent} = \frac{\text{Amount Saved}}{\text{Regular Price}}$$

(where amount saved = regular price − discount price)

Suppose your family wants to do some floors over (*see* Sec. 1 of this part, "How-to Math"). You see an ad for different kinds of floor coverings on sale. The ad says that parquet tile is on sale for $1.89 per square foot. The ad also indicates that the regular price is $2.49 per square foot and that the saving is 24 percent. You check. You find the saving by subtracting $1.89 from $2.49, giving 60¢; then you divide the saving by the regular price.

$$60¢ \div \$2.49 = 24.09\%$$

The ad also claims 25-percent savings for ceramic tile. The price has been reduced from $1.89 to $1.42 per square foot. If you want to check the accuracy of the ad, you have an alternate way to go. Saving 25 percent means you will pay 75 percent of the regular price.

$$75\% \times \$1.89 = \$1.41\frac{3}{4}$$

The ad does not exaggerate.

Now notice the ad for quarry tile. The ad claims $\frac{1}{3}$ savings for tiles on prices normally ranging from $1.29

An example of sale offers expressed in the language of discounts and of other offers that can be converted.

to $1.59. A quick check shows that $\frac{1}{3}$ of the first price gives 43¢, so $\frac{2}{3}$ would be 86¢. Likewise, $\frac{1}{3}$ of $1.59 is 53¢, so $\frac{2}{3}$ would be $1.06. This tells you that the tiles at the upper and lower limits of the price range are discounted at $33\frac{1}{3}$ percent. It does not show the same for tiles priced in between. (Chances are that those are also reduced, but run the same kind of quick math check when you go to the store.)

Now you see ceiling paneling on sale for 50 percent off. The ad says that it normally sells for 99¢ a square foot and is on sale for 49¢. Your saving would be close to $\frac{1}{2}$ the regular price. But clear plastic paneling for windows is on sale at $4.15 instead of the regular $4.99—a 16-percent saving. You compute the money saved at 80 cents a unit and divide that by $4.99, coming out with an actual saving of 16.8 percent.

Now you should be able to compute your savings even when you lack some information. How much of a discount are you getting on the ratchet tool system that is on sale at $2.99? The manufacturer's "suggested list" price is $10.75.

The answer is you are saving $7.76 from the list price. Dividing that figure by the list price gives a 72-percent discount even though the ad does not say that in so many words.

Some ads contain multiple offers. It may look as if anything you buy will be discounted. For example, the ad announcing ceiling and quarry tile savings may give prices on circular fluorescent bulbs as well. But you see only the price you will pay now. You can't conclude that the bulbs are being sold at a discount. You may only think they are because their ad is surrounded by discounted items. Be on the lookout for devices like this to get you to buy.

Another device is to inflate the list price to make the price your family will pay look like a saving. The manufacturer's suggested price may be the maximum charged by the most elite shops. In truth, most department or speciality stores are probably selling below that inflated price as well. It pays to be familiar with what you are buying and do a little comparison shopping.

A different kind of true discount is called a *chain discount*. In a wholesale-retail store, an item may be offered at a 50-percent discount, with a further discount of 10 percent. But the $\frac{1}{2}$ discount is for the wholesale customers, the $\frac{1}{10}$ discount for everyone.

If an item lists at $10.00, how much would you, as a wholesale customer, pay with the chain discount? Do *not* add up the two figures to get a 60-percent discount.

Multiply the 50-percent discount by the list price first, giving a discounted price of $5.00. Then multiply the second discount by this price: 10 percent of $5.00 is 50¢, so the final price is $4.50; or 90 percent of $5.00 is $4.50.

What is involved is a chain calculation.

$10.00 × 50% × 90% = $4.50

Obviously, if you want to do each multiplication separately, it doesn't matter in which order you perform these operations.

Bulk buying

You already know about some ways to use math to save money on what you buy. Now your family may want to consider combining some of these techniques.

You've done your shopping homework. You've found, in comparing prices at different stores, that one offers outstanding savings on canned goods. Where this occurs, it may pay to buy in bulk even if you do not use all the items right away. Another good reason for buying in bulk is inflation. Goods bought at today's prices can mean money saved tomorrow.

You have choices when buying in quantity. One approach is to go to a discount store. There, you can frequently save on items that more expensive retail stores carry.

Suppose you have a choice between a T-shirt that sells for $2.50 at a retail store and another that is three for $6 at a discount store. How much can you save if you buy in bulk? Assume that the two brands are equal in quality. If you bought a dozen at the higher price, you would pay $30; a dozen of the "discounted" T-shirts would be $24, a saving of $6 per dozen. Buying two dozen saves $12—you would pay $48 instead of $60.

Quality has to be taken into account. If the more expensive T-shirt is made better and could be expected to last twice as long, you would need two dozen of the cheaper T-shirts to last as long as one dozen of the more expensive ones: $48 as opposed to $30. In buying the cheaper shirts, you would not really save but would end up spending more.

How can you compare the two brands, taking both price and durability into account? The appropriate cost-per-unit comparison here is cost-per-year. This is expressed as the following ratio

Price/Durability = Dollars/Number of Years

If the more expensive T-shirt costs $2.50 and lasts 2 years, the cost-per-year is $1.25. The less expensive T-shirt costs $2.00 ($6 ÷ 3 = $2.00) and lasts 1 year; so the cost-per-year is $2.00. The real cost-per-year for the cheaper T-shirt is higher rather than less. The durability comparison is the same, whether you buy and wear one T-shirt or a dozen.

Buying on credit

Using a credit card makes buying goods or services easy: if you don't have enough cash with you, you can "charge it." You then pay the bill over a period of time. The period may be a month, if the credit agreement indicates that, or it may be an indefinite period. The second kind is called a *revolving credit account*.

Whatever kind of credit arrangement your family has, you should remember that you are, in effect, borrowing money when you use credit to purchase merchandise or obtain a service. Borrowing money usually costs money. The charge for borrowing money is referred to as *interest*. The lender may charge you in other ways for borrowing, for example, requiring that you buy credit life insurance if a major purchase is involved. All such charges may be lumped together under the term *finance charge*.

Besides finance charges, your family may be paying hidden charges for using credit. It costs the credit card issuer money to handle your credit. The merchant passes along that additional cost as higher prices on some merchandise. Some merchants, especially those who accept gasoline credit cards, offer discounts if you pay cash. Others no longer accept credit cards at all.

For budget reasons, you'll want to know how much using your credit card costs you. Many cards now charge an annual fee just to issue a card. But finance charges? Math can help you calculate them.

Most lenders charge on a yearly basis, using an *annual percentage rate* (APR). Credit cards with a revolving agreement are required by federal regulation to state the finance charge in APR terms; nonrevolving, or regular, agreements are not required to do so. Until the stipulation became law, you were informed only of the monthly finance charge in either case.

Suppose you have a credit card that assesses a finance charge on your unpaid balance of $550. If the monthly finance charge is $1\frac{1}{2}$ percent for the first $200 and 1 percent on anything above that, what is the finance charge in dollars? What is the APR?

A balance of $550 has an APR that is a combination of the APR for the first $200 and the APR for the remaining $350. If you owed only $200, the APR would be computed as the monthly finance charge multiplied by 12 months.

$$1\frac{1}{2}\% \times 12 = 18\% \text{ annually}$$

Any amount above $200 has an APR of 1 percent $\times$ 12 = 12 percent annually.

To compute this combined APR, you first compute the finance charge in dollars and cents for that month. Compute the monthly charge for the first $200.

$$1\frac{1}{2}\% \times \$200 = \$3.00$$

Now compute the monthly charge for the remaining $350.

$$1\% \times \$350 = \$3.50$$

The monthly finance charge is $3.00 + $3.50 = $6.50. And the total amount due is $556.50.

To calculate the combined annual rate, first figure the combined finance charge percentage for the current month. You do so by dividing the finance charge by the amount in the balance on which the charge is computed.

$$\$6.50 \div \$550 = 1.18\%$$

To find the annual rate based on the rate for this month, multiply that figure by 12.

$$12 \times 1.18\% = 14.16\%$$

Now you have the true rate for borrowing money on your credit card, and it's not $1\frac{1}{2}$ percent or 1 percent.

What does all this mean? It means that, if you consider nothing else, it would cost you $77.88 over a period of 1 year to retain $550 as your credit card balance ($14.16\% \times \$550 = \$77.88$).

This does not account for the fact that you must make a payment each month on your credit card balance. Each payment reduces the amount loaned, or *principal*, and therefore also the monthly finance charge. Suppose you decide to make 12 equal payments on the principal, or $45.83 ($550 ÷ 12 = $45.83), plus the monthly finance charge.

You can estimate the total finance charges for the year by figuring the average finance charge for each month. Just add the finance charges for the first month and for the last month and divide by 2.

As noted, the finance charge for the first month is $6.50. If the balance for the last month is approximately $45.83, the finance charge of $1\frac{1}{2}$ percent would be 69¢. The average finance charge would therefore be $3.60.

$$\$6.50 + .69 = \$7.19; \$7.19 \div 2 = \$3.595$$

Now you can multiply your answer by 12 to get a total finance charge of $43.14 for the year. Divided by the principal of $550, this equals 7.84 percent, the real APR for paying in 1 year.

Note that this estimate is based on the decision to make 12 equal payments plus finance charges. Most credit card invoices show a minimum payment. That minimum, in most cases, will not match the amount your family has chosen to pay. That means that you need not pay off what you owe as quickly as possible. The longer you take to pay, the higher your finance charge each month.

All this makes for a hidden cost of credit. Here is another hidden cost. If the monthly finance charge rate declines to 1 percent as the balance exceeds $200, the combined APR goes below 18 percent. Your family may think that you are paying less for credit. But the more you borrow, the more you have to pay in actual dollars.

Note another hidden cost of credit: the average daily balance. The balance left unpaid in your account is recorded for each day of the month. Then the balances for each day are added up, and the total is divided by the number of days in that month. If you make a payment at the beginning of the month, you have reduced the daily balance by that amount for that many days, and your average daily balance will be lower. If you pay at the end of the month, your average daily balance will, obviously, be higher.

Is it cheaper to use a credit card or simply to borrow money? As indicated, the costs of using a credit card can vary. But you know how to figure those costs. You will learn soon how to figure the cost of a loan from a bank, finance company, or credit union. Then you can decide which is better in any particular case. But in general, your family is better off not using the credit card. Unless you are careful and disciplined, you may let your debts increase and pay high finance charges month after month.

Sales taxes

On most merchandise you have to pay a sales tax in addition to a purchase price. Unlike income taxes, sales taxes are usually set at a flat rate, say 5 percent. In some states, some categories of items may have differential tax rates. For example, medicines may be taxed at lower rates than food, or food may not be taxed at all. In addition to state taxes, some items may have federal and local taxes. What is the state sales tax in your area? What other taxes on merchandise or services is your family paying?

Do you know how much your family pays in sales taxes each year? You can find the answer by itemizing.

To itemize, keep a record, daily or weekly, in which you write each purchase, with the sales tax rate and the amount paid. Both are generally easy to find. On a grocery receipt, a restaurant check, or an automobile sales invoice, the tax entry appears separately. If that information is not available, you can compute the tax from the price of the item. But remember that you have to know the tax rate.

Say the rate is 5 percent in your state. Shopping for a sweater, you buy one for $20.00. How much tax do you pay? Since 5 percent is half of 10 percent, you can figure the answer in your head; $\frac{1}{10}$ of $20.00 is $2.00, and half of that is $1.00. The total amount paid is $21.00.

The total amount paid is also 105 percent of the cost of the item. If you know only the total amount, how do you figure the tax? Divide the total amount by 105 percent, or 1.05. For the sweater, divide $21.00 by 1.05 to get $20.00; then subtract that from the total. The answer is $1.00.

How about your family's phone bill last month? The monthly service and long-distance charges came to

$40. How much tax were you charged on that amount if the federal tax is 3 percent, the state tax is 2 percent, and the city tax is 5.8 percent? Multiplying the phone bill by each of these percentages gives $1.20, $.80, and $2.32, for a total tax of $4.32. Alternately, you could add the tax percentages to get 10.8 percent, then multiply that by the phone charge to get $4.32.

The Math of Money Manage- ment

The money you and your family manage can be described in a simple equation.

Money Earned − Money Spent = Money Saved

The consumer math described in the first part of this section has pointed out ways of reducing spending, thereby making possible more savings. The saved money can be described in another equation.

Money Saved = Emergency Money + Invested Money

Now you have divided your savings into two kinds of money. The first constitutes a "liquid," or readily available, fund for normal spending or emergencies or special purposes such as a Christmas account. The second is money you have tied up so it can earn more money. Ideally, the more money earned, the more money you can spend, save, and invest.

Banking

However you plan to spend your money, you need someplace to keep it while you are deciding what to do with it. Banks serve that "keeping" purpose. Your family probably pays most bills by check, so checking accounts are a basic tool in managing money.

A checking account, in brief, is a source of liquid money. To use that money, all you have to do is write a check. You have two ways of knowing how much you have written in checks and how much you have left in the checking account: (1) You can add up your checks and deposits or (2) you can examine the statement received from the bank each month.

Either addition or subtraction comes into play with each deposit or check written. Over the course of a month, mistakes can occur in either of these operations. When you examine the monthly statement, you should check to see whether your bookkeeping matches the bookkeeping at the bank. If the balance

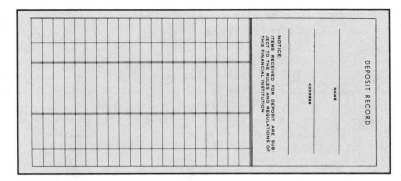

A deposit record shows all deposits. Be sure to get a receipt from the bank for each deposit made.

A check record shows deposits and checks as well as check fees, if any. Depositors can use a one-line method, in which each entry is recorded on one line. In a two-line method, the second line shows the purpose of the check or the source of the deposit.

doesn't agree with the bank statement, and you've done your checking properly, the bank may be in error.

With each statement most banks also send you the canceled checks. If time allows, compare each of these with the corresponding entry in the check record. Ideally, all the deposits made and checks written are noted on the statement.

You can calculate the final balance of the statement with this equation.

Final Balance = Initial Balance + Total Deposits
− Total Checks − Total Charges

Total each of these categories for this month. Insert each answer into the equation. If the final figure disagrees with the last balance in the checkbook, take these steps.

1. First, check for any charges assessed on the statement but not entered into the record. These might include a monthly service charge, a penalty for an overdraft, or charges for ordering new checks.

| | | COMMONWEALTH NATIONAL BANK | | ACCOUNT NO. |
| | | | | |

Ms. Marguerite Mitchell
2515 State St.
Chicago, IL 60613

ACCOUNT NO.
723 304322

Closing Date: 04/30/90

	Date Forwarded 04/01/90		Balance Forwarded $741.50	
Date	Check No.	Amount	Deposits	Balance
3/05			125.00	866.50
3/12	152	80.00		786.50
3/22	151	17.25	85.25	854.50
3/24	154	50.00		804.50

A bank statement for a checking account.

2. Second, look for checks written but not canceled. Add these back into the final balance, since they have not been subtracted yet by the bank.
3. Finally, on the check record look for errors in adding deposits or in subtracting checks or fees. If you find no errors, give the bank a call. The bank should answer your questions.

Simple and compound interest

Banks do other things besides handle checking accounts. Your family can also borrow money from them. Or you can put money in a savings account, in which case banks are borrowing from you. (For checking accounts, banks are also borrowing your money but without paying for the privilege, unless you have one of the newer types of checking accounts that earn interest on money deposited until the balance drops below a certain level.)

The subject of interest generally arouses interest. When money draws interest, it's "working" for you and your family. Of course, interest also determines the price you must pay for borrowing money, as you've already seen in the case of credit cards.

Savings accounts and investments earn two kinds of interest: simple and compound. Typically, a bank charges simple interest when you want to borrow money. The bank pays compound interest when you have a savings account. Let's simplify by starting with simple interest.

Simple interest

You can compute the interest on a loan by using a simple formula.

$$I = P \times r \times t$$

I stands for the amount of interest charged. P is the principal, or amount borrowed. The letter r stands for the annual rate of interest (remember APR, annual percentage rate?). And t represents time, specifically the number of years or fractions of years.

Suppose your family wants to borrow $550 with a cash loan at 8-percent annual interest for 1 year. How much interest would you be charged, and what would be your total repayment of the loan? Insert the figures into the formula.

$$I = \$550 \times 8\% \times 1 \text{ year} = \$44$$

Your total repayment would be $P + I = \$594$.

What if you want to borrow the $550 for 2 years? You have a choice of how to repay the loan. You can repay the entire sum at the end of 2 years or you can make periodic payments. If you make one payment, your interest would be calculated this way.

$$I = \$550 \times 8\% \times 2 = \$88$$

Obviously, this is twice the amount for a 1-year loan. If you decide to pay off half the loan after 1 year and the other half after 2 years, here is where you stand: you are borrowing the entire amount for 1 year but only half that total for the second year. So you would pay the full interest for the first year, or $44. For the second year, you would pay the interest for 1 year on $275 of principal.

$$I = \$275 \times 8\% \times 1 = \$22$$

So the total interest is $66, instead of $88.

Sounds simple? Well, it can become more complex. Suppose the bank offers a loan for 2 years at 8 percent annually; you want to pay it back in 24 monthly payments. You already know the interest will be $88 for 2 years at 8 percent.

Sounds fair enough. But is it? Your family will be paying what is called *add-on interest,* which is based on the false impression that you pay off none of the loan until the end of the loan period.

But you *will* be paying off the loan gradually. By the last payment, you will have paid off all but $\frac{1}{24}$ of the principal and $\frac{1}{24}$ of the interest. What is the actual rate of interest you would be paying? You find this by calculating the average monthly principal that is subject to interest. You take the principal for the first month, $550, and the last month, $22.92 ($550 ÷ 24 = $22.92), sum them, and divide by 2.

$$(\$550 + \$22.92) \div 2 = \$572.92 \div 2 = \$286.46$$

To find r, the rate, recall that $I = P \times r \times t$.

$$r = \frac{I}{P \times t} = \frac{\$88}{\$286.46 \times 2} = 15.36\%$$

Here, P is the average monthly principal as computed above. Thus 15.36 percent is a little more than your family bargained for.

Compound interest table (value of $1)

Number of periods	1.5%	2%	2.5%	3%	3.5%	4%
1	1.0150	1.0200	1.0250	1.0300	1.0350	1.0400
2	1.0302	1.0404	1.0506	1.0609	1.0712	1.0816
3	1.0457	1.0612	1.0769	1.0927	1.1087	1.1248
4	1.0614	1.0824	1.1038	1.1255	1.1475	1.1699
5	1.0773	1.1041	1.1314	1.1593	1.1877	1.2167
6	1.0934	1.1262	1.1597	1.1941	1.2293	1.2653
7	1.1098	1.1487	1.1887	1.2299	1.2723	1.3159
8	1.1265	1.1717	1.2184	1.2668	1.3168	1.3686
9	1.1434	1.1951	1.2489	1.3048	1.3629	1.4233
10	1.1605	1.2190	1.2801	1.3439	1.4106	1.4802
11	1.1779	1.2434	1.3121	1.3842	1.4600	1.5395
12	1.1956	1.2682	1.3449	1.4258	1.5111	1.6010
13	1.2136	1.2936	1.3785	1.4685	1.5640	1.6651
14	1.2318	1.3195	1.4130	1.5126	1.6187	1.7317
15	1.2502	1.3459	1.4483	1.5580	1.6753	1.8009
16	1.2690	1.3728	1.4845	1.6047	1.7340	1.8730
17	1.2880	1.4002	1.5216	1.6528	1.7947	1.9479
18	1.3073	1.4282	1.5597	1.7024	1.8575	2.0258
19	1.3270	1.4568	1.5987	1.7535	1.9225	2.1068
20	1.3469	1.4859	1.6386	1.8061	1.9898	2.1911
21	1.3671	1.5157	1.6796	1.8603	2.0594	2.2788
22	1.3876	1.5460	1.7216	1.9161	2.1315	2.3699
23	1.4084	1.5769	1.7646	1.9736	2.2061	2.4647
24	1.4295	1.6084	1.8087	2.0328	2.2833	2.5633
25	1.4509	1.6407	1.8539	2.0938	2.3673	2.6658

Which is the cheaper form of credit, a credit card or a bank loan? The answer: it depends on the kind of loan. Even simple interest is not so simple.

Compound interest

If you put money into a savings account, chances are that you will want to keep it there awhile. You want it to earn interest. Will the bank pay you as much interest for saving as it charges you for borrowing? Not likely. But to sweeten the deal and stimulate your "interest" in saving, the bank will *compound* the interest on your savings.

With compound interest, the interest earned on your principal is added to your principal at the end of a specific period. Then in the next period, this new total earns interest. With each new period, the amount of interest climbs. Your interest is earning interest.

5%	6%	7%	8%	9%	10%
1.0500	1.0600	1.0700	1.0800	1.0900	1.1000
1.1025	1.1238	1.1449	1.1664	1.1881	1.2100
1.1576	1.1910	1.2250	1.2597	1.2950	1.3310
1.2155	1.2625	1.3108	1.3605	1.4116	1.4641
1.2763	1.3382	1.4026	1.4693	1.5386	1.6105
1.3401	1.4186	1.5007	1.5869	1.6771	1.7716
1.4071	1.5036	1.6058	1.7138	1.8280	1.9487
1.4775	1.5938	1.7182	1.8059	1.9926	2.1436
1.5513	1.6895	1.8385	1.9990	2.1719	2.3679
1.6289	1.7908	1.9672	2.1589	2.3674	2.5937
1.7103	1.8983	2.1049	2.3316	2.5804	2.8531
1.7959	2.0122	2.2522	2.5182	2.8127	3.1384
1.8856	2.1329	2.4098	2.7196	3.0658	3.4523
1.9799	2.2609	2.5785	2.9372	3.3417	3.7975
2.0789	2.3966	2.7590	3.1722	3.6425	4.1772
2.1829	2.5404	2.9522	3.4259	3.9703	4.5950
2.2920	2.6928	3.1588	3.7000	4.3276	5.0545
2.4066	2.8543	3.3799	3.9960	4.7171	5.5599
2.5270	3.0256	3.6165	4.3157	5.1417	6.1159
2.6533	3.2071	3.8697	4.6610	5.6044	6.7275
2.7860	3.3996	4.1406	5.0338	6.1088	7.4003
2.9253	3.6035	4.4304	5.4365	6.6586	8.1403
3.0715	3.8198	4.7405	5.8715	7.2579	8.9543
3.2251	4.0489	5.0724	6.3412	7.9111	9.8497
3.3864	4.2919	5.4274	6.8485	8.6231	10.8347

Interest can be compounded annually, semiannually, quarterly, or daily. With a deposit of $100, let's say you have opened a savings account that compounds at 5.5 percent annually. How much money will the account contain at the end of 3 years, with no new deposits or withdrawals? To find the compounded amount, A, use this formula.

$$A = P(1 + r)^n$$

Here n is the number of years, P represents the principal, and r is the annual rate. You compute it this way.

$$A = \$100(1 + .055)^3 = \$100(1.1742) = \$117.42$$

The total interest earned over 3 years is $117.42 − $100 = $17.42.

Most savings accounts use a quarterly compounding formula. Say you have $400 in such an account at 6-percent interest. At the end of 1 year, how much has compounding yielded in actual interest income (the annual yield)?

The table on the previous page shows you how to find the answer. Quarterly compounding means there are 4 "add-up" periods during the year, so you find the *4* in the periods column. With 6 percent earned over a year, $\frac{1}{4}$ of that is earned in a quarter, or 6 percent ÷ 4 = 1.5 percent. Looking down the 1.5-percent column, you find that $1 ends up as $1.0614 after 4 periods. Multiplying that by $400, your balance ends up as $424.56 after 1 year. The actual annual yield is 6.14 percent ($24.56 ÷ $400 = 6.14%).

Calculator Shortcuts

As you've noticed, percents "figure" importantly in this section. You need to know how to figure percents with your calculator.

Suppose you are calculating the amount of interest you would pay on a 2-year loan for $550 at 8 percent. The formula for simple interest was $I = P \times r \times t$. Computing with percents, it's easy to use decimals. Just remember that to convert percentages to decimals you move the decimal point two places to the left.

When you use decimals, it doesn't matter in what order you enter the numbers for P, r, and t into your calculator.

$$I = \$550 \times .08 \times 2 = \$88$$

This order gives the same answer.

$$I = .08 \times 2 \times \$550 = \$88$$

If you bought a calculator that has a percent key, you may find that you are more relaxed using it instead. What happens if you use this sequence?

| 8 | % | × | 550 | × | 2 | = |

Did you get $88 again? Probably not, though calculators differ in their reaction to this kind of entry.

What may have happened is this. When you pressed the percent key, a 0 showed up on your readout. When you tried to multiply, it remained 0. If you went on to press 550, you had 0 again.

To multiply with percents, first enter a nonpercent.

| 550 | × | 8 | % | × | 2 | = |

After entering the first three keys, the moment you press the percent key, a 44 shows up on the readout. Now you have an ordinary figure that you can multiply by 2 to get 88.

This eliminates any operation on your calculator that begins with a percent figure. You say you want to divide 66 percent by 3? You must either say $\frac{1}{3} \times 66$ percent or use decimals.

Figuring income taxes

Not everyone has to pay federal income taxes. People with an income below a certain level don't have to file a tax return. For example, a married person under age 65 who files a joint return and whose income is below $8,900 pays nothing. This is also true for a single person under age 65 who is a head of household who earns less than $6,350.

Those who have to file have a choice of forms. Single taxpayers under 65 with no dependents can use Form 1040EZ if they could have filed Form 1040A. All others who earn less than $50,000 per year and have no itemized deductions can use Form 1040A if other requirements are met. Otherwise, Form 1040 is used.

You want to select the simplest form possible, but you don't want to miss any opportunity to reduce the taxes that have to be paid. There may be exemptions and deductions that will lower the taxable income, and you must select the income tax form that permits you to show them.

A quick, basic method to fill out a Form 1040EZ is described in the following discussion. Only the sim-

Taxes, Mortgages, Insurance, and Investments

Department of the Treasury - Internal Revenue Service

Form 1040EZ

Income Tax Return for Single filers with no dependents (0) **1988**

Name & address

Use the IRS mailing label. If you don't have one, please print.

L A B E L   H E R E

Print your name above (first, initial, last)

Present home address (number, street, and apt. no.). (If you have a P.O. box, see back.)

City, town, or post office, state, and ZIP code

Please print your numbers like this:

`0 1 2 3 4 5 6 7 8 9`

Your social security number

Please read the instructions on the back of this form. Also, see page 13 of the booklet for a helpful checklist.

Presidential Election Campaign Fund
Do you want $1 to go to this fund?

Note: Checking "Yes" will not change your tax or reduce your refund.

Yes No

Dollars   Cents

Report your income

Attach Copy B of Form(s) W-2 here

1 Total wages, salaries, and tips. This should be shown in Box 10 of your W-2 form(s). (Attach your W-2 form(s).) **1**

2 Taxable interest income of $400 or less. If the total is more than $400, you cannot use Form 1040EZ. **2**

3 Add line 1 and line 2. This is your **adjusted gross income.** **3**

Note: You must check Yes or No.

4 Can your parents or someone else claim you on their return?
☐ **Yes.** Do worksheet on back; enter amount from line E here.
☐ **No.** Enter 3,000 as your standard deduction. **4**

5 Subtract line 4 from line 3. If line 4 is larger than line 3, enter 0. **5**

6 If you checked the "Yes" box on line 4, enter **0.**
If you checked the "No" box on line 4, enter **1,950.**
This is your **personal exemption.** **6**

7 Subtract line 6 from line 5. If line 6 is larger than line 5, enter 0. This is your **taxable income.** **7**

Figure your tax

8 Enter your Federal income tax withheld from Box 9 of your W-2 form(s). **8**

9 Use the **single** column in the tax table on pages 37–42 of the Form 1040A/1040EZ booklet to find the **tax** on the amount shown on **line 7** above. Enter the amount of tax. **9**

Refund or amount you owe

Attach tax payment here

10 If line 8 is larger than line 9, subtract line 9 from line 8. Enter the **amount of your refund.** **10**

11 If line 9 is larger than line 8, subtract line 8 from line 9. Enter the **amount you owe.** Attach check or money order for the full amount, payable to "Internal Revenue Service." **11**

Sign your return

I have read this return. Under penalties of perjury, I declare that to the best of my knowledge and belief, the return is true, correct, and complete.

Your signature   Date

For IRS Use Only—Please do not write in boxes below.

For Privacy Act and Paperwork Reduction Act Notice, see page 3.

Form **1040EZ** (1988)

Form 1040EZ.

plest parts will be considered because there are so many variables in preparing tax forms. But there are many excellent books and articles, including those from the IRS, on how to file income taxes. After you've mastered the basic techniques described here, you should refer to a more complete source for information on how to prepare more difficult tax returns.

The process for filing a 1040EZ, as well as any other tax form, can be compared to an assembly line. Before looking in the tax table, you run your total income through this assembly line, which can be described with this equation:

**Tax-table Income = Total Income − Exemptions −
Adjustments − Deductions**

The first part of the assembly line involves determining the number of exemptions. This refers to the number of dependents in the family. Let's say you are a single adult. You have no other dependents. That means you have one exemption: yourself. You are filing Form 1040EZ, which has already figured out, on line 6, what your exemption is.

Let's say you have a wage income of $12,000, according to the W-2, or withholding tax form you received from your employer. You enter this amount on line 1. Your bank has informed you that your savings account earned $24 in interest. You enter this income on line 2. Line 3 is the sum of these, $12,024, and represents the adjusted gross income, or the total income.

At the next stage of the assembly line, you deduct the single exemption of $1,950. Now you write the taxable income on line 7: $10,074. The tax table tells you that a single person with your income has a tax of $1,511, which you enter on line 9.

How much do you owe the government? Or does the IRS owe you a refund? Your W-2 form indicates that $1,600 was withheld from your pay during the year. You enter this figure on line 8. You subtract line 9 from line 8, obtaining the refund due you—$89—on line 10.

Mortgages and housing

Because a house is usually the biggest of a family's "big ticket" items, most purchases involve a mortgage of some type. Many people are frightened by the language of mortgages, especially with so many kinds of "alternative financing" available today. But just keep in mind that a *mortgage* is simply a loan taken for a long period of time. And your family has to pay interest for the privilege of borrowing the principal.

A list of terms in this section will give you a brief rundown of the different mortgage types so you can recognize them. You will learn how to figure the actual

Form **1040A**
Department of the Treasury—Internal Revenue Service
U.S. Individual
Income Tax Return (0) **1988**

OMB No. 1545-0085

Step 1
Label
Use IRS label. Otherwise, please print or type.

L A B E L   H E R E

Your first name and initial (if joint return, also give spouse's name and initial)   Last name

Present home address (number, street, and apt. no.). (If you have a P.O. Box, see page 13 of the instructions.)

City, town or post office, state, and ZIP code

Your social security no.

Spouse's social security no.

For **Privacy Act and Paperwork Reduction Act Notice, see page 3.**

Presidential Election Campaign Fund

Do you want $1 to go to this fund? . . . . □ Yes   □ No
If joint return, does your spouse want $1 to go to this fund? □ Yes   □ No

Note: *Checking "Yes" will not change your tax or reduce your refund.*

Step 2
Check your filing status
(Check only one)

1 □ Single (See if you can use Form 1040EZ.)
2 □ Married filing joint r
3 □ Married filing separa and spouse's full nam
4 □ Head of household (v but not your depende
5 □ Qualifying widow(er

Step 3
Figure your exemptions
(See page 16 of instructions.)

6a □ **Yourself** If someone (su return, do not
6b □ **Spouse**

c **Dependents:**
1. Name (first, initial, and last nam

If more than 7 dependents, see page 19.

Attach Copy B of Form(s) W-2 here.

d If your child didn't live under a pre-1985 agreem
e Total number of exempt

Step 4
Figure your total income

Attach check or money order here.

7 Wages, salaries, tips, etc form(s). (Attach Form(s
8a **Taxable** interest incom and attach Schedule 1, F
b Tax-exempt interest i (DO NOT include on lin

9 Dividends. (If over $400,

10 Unemployment compen

11 Add lines 7, 8a, 9, and 10

Step 5
Figure your adjusted gross income

12a Your IRA deduction fro Rules for IRAs begin on
b Spouse's IRA deduction Rules for IRAs begin on
c Add lines 12a and 12b. E **adjustments.**

13 Subtract line 12c from l **gross income.** (If this you, see "Earned Income

Form 1040A.

Form **1040**
Department of the Treasury—Internal Revenue Service
U.S. Individual Income Tax Return **1988** (0)

For the year Jan.–Dec. 31, 1988, or other tax year beginning   , 1988, ending   , 19

OMB No. 1545-0074

Label
Use IRS label. Otherwise, please print or type.

L A B E L   H E R E

Your first name and initial (if joint return, also give spouse's name and initial)   Last name

Present home address (number, street, and apt. no. or rural route). (If a P.O. Box, see page 6 of Instructions.)

City, town or post office, state, and ZIP code

Your social security number

Spouse's social security number

For **Privacy Act and Paperwork Reduction Act Notice, see Instructions.**

Presidential Election Campaign

Do you want $1 to go to this fund? . . . . □ Yes   □ No
If joint return, does your spouse want $1 to go to this fund?. □ Yes   □ No

Note: *Checking "Yes" will not change your tax or reduce your refund.*

Filing Status
Check only one box.

1 □ Single
2 □ Married filing joint return (even if only one had income)
3 □ Married filing separate return. Enter spouse's social security no. above and full name here.
4 □ Head of household (with qualifying person). (See page 7 of Instructions.) If the qualifying person is your child but not your dependent, enter child's name here.
5 □ Qualifying widow(er) with dependent child (year spouse died ▶ 19   ). (See page 7 of Instructions.)

Exemptions
(See Instructions on page 8.)

6a □ **Yourself** If someone (such as your parent) can claim you as a dependent, do not check box 6a. But be sure to check the box on line 33b on page 2. . . . .
b □ **Spouse**

c **Dependents:**	(2) Check if under age 5	(3) If age 5 or older, dependent's social security number	(4) Relationship	(5) No. of months lived in your home in 1988
(1) Name (first, initial, and last name)				

If more than 6 dependents, see Instructions on page 8.

No. of boxes checked on 6a and 6b

No. of your children on 6c who:
● lived with you
● didn't live with you due to divorce or separation

No. of other dependents listed on 6c

d If your child didn't live with you but is claimed as your dependent under a pre-1985 agreement, check here . . ▶ □
e Total number of exemptions claimed . . . .

Add numbers entered on lines above ▶

Income
Please attach Copy B of your Forms W-2, W-2G, and W-2P here.
If you do not have a W-2, see page 6 of Instructions.

7 Wages, salaries, tips, etc. (attach Form(s) W-2) . . . . | 7
8a **Taxable** interest income (also attach Schedule B if over $400) . . . . | 8a
b **Tax-exempt** interest income (see page 11). DON'T include on line 8a | 8b
9 Dividend income (also attach Schedule B if over $400) . . . . | 9
10 Taxable refunds of state and local income taxes, if any, from worksheet on page 11 of Instructions . | 10
11 Alimony received . . . . | 11
12 Business income or (loss) (attach Schedule C). . . . . | 12
13 Capital gain or (loss) (attach Schedule D) . . . . | 13
14 Capital gain distributions not reported on line 13 (see page 11) . . . . | 14
15 Other gains or (losses) (attach Form 4797) . . . . | 15
16a Total IRA distributions . . | 16a | 16b Taxable amount (see page 11) | 16b
17a Total pensions and annuities | 17a | 17b Taxable amount (see page 12) | 17b
18 Rents, royalties, partnerships, estates, trusts, etc. (attach Schedule E) . . . . . | 18
19 Farm income or (loss) (attach Schedule F) . . . . | 19
20 Unemployment compensation (insurance) (see page 13) . . . . | 20
21a Social security benefits (see page 13) . . . . . . | 21a |
b Taxable amount, if any, from the worksheet on page 13 . . . . | 21b
22 Other income (list type and amount—see page 13) . . . . | 22
23 Add the amounts shown in the far right column for lines 7 through 22. This is your **total income** ▶ | 23

Adjustments to Income
(See Instructions on page 13.)

Please attach check or money order here.

24 Reimbursed employee business expenses from Form 2106, line 13 . | 24
25a Your IRA deduction, from applicable worksheet on page 14 or 15 | 25a
b Spouse's IRA deduction, from applicable worksheet on page 14 or 15 | 25b
26 Self-employed health insurance deduction, from worksheet on page 15 . | 26
27 Keogh retirement plan and self-employed SEP deduction . . . | 27
28 Penalty on early withdrawal of savings . . . . | 28
29 Alimony paid (recipient's last name and social security no. ▶   ) | 29
30 Add lines 24 through 29. These are your **total adjustments** . . . . | 30

Adjusted Gross Income

31 Subtract line 30 from line 23. This is your **adjusted gross income.** If this line is less than $18,576 and a child lived with you, see "Earned Income Credit" (line 56) on page 19 of the Instructions. If you want IRS to figure your tax, see page 16 of the Instructions ▶ | 31

Form 1040.

---

cost of a mortgage loan. You can compare different mortgage packages or you can examine different terms of the same mortgage. With this math skill, your family can shop for a mortgage and understand what you are looking at.

You have a choice of a variety of mortgages, besides the *standard* one with fixed payments. The *grad-*

Page 37

Section 4—1988 Tax Table

For persons with taxable incomes of less than $50,000

Example: Mr. and Mrs. Green are filing a joint return. Their taxable income on line 19 of Form 1040A is $23,250. First, they find the $23,250–23,300 income line. Next, they find the column for married filing jointly and read down the column. The amount shown where the income line and filing status column meet is $3,491. This is the tax amount they must write on line 20 of Form 1040A.

At least	But less than	Single (and 1040EZ filers)	Married filing jointly *	Married filing sepa-rately	Head of a house-hold
		Your tax is—			
23,200	23,250	4,183	3,484	4,569	3,484
23,250	23,300	4,197	(3,491)	4,583	3,491
23,300	23,350	4,211	3,499	4,597	3,499
23,350	23,400	4,225	3,506	4,611	3,506

If 1040A, line 19, OR 1040EZ, line 7 is—		And you are—			
At least	But less than	Single (and 1040EZ filers)	Married filing jointly *	Married filing sepa-rately	Head of a house-hold
		Your tax is—			
$0	$5	$0	$0	$0	$0
5	15	2	2	2	2
15	25	3	3	3	3
25	50	6	6	6	6
50	75	9	9	9	9
75	100	13	13	13	13
100	125	17	17	17	17
125	150	21	21	21	21
150	175	24	24	24	24
175	200	28	28	28	28
200	225	32	32	32	32
225	250	36	36	36	36
250	275	39	39	39	39
		43	43	43	43

If 1040A, line 19, OR 1040EZ, line 7 is—		And you are—			
At least	But less than	Single (and 1040EZ filers)	Married filing jointly *	Married filing sepa-rately	Head of a house-hold
		Your tax is—			
1,400	1,425	212	212	212	212
1,425	1,450	216	216	216	216
1,450	1,475	219	219	219	219
1,475	1,500	223	223	223	223
1,500	1,525	227	227	227	227
1,525	1,550	231	231	231	231
1,550	1,575	234	234	234	234
1,575	1,600	238	238	238	238
1,600	1,625	242	242	242	242
1,625	1,650	246	246	246	246
1,650	1,675	249	249	249	249
1,675	1,700	253	253	253	253
~7		257			

If 1040A, line 19, OR 1040EZ, line 7 is—		And you are—			
At least	But less than	Single (and 1040EZ filers)	Married filing jointly *	Married filing sepa-rately	Head of a house-hold
		Your tax is—			
2,700	2,725	407	407	407	407
2,725	2,750	411	411	411	411
2,750	2,775	414	414	414	414
2,775	2,800	418	418	418	418
2,800	2,825	422	422	422	422
2,825	2,850	426	426	426	426
2,850	2,875	429	429	429	429
2,875	2,900	433	433	433	433
2,900	2,925	437	437	437	437
2,925	2,950	441	441	441	441
2,950	2,975	444	444	444	444
2,975	3,000	448	448	44^	148

A segment of a tax table showing exemptions.

uated payment mortgage (GPM) starts with smaller payments that increase over the years. Many experts believe the GPM is the best bet for a family buying its first home. The *variable rate mortgage* (VRM) has an interest rate that may increase or decrease within limits during the period of the loan. Experts say to avoid this type. It will probably never decrease. A *rollover mortgage* is a short-term loan that can be renegotiated. This is more advantageous than the variable rate mortgage because you can take part in the negotiations. In a *price level adjusted mortgage,* the interest rate remains constant, but the size of the payment varies with a price index. Again, experts advise to avoid this one. Payments can vary from month to month—a tough challenge if you have a tight budget.

Payments and balance due will vary with the type of mortgage your family selects, the percent of interest charged on the mortgage, and the amount of the mortgage. Banks and title and trust companies have pamphlets explaining these variables. If you are considering a mortgage, you should study the pamphlet and discuss it in detail with your real estate loan officer until you are sure you understand all the possibilities. Then make your choice.

Your family has decided to look for a standard (straight) mortgage. You still have to consider carefully the terms of the mortgage because they will call for a substantial monthly payment for a number of years. You will also have other expenses, such things as heating and cooling bills; water, sewer, and electricity charges; and repairs and alterations. You should take all these items into account in your family's home budget.

Consider the role of the mortgage in your budget. Mortgages can vary with regard to the length of the loan term and the annual rate of interest. Together, these two factors tell you how much your monthly payment will be.

Amount of monthly interest per $1,000 principal

Interest rate	Length of mortgage		
	20 years	25 years	30 years
7.5%	$8.06	$7.39	$7.00
8.0	8.37	7.72	7.34
8.5	8.68	8.06	7.69
9.0	9.00	8.40	8.05
9.5	9.33	8.74	8.41
10.0	9.66	9.09	8.78
10.5	9.99	9.45	9.15
11.0	10.33	9.81	9.53
11.5	10.67	10.17	9.91
12.0	11.02	10.54	10.29
12.5	11.37	10.91	10.68
13.0	11.72	11.28	11.07
13.5	12.08	11.66	11.46
14.0	12.44	12.04	11.85
14.5	12.80	12.43	12.25
15.0	13.17	12.81	12.65

Your family wants to move. You are looking at a $60,000 house. Your banker offers you a mortgage with a 11.5 percent interest rate. You can choose between terms of 20, 25, or 30 years. If you choose 20 years, for each $1,000 in the principal, you will pay $10.67 for each monthly payment. For a $60,000 house, your monthly payment would be figured this way.

$$60 \times \$10.67 = \$640.20$$

How much in total payments would this be? Well, 20 years $\times$ 12 months/year = 240 payments.

$$240 \times \$640.20 = \$153,648.00$$

You would be paying $93,648.00 in excess of the closing price for the convenience of paying on time.

A 30-year term means a monthly payment of $9.91 per $1,000 of principal, or a monthly payment of $594.60. With 360 payments (30 × 12 months = 360), your total payments would be $214,056.00, or $154,056.00 over the cost of the house. You can look at any mortgage in the same way to see what your final costs will be.

Buying insurance

The following discussion will introduce important factors to consider when purchasing life, automobile, and health insurance. As with income taxes, the discussion is limited due to the complexity of the many insurance policies available. Expert advice, via good reference books or an advisor, is important anytime your family is considering purchasing a major insurance policy.

Insurance has been called a form of gambling. Every time your family pays a premium on an insurance policy, you are placing a bet, or making a partial payment on a bet, with the insurance company. If you "win" the bet, the insurance company has to pay off.

A risky business? Yes, insurance always involves taking a risk by paying for protection against possible problems. Insurance companies compute the probabilities that they will have to "pay off." The probabilities then determine the size of the premiums.

Life insurance

Are you gambling with your life when you buy life insurance? Not really. After all, everyone eventually loses the game of life. But where a life is insured, a family or other *beneficiary* "wins" by receiving the *face value* of the policy, the amount of the insurance. The person who lives a long life simply has to pay more premiums.

You could think of life insurance as a bet on the number of premiums the buyer will have to pay before the beneficiary collects. The younger the buyer the greater the number of premiums. The insurance company will collect more payments, so it can afford to charge younger people lower premiums.

It sounds simple, but insurance companies offer a variety of life insurance policies. With *term insurance,* the buyer is insured for a specific term, say 5 years. At the end of that time, the premium goes up for the next

Approximate annual premiums per $1,000 of insurance

Age		Term		Straight Life	Limited-payment		Endowment	
Male	Female	10-year	15-year		20-year	30-year	20-year	30-year
15				$10.11	17.97	$13.80	$42.47	$25.90
20	23	$ 4.99	$ 5.42	11.55	19.84	15.26	42.55	26.15
25	28	5.19	5.63	13.35	22.07	17.03	42.69	26.50
30	33	5.77	6.20	15.65	24.73	19.20	43.01	26.92
35	38	7.09	7.42	18.61	27.93	21.93	43.63	27.50
40	43	9.18	9.67	22.55	31.80	25.38	44.76	29.85
45	48	12.74	13.44	27.58	36.49	29.79	46.67	33.33
50	53	18.59	19.03	33.61	42.19	35.52	49.65	37.77
55	58	24.89		41.57	42.25		54.14	
60	63			52.71	58.68		61.26	

Reproduced with permission from CONSUMER MATH AND YOU by R. Robert Rosenberg and Joy Risser. © 1979 by McGraw-Hill, Inc., p. 296.
Policies under $10,000 are a little higher in premiums. Premiums are lower for policies of $25,000 and over. Policies for women are lower because women generally live longer.

term. The premium is low for a young, healthy person. *Straight life insurance* insures you for your whole life. It builds up a cash value in case you decide you want to borrow back some of your money. The premium is higher initially than for term insurance but remains the same throughout your life. A *limited-payment policy* is the same as straight life except that you pay a premium for a set period, say 20 or 30 years. An *endowment policy* resembles straight life, but it pays off after you reach a specified age. The payments come in either a lump sum or monthly payments. You have in effect a savings or investment plan, but with a relatively low percentage of return or yield.

Choosing a policy can be a challenge. The experts suggest that when you are young, you should consider a term policy. Why? You can eliminate the endowment type because you will have inadequate return on your investment. The other policies may commit you to pay too much in premiums too soon.

Suppose you are 20 years old and want $10,000 worth of coverage. The table shows you how to compute your annual premium. Multiply by the number of thousands of dollars. On a 10-year term policy, your premium would be $49.90 per year until age 30, $57.70 until age 40, $91.80 until age 50, and $185.90 until age 60: a total of $3,853 in premiums. For straight life, the annual premium would be $115.50, for a total of $4,620 to age 60. A 20-year limited payment policy costs $198.40 a year for 20 years, totaling $3,968. The term policy costs least.

Automobile insurance

How does your family play the gambling game with the insurance of your car? By examining the policies available and by comparing. A special area of concern in car insurance is the *deductible* allowance, the maximum repair charge that you would have to pay before the insurance company would pay the remainder.

For example, on collision coverage, the higher the deductible, the lower your premium for that part of the coverage. You can reasonably gamble that the savings on premiums will exceed the higher deductible that your family would have to pay in case of an accident. (Remember too that you have some control of the risks if all the drivers in the family practice sensible driving habits.)

Does your family have an older car? You may want to eliminate the collision coverage altogether. Because of depreciation, the dollar value of the car might be so low that the car wouldn't be worth fixing or replacing. (*Depreciation*, or the lessening in value of an item over time, will be explained in more detail in Sec. 5, "Business Math," of this part.)

Health insurance

Most health care coverage also starts with a deductible allowance. You pay a certain part of your medical bill, say $100, and the insurance company pays a percentage, say 80 percent, of the rest. If you had a bill of $500, how much of it would you pay? First, you have to pay the $100 deductible. Then you pay 20 percent of the remainder.

$$20\% \times \$400 = \$80$$

You would pay $180 of the original $500 bill.

Shopping for health insurance today involves almost endless complexities. For most persons, a reliable company and a trusted insurance agent offer basic protection.

Investments

Your family wants to invest, to use money saved to make additional money. You know that placing money in a savings account regularly can produce a nest egg after a number of years. For example, $10 deposited monthly, earning 6 percent annually, compounded

Earnings on $10 savings deposited per month, at selected interest rates, compounded monthly.

No. of years	4.5%	5%	Interest rates 5.5%	6%	6.5%
1	$ 122.96	$ 123.29	$ 123.62	$ 123.95	$ 124.29
2	251.54	252.86	254.18	255.52	256.86
3	386.01	389.03	392.07	395.15	398.25
4	526.63	532.13	537.71	543.35	549.06
5	673.68	682.53	691.52	700.65	709.92
6	827.47	840.59	853.96	867.60	881.49
7	988.29	1,006.70	1,025.53	1,044.79	1,064.49
8	1,156.48	1,181.28	1,206.73	1,232.86	1,259.68
9	1,332.36	1,364.74	1,398.10	1,432.46	1,467.66
10	1,516.29	1,557.56	1,600.22	1,644.32	1,689.91
11	1,708.64	1,760.20	1,813.68	1,869.17	1,926.75
12	1,909.79	1,973.16	2,039.13	2,107.83	2,179.37
13	2,120.15	2,196.97	2,277.24	2,361.12	2,448.80
14	2,340.13	2,432.18	2,528.71	2,629.97	2,736.19
15	2,570.19	2,679.38	2,794.31	2,915.30	3,042.71
16	2,810.77	2,939.17	3,074.82	3,218.15	3,369.65
17	3,062.36	3,212.19	3,371.07	3,539.58	3,718.36
18	3,325.46	3,499.13	3,683.96	3,880.74	4,090.30
19	3,600.61	3,800.68	4,014.42	4,242.83	4,487.01
20	3,888.35	4,117.59	4,363.43	4,627.14	4,910.14

monthly, would result in a balance of $4,627.14 after 20 years. A deposit of $50 a month would produce 5 times that amount, or $23,135.70.

The effects of inflation, however, would diminish the actual earnings. To use the language of investment, savings are no hedge against inflation. Savings can lose value faster than they earn interest. But savings serve a valid purpose in the short term. The money in a savings account is highly liquid (quick and easy to withdraw), so some of it can be "poured" into other investments that will earn at a higher rate. At the same time, the savings account is earning interest.

Now consider the characteristics of some of the investments your family can make. You would want to select any investment on the basis of such characteristics.

Very few, if any, investments are highly desirable on all characteristics. You would want to choose the kind of investment that suits your purpose. A common strategy is to diversify your investments so that each investment item will share some of each of these characteristics. As an inflation hedge (because its value

Investment category	Expected return	Risk	Inflation hedge	Liquidity	Tax liabilities	Management required
U.S. Treasury Bills (1-year bills)	7.13%	None	None	Good	Federal	None
U.S. Treasury Bonds	8.98%	None	None	Good	Federal	None
Municipal Bonds (Aaa)	7.36%	Little	None	Good	State	None
Corporate Bonds (Aaa)	9.71%	Little	None	Good	Federal & state	None
Corporate Bonds (A)	10.24%	More	None	Good	Federal & state	None
Preferred Stock	8.37%	More	Some	Good	Federal & state	Some
Common Stock	12.10%	Greatest	Hopeful	Fair	Federal & state	Some

could rise with inflation), you might have some common stock even though the risk is higher. You might also have United States Treasury bills or bonds as low-risk investments, even though they don't protect you against inflation. By diversifying, you are "covering all bets." Clearly, insurance is not the only purchase involving risks.

Stocks

Generally, *brokers* buy and sell stocks—trade them—on stock exchanges. The broker charges a commission on each purchase or sale; the commission figures as part of the price. A typical transaction involves 100 shares or a multiple of 100. If less than $100 is involved, the commission is usually 7.5 percent; it's about 2.4 percent for $100 to $800, with a "sweetener" of $7.50; 1.5 percent plus $15 is charged for purchases up to $2,500; and 1.1 percent plus $26 is charged for $2,500 to $5,000. These are only average fees; stock commissions are negotiable.

If your family bought 100 shares of MNO stock with a value of $12 a share, what was your total purchase cost? First, the shares cost $100 \times \$12 = \$1,200$. A commission of 1.5 percent plus $15 was assessed.

$$1.5\% \times \$1,200 = \$18; \$18 + \$15 = \$33$$

The total price, then, was $1,233. Three years later the value of 1 share of the stock has risen to $24, for a total value of $2,400.

The same commission will be charged if you sell your MNO stock.

$$.015 \times \$2,400 = \$36; \$36 + \$15 = \$51$$

But your family has made some money. You received the stock price *minus* the commission, or $2,349. Over three years the stock earned $2,349 − $1,233 = $1,116. You made 1,116/1,233 = 90.5 percent. Under tax law the profit represents a long-term capital gain, and an individual is allowed a tax deduction of 60 percent of his net long-term capital gain. This is another good reason for investing in stocks.

While you held your MNO stock you collected a dividend of $1.50 per share annually. For 100 shares, that's $150. The "yield" or annual rate of return is the quotient.

$$\frac{\text{total dividend}}{\text{total cost}} = \$150 \div \$1,233 = 12.2\%$$

That is an excellent yield indeed.

Bonds and IRA's

You can calculate the yield on a bond in the same way. Suppose you bought a bond at *par value* (true or face value), $1,200, and it pays 9.5-percent interest. That comes to 9.5 percent × $1,200 = $114. For a par value purchase, the yield is the same as the interest.

$$\text{Yield} = \$114 \div \$1,200 = 9.5\%$$

If you paid $1,000 for the bond, the *interest* would still be computed on the par value, $114. But the *yield* is computed on the purchase price, or $114 ÷ $1,000 = 11.4 percent.

The United States government permits various kinds of *tax shelters,* ways to invest money and not pay taxes on it, including the Individual Retirement Account, or IRA. With an IRA you can set aside so much money annually, exempt from taxes, and invest it. If you set aside $2,000 every year and invest it in an IRA savings account at 6 percent, the balance will compound after 25 years to give you a nest egg of $116,314. But you cannot withdraw your money from an IRA without paying a penalty until you are $59\frac{1}{2}$.

You have a choice of how to invest your IRA money, so you are not limited to 6-percent earnings. Remember inflation.

An IRA plan and how it grows

Years elapsed	Contribution this year	Amount available from previous yr.	Total nest egg at work this yr.	Int. earned this year (no tax)	Total nest egg available to go to work next year
1	$2,000	$ 0	$ 2,000	$ 120	$ 2,120
2	2,000	2,120	4,120	247	4,367
3	2,000	4,367	6,367	382	6,749
4	2,000	6,749	8,749	525	9,274
5	2,000	9,274	11,274	676	11,950
6	2,000	11,950	13,950	837	14,787
7	2,000	14,787	16,787	1,007	17,794
8	2,000	17,794	19,794	1,188	20,982
9	2,000	20,982	22,982	1,379	24,361
10	2,000	24,361	26,361	1,582	27,943
11	2,000	27,943	29,943	1,797	31,740
12	2,000	31,740	33,740	2,024	35,764
13	2,000	35,764	37,764	2,266	40,030
14	2,000	40,030	42,030	2,522	44,552
15	2,000	44,552	46,552	2,793	49,345
16	2,000	49,345	51,345	3,081	54,426
17	2,000	54,426	56,426	3,386	59,812
18	2,000	59,812	61,812	3,709	65,521
19	2,000	65,521	67,521	4,051	71,572
20	2,000	71,572	73,572	4,414	77,986
21	2,000	77,986	79,986	4,799	84,785
22	2,000	84,785	86,785	5,207	91,992
23	2,000	91,992	93,992	5,640	99,632
24	2,000	99,632	101,632	6,098	107,730
25	2,000	107,730	109,730	6,584	116,314

Assessing your financial situation

Effective money management means keeping good records of the money you earn and spend. Remember the basic equation, Money Earned − Money Spent = Money Saved? Concentrate for a moment on the left side of the equation. If you itemize all your family's income and expenses for the past year, you should come up with something like the chart on page 754.

Some basic math is useful here. For each entry in the annual column, divide by 12 and enter the answer in the monthly column. Now you have an average for that transaction on a monthly basis. With the monthly figure, you have a kind of motion picture of your finances for the past year.

INCOME

	Annual*	Monthly
TOTAL TAKE-HOME INCOME,	$_____	$_____
WAGE INCOME	_____	_____
INCOME from interest, dividends, etc.	_____	_____
OTHER INCOME	_____	_____
TOTAL	$_____	$_____

EXPENSES

	Annual*	Monthly
FIXED EXPENSES		
Taxes not withheld from income	$_____	$_____
Savings	_____	_____
Investments	_____	_____
Insurance premiums _____	_____	_____
(Types of coverage) _____	_____	_____
_____	_____	_____
Mortgage or rent	_____	_____
Loan payments	_____	_____
Other credit payments	_____	_____
TOTAL FIXED EXPENSES:	$_____	$_____
VARIABLE EXPENSES		
Food and beverages	$_____	$_____
Supplies	_____	_____
Utilities: Gas or oil	_____	_____
Electricity	_____	_____
Telephone	_____	_____
Water and sewer	_____	_____
Household operation and maintenance	_____	_____
Transportation: Automobile expenses	_____	_____
Public transportation	_____	_____
Clothing purchases	_____	_____
Laundry, cleaning	_____	_____
Medical care	_____	_____
Dental care	_____	_____
Gifts and contributions (charity)	_____	_____
Educational expenses	_____	_____
Personal expenses	_____	_____
Family allowances	$_____	$_____
Vacations	$_____	$_____
Miscellaneous expenses	_____	_____
TOTAL VARIABLE EXPENSES:		
TOTAL EXPENSES, Fixed and Variable:		

*Other period if different from annual.

A sample chart for recording last year's financial transactions.

Are you satisfied with what you see? Would you like to improve things? Why not set up a family budget? Here you can and should indicate what the anticipated monthly income and expenses will be. How do your fixed payments vary from month to month? How about income? In what month will you encounter a tight squeeze, and what months will show a surplus? If you find a surplus, what can you do about eliminating the tight times? Using the workup for last year, what expenses did you find, and didn't realize before, that the family could cut down on? By planning, you can actually find ways to reduce expenses.

But expenses are only one element of money management. To give your finances a more complete health checkup, you need to look at your net worth. *Net worth* is defined by this equation.

Net Worth = Assets − Liabilities

Net Worth Statement   Year _____

ASSETS

Cash: amount on hand $_____

      savings accounts   _____

      checking accounts   _____

House, current market value   _____

Other real estate, market value   _____

Household furnishings, value   _____

Life insurance, cash value   _____

Automobile, current retail value   _____

Stocks and bonds, current value   _____

Money owed you   _____

Other assets   _____

              TOTAL $_____

LIABILITIES

Mortgages, balance due $_____

Installment debts, balance due   _____

Credit card purchases, balance due   _____

Charge accounts, current balance   _____

Other debts, total amount owed   _____

              TOTAL $_____

NET WORTH

Assets minus liabilities $_____

A simple net worth statement.

Assets are everything you own and everything that is owed to you. Liabilities are everything you owe to others.

Your statement of net worth shows the results of various transactions. To simplify discussion, say you are a single adult who bought an automobile for $5,000. Then you have an asset worth $5,000 less depreciation. If you study the loan agreement, you will probably find that you have a responsibility to repay a total loan of something near $5,900. Now tally up the rest of your assets and liabilities to find your net worth.

Ideally, your net worth is positive; your assets exceed your liabilities. If they do not, you know where to make changes. Identify the items that you can change to increase your net worth. You already know ways to cut expenses. Money not spent is money saved.

5

Business Math

Do you want to know how math is used to run a business? To make more money and cut costs? Read on.

Section 4 of this part showed you how to use math in making personal financial decisions. Business involves countless financial decisions. As you'll see, the techniques of ''money math'' are as important to running a business as they are to running a household.

Businesspersons selling to consumers have to have certain information. If you owned an auto dealership you would have to know what you paid for the cars you sold. You would have to calculate quickly what the consumer can only guess, what markup, or profit, you would charge on a car. As a merchant, you would have to know how to figure discounts, the same as you did in ''Money Math.'' You would have to figure sales taxes accurately. If you sold on credit, you would have to figure the cost of credit you would charge a customer.

Business math uses the principles of consumer math, in part. But it also involves the fundamentals of money management math. Previous sections of this part have discussed household and personal math. And what is a business but a special kind of "household" to be managed? Just as your family turns to math to invest and save, to cut expenses and increase savings, a business uses math every day for much the same purposes. As an individual or family, you have "net worth"; a business has "capital." This is expressed in this equation: Capital = Assets − Liabilities.

This section considers some of the ingredients that can go into this equation. You will learn how to deal with each ingredient separately and how to use math to put the ingredients together. You can then make informed business decisions.

Income ingredients, or assets, are considered first. Income for employees usually takes the form of commissions or salaries. If you are self-employed, your earnings may take the form of commissions. As an employer, you would have to be able to figure the gross amount of income and the net earnings for each employee; you would deduct everything that must be deducted. The income of your business would emerge as gross and net profit.

The second major ingredient is costs, or liabilities. One major cost has been noted: labor, or total payroll. Another major cost in business and industry is equipment. This cost has a time dimension called depreciation.

Simple accounting (math) principles help you put together the ingredients. Once you know how to record the figures you need, you can plug them into basic equations like the one given previously. You can judge the financial health of your company or of any company you care to investigate.

You can use the same kind of information for another purpose: to set up a budget for planning the day-to-day and future operations of a business. *Your* business perhaps.

Salaries and Commissions

The income you work for can be figured in different ways. If you are paid by the hour or by some other unit of time, you are paid a *wage*. You may receive a *salary*, a fixed amount weekly, monthly, or annually. If you are paid by the amount of work or product you turn out, you work on a *piecework* system. If you are paid a percentage of everything you sell, you have a *commission* arrangement.

Wages and salaries

Most often, an employer figures and pays wages on an hourly basis. If one employee earns $5 per hour and works 35 hours a week, what is the weekly salary?

$5/hr. × 35 hr./wk. = $175/wk.

If the employee works 50 weeks a year, what is the yearly salary? Multiplying the weekly salary by 50, you arrive at $8,750. These figures are a person's gross wage on a weekly and yearly basis.

An employer advertises a job that pays an annual salary of $15,000. Can you figure out how much the weekly or hourly rate is? Assuming a 50-week work year, you divide the annual figure by 50 to get $300 per week. Dividing $300 by 35 hours, you get an hourly salary rate of $8.57 per hour.

What would the hourly rate be if the employee had to work an average 40-hour week? A 50-hour week?

Obviously, in a particular week an employee paid an hourly wage may work less than a full 35- or 40-hour week. Another employee might work more than the regular time and is paid *overtime* for the extra hours. For this and other reasons, it's necessary to keep a record of the time put in each week by each employee. A payroll ledger serves that purpose.

Payroll ledger

Employee	Marital status	S	M	T	W	Th	F	S	Total hours Reg.	O.T.	Rate per hour	Gross pay Reg.	O.T.	Total	No. ex-emp-tions	FITW	FICA	Other	Total	Net pay
Adams	S		8	8	9	9	6	2			5.00				1					
Green	M		8	8	8	8	8				5.20				2					
Wilson	M		8	9	7	9	9	4			4.90				3					
TOTAL																				

Employee Adams has put in the number of hours indicated on the payroll ledger: 8, 8, 9, 9, 6, and 2. The regular workweek at this business is 35 hours. How many regular hours and overtime hours has Adams put in? Simple addition shows that Adams has put in a total of 42 hours: 35 at regular time, 7 on overtime.

Overtime is usually paid at the rate of time and a half or double time. At time and a half, $1\frac{1}{2}$ times the regular hourly rate is paid for all hours worked over the regular workweek. That means the overtime rate of pay for Adams is 1.5 × $5 = $7.50/hour. Now you can calculate Adams' gross salary. The regular salary for 35 hours is 35 × $5 = $175. The overtime salary for 7 hours is figured this way.

7 hr. × $7.50/hr. = $52.50

That yields a total gross salary of $227.50 for that week. Now try to figure the gross wages for the other two employees before reading on.

You should have found that Green worked an extra 5 hours, at $1\frac{1}{2}$ times $5.20, or $7.80/hour. Green's regular salary is $182/week. Overtime for Green comes to this amount.

5 hr. × $7.80/hr. = $39

This gives a total salary of $221.

Wilson worked 11 hours overtime: 1.5 × $4.90 = $7.35/hr.

11 hr. × $7.35/hr. = $80.85

That yields a total gross salary for Wilson of $252.35 for the week.

How much did the three employees receive in overtime pay that week? The regular salary total was $528.50; the total salary was $700.85, giving a difference of $172.35.

Piecework

A few companies pay according to a piecework system. The companies feel that this system gives a worker more incentive to produce. A ball bearing company might pay each employee 20¢ to finish one bearing. How much does an employee make when producing 1,350 bearings in one week?

1,350 × $.20 = $270 (Gross Pay)

Likewise, if an employee earned $300 in one week, how many bearings were produced? Dividing $300 by $.20, you can readily calculate that the total was 1,500 bearings.

Commissions

The commission is a form of piecework. It too provides an incentive to produce more. Used typically in sales, it may be the only form of payment. But many salespersons receive a salary or "draw" (advance) as well. Some employees earn income from customers or clients in the form of commissions; an example is a stock broker.

Say you own a clothing store. Your sales clerks receive a commission of 4 percent. Selling a $150 suit, how much commission does a salesperson earn? You calculate this way

$$\$150 \times 4\% = \$6$$

Knowing the commission rate, you can figure a commission from a sale or do the reverse, compute the size of the sale from the size of the commission. The first problem is solved with this equation.

Amount of Commission
= Sale × Commission Rate

To find the sale, you use this formula

$$\textbf{Sale} = \frac{\textbf{Amount of Commission}}{\textbf{Commission Rate}}$$

Commission collected by a factor.

MICHAELS AND MICHAELS, COMMISSION AGENTS
CHICAGO, IL 60606

ACCOUNT
SALES

FOR: SKLAREWITZ Hardware, Inc.
9453 Longwood Dr.
Beverly, IL 60402

DATE: JAN. 10, 1990

Dec. 12	200 Boxes Nails, assorted @ $3.75	$ 750.00		
18	150 Boxes Screws @ $3.50	525.00		
27	100 Cans S & J Paint @ 8.50	850.00		
Jan. 3	400 Plastic Buckets @ 1.75	700.00		
9	200 Boxes Brads @ 2.15	430.00		
	Gross Proceeds		$3,255.00	
	Charges:			
	Freight	118.25		
	Storage	42.75		
	Commission, 4% of $3,255.00	130.20	291.20	
	Net Proceeds		$2,963.80	

Suppose you are a salesperson yourself. Your goal in commissions for a week is $300. You want to figure how much you have to sell to reach that goal. Divide the target commission total, $300, by the commission rate, 4 percent, to get $7,500 in merchandise. If your yearly goal is $20,000 in commissions, you will try to sell $20,000 ÷ 4 percent = $500,000.

Some businesses depend on commissions for their incomes. One kind of business, *factoring,* sells for manufacturers. The factor, or agent, deducts commissions from the gross proceeds paid to the manufacturer, leaving the manufacturer the net proceeds. If the factor handles storage and freight, those expenses are also deducted from the gross proceeds.

Factoring service saves the manufacturer the expense of carrying a sales force. The manufacturer thus does not have to pay fringe benefits or social security taxes for sales employees.

Do you recall the example of stock transaction commission in Section 4, "Money Math"? In that case the commission rate decreased with the size of the transaction so that investors would be encouraged to place larger orders.

If you go into selling, chances are that you will work on commission. Perhaps your income will be in "finder's fees." In a typical situation, someone with a business to sell asks you to find a buyer. Your finder's fee could be 10 percent of the gross proceeds of the sale. Your incentive is, the more you can get for the business, the more you will make. You find someone who will pay $100,000 for the business and collect $10,000, or 10% of $100,000, for your assistance.

Gross and Net Earnings

As the payroll ledger on page 759 shows, as an employer, you could calculate the weekly earnings of each of your employees. You note that "pay" is listed under two headings: gross pay and net pay. The relationship between the two is stated in this equation.

Net Pay = Gross Pay − Total Deductions

In the ledger, three kinds of deductions are listed: (1) federal income tax withheld (FITW), (2) social security and disability taxes (Federal Insurance Contributions Act, or FICA), and (3) other. The first two are the most important deductions, since they are generally the largest of payroll deductions.

Withholding tax

As an employee, you must *prepay* your income taxes in installments taken from each paycheck. (The self-employed person makes a quarterly *estimated tax payment*.) Your employer withholds a certain proportion of your gross pay from each paycheck—hence the name "withholding tax," or FITW. Payroll periods may be weekly, biweekly, semimonthly, or monthly, so the amount withheld is calculated accordingly.

Remember from "Money Math" how you entered the total taxes withheld for the year? This information was supplied to you by your employer on the W-2 Form, which you attached to your tax return form.

If you are an employer yourself, you have a choice of methods for computing the withholding tax for your employees. Under one method, you compute a percentage of each employee's gross pay. With a second method, the "wage bracket" method, tables tell you at a glance the withholding tax that has been computed for a given level of pay. Both methods of figuring the tax are available for all payroll periods.

Tables for computing withholding taxes under the percentage method.

(For Wages Paid After December 1988)

Alternative 1.—Tables for Percentage Method Withholding Computations

Table A(1)—WEEKLY PAYROLL PERIOD (Amount for each allowance claimed $38.46)

	Single Person					Married Person		
If the wage in excess of allowance amount is:		The income tax to be withheld shall be:			If the wage in excess of allowance amount is:		The income tax to be withheld shall be:	
Over—	But not over—	Of such wage—	From/to product		Over—	But not over—	Of such wage—	From/to product
$0	—$21	0			$0	—$62	0	
$21	—$378	15% less	$3.15		$62	—$657	15% less	$9.30
$378	—$885	28% less	$52.29		$657	—$1,501	28% less	$94.71
$885	—$2,028	33% less	$96.54		$1,501	—$3,695	33% less	$169.76
$2,028	—	28% PLUS	$4.86		$3,695	—	28% PLUS	$14.99

Table B(1)—BIWEEKLY PAYROLL PERIOD (Amount for each allowance claimed $76.92)

	Single Person					Married Person		
If the wage in excess of allowance amount is:		The income tax to be withheld shall be:			If the wage in excess of allowance amount is:		The income tax to be withheld shall be:	
Over—	But not over—	Of such wage—	From/to product		Over—	But not over—	Of such wage—	From/to product
$0	—$42	0			$0	—$123	0	
$42	—$756	15% less	$6.30		$123	—$1,313	15% less	$18.45
$756	—$1,769	28% less	$104.58		$1,313	—$3,002	28% less	$189.14
$1,769	—$4,055	33% less	$193.03		$3,002	—$7,389	33% less	$339.24
$4,055	—	28% PLUS	$9.72		$7,389	—	28% PLUS	$30.21

Table C(1)—SEMIMONTHLY PAYROLL PERIOD (Amount for each allowance claimed $83.33)

	Single Person					Married Person		
If the wage in excess of allowance amount is:		The income tax to be withheld shall be:			If the wage in excess of allowance amount is:		The income tax to be withheld shall be:	
Over—	But not over—	Of such wage—	From/to product		Over—	But not over—	Of such wage—	From/to product
$0	—$46	0			$0	—$133	0	
$46	—$819	15% less	$6.90		$133	—$1,423	15% less	$19.95
$819	—$1,917	28% less	$113.37		$1,423	—$3,252	28% less	$204.94
$1,917	—$4,393	33% less	$209.22		$3,252	—$8,005	33% less	$367.54
							28% PLUS	

Say you are figuring the withholding tax weekly for one person whose gross pay last week was $220. You have to know two things in order to figure the tax: the amount of pay and the employee's marital status. The first you already know. Suppose that this employee is single. How much do you withhold?

First, figure the tax using the percentage method of computation. You would find the appropriate payroll period, which is weekly. Look at the part of the table on page 763 that deals with single persons, the left side. Now locate the line on which your employee's weekly pay falls. It shows a pay range of $21 to $378. Perform the appropriate calculations

$$(\$220 \times .15) - \$3.15 =$$
$$\$33 - \$3.15 = \$29.85$$

How much net pay does that leave, just deducting withholding tax? The answer is $220 − $29.85 = $190.15.

The tax bracket method involves finding the appropriate column and line in the weekly withholding tax tables. Look at the Single Persons section of the Wage Bracket Percentage Method Table. In "Money Math," remember, you noted that one tax exemption is allowed for each person the taxpayer supports. Because a single taxpayer may support others besides himself, you will find different columns for "the number of withholding allowances claimed." If the employee supports only himself, the tax appears in the "1" row.

Looking across this row, find the tax bracket that fits a paycheck of $220. What is the tax, $59.46 or $225.21? You're right if you picked $59.46. Deducting this from the gross pay leaves a remainder of $160.54, which is then multiplied by 15.0% for a product of $24.08. Deducting this product from the gross pay leaves a net pay of $195.92. The second method has left a larger net pay for your employee.

If more tax is withheld every paycheck, the taxpayer may be able to claim a refund from the Internal Revenue Service. With this approach, the employee can conveniently budget tax payments over the year, without paying a lump sum at the end of the year. This approach has a disadvantage, however. The IRS has in effect borrowed the employee's money interest free. The employee could have deposited that money in a

(For Wages Paid After **December 1988**)

Wage Bracket Percentage Method Table for Computing
Income Tax Withholding from Gross Wages

Weekly Payroll Period

If the number of allowances is–	Single Persons				Married Persons			
	And gross wages are–		from/to gross wages [1]	Multiply result by–	And gross wages are–		from/to gross wages [1]	Multiply result by–
	Over	But not over			Over	But not over		
	A	**B**	**C**	**D**	**A**	**B**	**C**	**D**
0	$0	$378.00	subtract $21.00	15.0%	$0	$657.00	subtract $62.00	15.0%
	378.00	885.00	subtract 186.75	28.0%	657.00	1,501.00	subtract 338.25	28.0%
	885.00	2,028.00	subtract 292.55	33.0%	1,501.00	3,695.00	subtract 514.42	33.0%
	2,028.00	....	ADD 17.36	28.0%	3,695.00	....	ADD 53.54	28.0%
1	$0	$416.46	subtract $59.46	15.0%	$0	$695.46	subtract $100.46	15.0%
	416.46	923.46	subtract 225.21	28.0%	695.46	1,539.46	subtract 376.71	28.0%
	923.46	2,066.46	subtract 331.01	33.0%	1,539.46	3,733.46	subtract 552.88	33.0%
	2,066.46	....	subtract 21.10	28.0%	3,733.46	....	ADD 15.08	28.0%
2	$0	$454.92	subtract $97.92	15.0%	$0	$733.92	subtract $138.92	15.0%
	454.92	961.92	subtract 263.67	28.0%	733.92	1,577.92	subtract 415.17	28.0%
	961.92	2,104.92	subtract 369.47	33.0%	1,577.92	3,771.92	subtract 591.34	33.0%
	2,104.92	....	subtract 59.56	28.0%	3,771.92	....	subtract 23.38	28.0%
3	$0	$493.38	subtract $136.38	15.0%	$0	$772.38	subtract $177.38	15.0%
	493.38	1,000.38	subtract 302.13	28.0%	772.38	1,616.38	subtract 453.63	28.0%
	1,000.38	2,143.38	subtract 407.93	33.0%	1,616.38	3,810.38	subtract 629.80	33.0%
	2,143.38	....	subtract 98.02	28.0%	3,810.38	....	subtract 61.84	28.0%
4	$0	$531.84	subtract $174.84	15.0%	$0	$810.84	subtract $215.84	15.0%
	531.84	1,038.84	subtract 340.59	28.0%	810.84	1,654.84	subtract 492.09	28.0%
	1,038.84	2,181.84	subtract 446.39	33.0%	1,654.84	3,848.84	subtract 668.26	33.0%
	2,181.84	....	subtract 136.48	28.0%	3,848.84	....	subtract 100.30	28.0%
	$0	$570.30	subtract $213.30	15.0%	$0	$849.30	subtract $254.30	15.0%
	570.30	1.077.30	subtract 379.05	28.0%	~~~ ~~	1,693.30	subtract 530.55	28.0%
			~tract		3.887 30		706.72	~

Part of wage bracket table used in calculating an employee's withholding tax.

savings account or used it for needed purchases. As an employer, you would not be affected; but your employees would.

Social security (FICA)

The Federal Insurance Contributions Act (FICA) governs payments of social security taxes, the second tax that the employer withholds regularly from employees' paychecks. The self-employed person pays self-employment tax quarterly when estimated tax payments are made.

However you pay your social security taxes, they involve having to contribute a certain percentage of income to the government annually. As the social security schedule on the next page shows, the percentage has increased somewhat over the years. In 1989, for example, it was 7.51 percent.

With social security taxes, a *ceiling* limits the amount of income that is subject to taxation. The ceil-

Social security tax rate schedule by year

Year	Maximum income subject to tax	Employer and employee tax (each) %	Maximum tax (each)	Self-employed tax (%)	Maximum tax
1984	$37,800	6.85	$2,589.30	11.30	$4,271.40
1985	39,600	7.05	2,791.80	11.80	4,672.80
1986	42,000	7.15	3,003.00	12.30	5,166.00
1987	43,800	7.15	3,131.70	12.30	5,387.40
1988	45,000	7.51	3,379.50	13.02	5,859.00
1989	48,000	7.51	3,604.80	13.02	6,249.60

ing (in the second column) rises regularly: in 1989 it was $48,000. The rise is based on an escalator provision, or a planned method of increase that is written into federal law.

Whatever amount the employer withholds from an employee's paycheck is matched by an equal sum contributed by the employer. Thus, in 1989 an amount totaling 15.02 percent (7.51% plus 7.51%) of the employee's gross pay was paid to the government during each payroll period. Half that sum came from the employee's paycheck. What about the self-employed person? In 1989, he was charged 13.02 percent of his self-employment income. So for an income of $10,000, the self-employment tax would be $1,302.

You can readily compute the amount of FICA tax to be withheld from an employee's paycheck. Using the percentage method, simply multiply the employee's gross pay for the pay period by the tax rate. If one week's gross pay in 1989 was $220, this would be the tax withheld.

$$\$220 \times 7.51\% = \$16.52$$

You could also use a table that has the tax figured out for different brackets.

The social security tax table has a series of income brackets. Your pay for a pay period falls within a particular range of figures—a bottom figure and a top figure. You can average these two figures, then multiply the average by the tax rate percentage to calculate the tax withheld.

As before, say your employee earned $220 in gross pay last week. But the table only goes up to $100. The lower right part of the table shows multiples of $100. At the tax rate of 7.51 percent, for $200 you would

Social Security Employee Tax Table for 1989
7.51% employee tax deductions

Wages at least	But less than	Tax to be withheld	Wages at least	But less than	Tax to be withheld	Wages at least	But less than	Tax to be withheld	Wages at least	But less than	Tax to be withheld
51 07	51 20	3 84	63 72	63 85	4 79	76 37	76 50	5 74	89 02	89 15	6 69
51 20	51 34	3 85	63 85	63 99	4 80	76 50	76 64	5 75	89 15	89 29	6 70
51 34	51 47	3 86	63 99	64 12	4 81	76 64	76 77	5 76	89 29	89 42	6 71
51 47	51 60	3 87	64 12	64 25	4 82	76 77	76 90	5 77	89 42	89 55	6 72
51 60	51 74	3 88	64 25	64 39	4 83	76 90	77 04	5 78	89 55	89 69	6 73
51 74	51 87	3 89	64 39	64 52	4 84	77 04	77 17	5 79	89 69	89 82	6 74
51 87	52 00	3 90	64 52	64 65	4 85	77 17	77 30	5 80	89 82	89 95	6 75
52 00	52 14	3 91	64 65	64 79	4 86	77 30	77 44	5 81	89 95	90 08	6 76
52 14	52 27	3 92	64 79	64 92	4 87	77 44	77 57	5 82	90 08	90 22	6 77
52 27	52 40	3 93	64 92	65 05	4 88	77 57	77 70	5 83	90 22	90 35	6 78
52 40	52 53	3 94	65 05	65 18	4 89	77 70	77 83	5 84	90 35	90 48	6 79
52 53	52 67	3 95	65 18	65 32	4 90	77 83	77 97	5 85	90 48	90 62	6 80
52 67	52 80	3 96	65 32	65 45	4 91	77 97	78 10	5 86	90 62	90 75	6 81
52 80	52 93	3 97	65 45	65 58	4 92	78 10	78 23	5 87	90 75	90 88	6 82
52 93	53 07	3 98	65 58	65 72	4 93	78 23	78 37	5 88	90 88	91 02	6 83
53 07	53 20	3 99	65 72	65 85	4 94	78 37	78 50	5 89	91 02	91 15	6 84
53 20	53 33	4 00	65 85	65 98	4 95	78 50	78 63	5 90	91 15	91 28	6 85
53 33	53 47	4 01	65 98	66 12	4 96	78 63	78 77	5 91	91 28	91 42	6 86
53 47	53 60	4 02	66 12	66 25	4 97	78 77	78 90	5 92	91 42	91 55	6 87
53 60	53 73	4 03	66 25	66 38	4 98	78 90	79 03	5 93	91 55	91 68	6 88
53 73	53 87	4 04	66 38	66 52	4 99	79 03	79 17	5 94	91 68	91 82	6 89
53 87	54 00	4 05	66 52	66 65	5 00	79 17	79 30	5 95	91 82	91 95	6 90
54 00	54 13	4 06	66 65	66 78	5 01	79 30	79 43	5 96	91 95	92 08	6 91
54 13	54 27	4 07	66 78	66 92	5 02	79 43	79 57	5 97	92 08	92 22	6 92
54 27	54 40	4 08	66 92	67 05	5 03	79 57	79 70	5 98	92 22	92 35	6 93
54 40	54 53	4 09	67 05	67 18	5 04	79 70	79 83	5 99	92 35	92 48	6 94
54 53	54 67	4 10	67 18	67 32	5 05	79 83	79 97	6 00	92 48	92 61	6 95
54 67	54 80	4 11	67 32	67 45	5 06	79 97	80 10	6 01	92 61	92 75	6 96
54 80	54 93	4 12	67 45	67 58	5 07	80 10	80 23	6 02			
54 93	55 06	4 13	67 58	67 71	5 08	80 23	80 36	6 03			
55 06	55 20	4 14	67 71	67 85	5 09	80 36	80 50	6 04			
55 20	55 33	4 15	67 85	67 98	5 10	80 50	80 63	6 05			
55 33	55 46	4 16	67 98	68 11	5 11	80 63	80 76	6 06			
55 46	55 60	4 17	68 11	68 25	5 12	80 76	80 90	6 07			
55 60	55 73	4 18	68 25	68 38	5 13	80 90	81 03	6 08			
55 73	55 86	4 19	68 38	68 51	5 14	81 03	81 16	6 09			
55 86	56 00	4 20	68 51	68 65	5 15	81 16	81 30	6 10			
56 00	56 13	4 21	68 65	68 78	5 16	81 30	81 43	6 11			
56 13	56 26	4 22	68 78	68 91	5 17	81 43	81 56	6 12			
56 26	56 40	4 23	68 91	69 05	5 18	81 56	81 70	6 13			
56 40	56 53	4 24	69 05	69 18	5 19	81 70	81 83	6 14			
		4 25	69 18	69 ??	5 20	81 83	81 96	6 ??			
						81 96	82 ??				

Wages / Taxes table (lower right corner):

Wages	Taxes
100	$7 51
200	15 02
300	22 53
400	30 04
500	37 55
600	45 06
700	52 57
800	60 08
900	67 59
1,000	75 10

Part of an employee FICA tax table.

withhold the amount of $15.02. For the last $20, you would withhold an additional $\frac{1}{10}$, or $1.50. The total tax withheld is $16.52.

If your employee's gross pay were $391, you would find the tax for the first $300 in the lower right corner. At the 1989 tax rate of 7.51 percent, that would come to $22.53. The remaining $91 falls in the bracket shown on the table: $90.88 to $91.02. You can now figure the tax on the median, or midpoint, for that bracket: $90.95.

$$\$90.95 \times 7.51\% = 6.83$$

Add this amount to $22.53 for a total social security tax withheld of $29.36 on $391 gross pay.

Other deductions

Total deductions from gross pay can now be described in an equation.

**Total Deductions = Withholding Tax
+ Social Security Tax
+ Other Deductions**

You already know about the first two items. What about the other deductions? They depend on three things: (1) In what state or city do you work? (2) What company do you work for? (3) What other choices do you have?

Your state or city may require certain additional deductions from your paycheck. Many states today impose their own income taxes. Very likely the taxes have to be withheld on a regular basis, as are federal taxes. Some cities may also have taxes of one kind or another. New York City, for example, has a payroll deduction of its own. Employers deduct these items automatically.

The same applies to deductions planned through the company itself. One important example is the company pension plan. Contributions to a pension fund may be made entirely by an employer; both employer and employee contribute under some plans. Another example applies to the unionized workforce. Here, using what is called a *checkoff* system, the employer deducts union dues in advance from each paycheck.

The employee may indicate some other optional deductions. These can include deductions for charities or for U.S. bonds bought under a payroll savings plan.

Assume the employee who earned $220 last week had only two paycheck deductions: the withholding tax and social security tax, figured using the percentage methods. What is the employee's net pay? The withholding tax was computed as $24.08; the social security deduction was figured at $16.52. The total deductions came to $40.60, leaving a net pay of $179.40.

Using averages

In "minding your business," as in other areas, you sometimes need special information. Statistics provide a way of summing up mathematical information in a compact and useful way. One kind of statistic is the *average,* or mean.

Suppose you employ three persons: Adams, Green, and Wilson. The gross salaries of these individuals appear on a weekly basis in your payroll ledger. What is the average salary, both regular and overtime, paid your employees? You've already encountered some examples of averages and know the procedure. First you add up the figures for all individual cases; then you divide the total by the number of cases. (For a complete discussion of averages, both mean and median, *see* the discussion about organizing data in Pt. III, Sec. 9, "Graphs and Statistics.")

What was the gross pay for your three employees in the payroll ledger? The regular pay for each came to $175, $182, and $171.50. To compute the average of these, find their sum, $528.50, then divide by the number of cases (3) to get $176.17, the average regular gross pay. Since each person worked at least the minimum number of hours to equal a regular workweek, the figure also represents the average regular gross pay for any week.

Now figure the average *total* pay, including overtime. The total pay for the three employees was $227.50, $221, and $252.35. That makes a total of $700.85, with an average of $233.62. Thus the group averaged $57.45 ($233.62 − $176.17) in overtime.

Can you think of some ways of using this kind of average? You can, as needed, compare averages for the group over a series of weeks; you may want to find out how the seasons of the year affect the amount of work time put in. You could also compare the yearly averages for the three workers. If an employee works 50 weeks, it takes 50 weekly salaries to compute an average for that one person. You can then tell whether, "on the average," one employee earns more money or works more each week than the other employees.

Gross and Net Profit

Profit is the standard that most businesses use to measure net, or after-costs, income. Very often, profit represents the differences between the selling price and the cost.

You are no doubt quite familiar with retail selling. This is where goods are sold in small quantities to the consumer—your family, perhaps. Retail sellers charge you more for the items than they have paid to obtain them. Generally, their source of purchase is manufacturers and distributors.

There are usually two kinds of costs to the retailer: (1) the initial cost of the item and (2) overhead, or all other costs. *Overhead,* the operating and handling costs, includes such items as salaries and commissions, transportation, storage, insurance, advertising, and taxes.

If there are two kinds of costs, that means the seller looks at two kinds of profit: gross profit and net profit. These two kinds of profit are defined in the following equations.

$$\textbf{Gross Profit} = \textbf{Selling Price} - \textbf{Cost of Goods}$$
$$\textbf{Net Profit} = \textbf{Selling Price}$$
$$- \textbf{Cost of Goods} - \textbf{Overhead}$$

Net profit, clearly, is always less than gross profit because it takes all costs into account.

Gross profit is the more familiar concept. It tells the seller how much an item should be marked up. But *net profit* is just as important. It tells whether the seller actually made money, lost money, or just broke even on a sale or series of sales.

Remember shopping for a car in "Money Math"? The estimate you made on the car's cost to the dealer allowed you to make an offer that would permit the dealer to make a net profit.

Figuring gross profit

Gross profit, as noted, accounts only for the cost of the goods and the selling price. As a seller, you could figure it in either of two ways, as a simple difference or as a percentage. If a department store buys an item for $1.20 and sells it for $2.40, the *markup* is $1.20. This simple difference represents the gross profit.

If you want to figure profit as a percentage rate, you calculate the percent of profit on the basis of either the cost or the selling price. Using cost as a basis for figuring in the example, you have this equation.

$$\textbf{Markup Rate} = \frac{\textbf{Markup}}{\textbf{Cost}} = \frac{\$1.20}{\$1.20} = 1 = 100\%$$

Using the selling price as a basis for figuring, you have this equation.

$$\textbf{Markup Rate} = \frac{\textbf{Markup}}{\textbf{Selling Price}} = \frac{\$1.20}{\$2.40} = 50\%$$

If you sell merchandise, chances are you'll be shopping around among manufacturers and distributors of goods. You want to estimate how much of a markup you could add to the price of an item. You know how much your competitors charge for this item, and you don't want them to undersell you. At the same time, you don't want to make too small a profit.

Profit chart

Cost	25%	30%	33⅓%	40%	45%	50%
		% Markup on selling price				
1.00	1.33	1.43	1.50	1.67	1.82	2.00
1.05	1.40	1.50	1.57	1.75	1.91	2.10
1.10	1.47	1.57	1.65	1.83	2.00	2.20
1.15	1.53	1.64	1.72	1.92	2.09	2.30
1.20	1.60	1.71	1.80	2.00	2.18	2.40
1.25	1.67	1.79	1.87	2.08	2.27	2.50
1.30	1.73	1.86	1.95	2.17	2.36	2.60
1.35	1.80	1.93	2.02	2.25	2.45	2.70
1.40	1.87	2.00	2.10	2.33	2.55	2.80
1.45	1.93	2.07	2.17	2.42	2.64	2.90
1.50	2.00	2.14	2.25	2.50	2.73	3.00
1.55	2.07	2.21	2.32	2.58	2.82	3.10
1.60	2.13	2.29	2.40	2.67	2.91	3.20
1.65	2.20	2.36	2.47	2.75	3.00	3.30
1.70	2.27	2.43	2.55	2.83	3.09	3.40
1.75	2.33	2.50	2.62	2.92	3.18	3.50
1.80	2.40	2.57	2.70	3.00	3.27	3.60
1.85	2.47	2.64	2.77	3.08	3.36	3.70
1.90	2.53	2.71	2.85	3.17	3.45	3.80
1.95	2.60	2.79	2.92	3.25	3.55	3.90
2.00	2.67	2.86	3.00	3.33	3.64	4.00
2.25	3.00	3.21	3.37	3.75	4.09	4.50
2.50	3.33	3.57	3.75	4.17	4.55	5.00
2.75	3.67	3.93	4.12	4.58	5.00	5.50
3.00	4.00	4.29	4.50	5.00	5.45	6.00
3.25	4.33	4.64	4.87	5.42	5.91	6.50
3.50	4.67	5.00	5.25	5.83	6.36	7.00
3.75	5.00	5.36	5.62	6.25	6.82	7.50
4.00	5.33	5.71	6.00	6.67	7.27	8.00
4.25	5.67	6.07	6.37	7.08	7.73	8.50
4.50	6.00	6.43	6.75	7.50	8.18	9.00
4.75	6.33	6.79	7.12	7.92	8.64	9.50
5.00	6.67	7.14	7.50	8.33	9.09	10.00
5.25	7.00	7.50	7.87	8.75	9.55	10.50
5.50	7.33	7.86	8.25	9.17	10.00	11.00
5.75	7.67	8.21	8.62	9.58	10.45	11.50
6.00	8.00	8.57	9.00	10.00	10.91	12.00

Let's say you are in a distributor's showroom. You are looking at a number of items for which you might place an order. You can select from two easy ways to figure your profit quickly from the markup rate. One is the *profit chart*. The other is the *profit wheel*.

Buying socks, you decide that you want to set a 30-percent markup on the selling price. Your competitor sells the same socks for $2.20 a pair. You can buy the socks from a supplier at $1.50. Can you sell them at the same or a lower price than your competitor and still make 30 percent? Looking at the profit chart, you run down the cost column until you come to $1.50. Moving along that row to the 30 percent column, you see that you would set the counter (selling) price at $2.14, a competitive price that still has the markup rate you want.

You can solve the same problem using the profit wheel. This device has a flat paper disc attached in the center to a somewhat larger disc. Both discs rotate. They carry a system of numbers that line up. Turn the inner disc to show a "cost each" of 150. This number can represent $.15, $1.50, $15.00, for example—just move the decimal point mentally. Then find 30 percent and the selling price indicated by the number system on the discs. Check your competitor's selling price the same way, and you will find that a selling price of $2.20 gives a profit of at least 32 percent.

Net profit as taxable income

How much money did your business actually make last year? If you used gross profit to determine your income, you would appear to have made more money than you actually did. You need to use net profit as your measure. As has been shown, net profit takes overhead into account.

The equations for gross and net profits apply to single items and the buying and selling prices on them. With another pair of equations you can calculate how much money you spent and made over a week, a month, or a year.

$$\text{Gross Income} = \text{Total Sales} - \text{Total Cost of Goods}$$
$$\text{Net Income} = \text{Total Sales} - \text{Total Cost of Goods}$$
$$- \text{Total Operating Costs}$$

You will want, of course, to pay income taxes on your net income. For one thing, that figure is lower. For another, that sum is all that you are legally required to pay the government.

Overhead or operating costs become even more important in determining net income in businesses where no goods are sold. These businesses generally supply a service. Businesses that supply services include consulting firms, accounting firms, public stenographers, and car rental agencies.

SCHEDULE C
(Form 1040)

Department of the Treasury
Internal Revenue Service

Profit or Loss From Business
(Sole Proprietorship)
Partnerships, Joint Ventures, Etc., Must File Form 1065.
▶ Attach to Form 1040, Form 1041, or Form 1041S.   ▶ See Instructions for Schedule C (Form 1040).

OMB No. 1545-0074

19**88**
Attachment
Sequence No. **09**

Name of proprietor | Social security number (SSN)

A Principal business or profession, including product or service (see Instructions) | B Principal business code (from Part IV) ▶

C Business name and address ▶ .... | D Employer ID number (Not SSN)

E Method(s) used to value closing inventory:
(1) ☐ Cost (2) ☐ Lower of cost or market (3) ☐ Other (attach explanation)

		Yes	No
F Accounting method: (1) ☐ Cash (2) ☐ Accrual (3) ☐ Other (specify) ▶			
G Was there any change in determining quantities, costs, or valuations between opening and closing inventory? (If "Yes," attach explanation.)			
H Are you deducting expenses for business use of your home? (If "Yes," see Instructions for limitations.)			
I Did you "materially participate" in the operation of this business during 1988? (If "No," see Instructions for limitations on losses.)			

J If this schedule includes a loss, credit, deduction, income, or other tax benefit relating to a tax shelter required to be registered, check here. ▶ ☐
If you check this box, you MUST attach **Form 8271.**

Part I Income

1a Gross receipts or sales	1a	
b Less: Returns and allowances	1b	
c Subtract line 1b from line 1a. Enter the result here	1c	
2 Cost of goods sold and/or operations (from Part III, line 8)	2	
3 Subtract line 2 from line 1c and enter the **gross profit** here	3	
4 Other income (including windfall profit tax credit or refund received in 1988)	4	
5 Add lines 3 and 4. This is the **gross income** ▶	5	

Part II Deductions

6 Advertising	6		23 Repairs	23	
7 Bad debts from sales or services (see Instructions)	7		24 Supplies (not included in Part III)	24	
8 Bank service charges	8		25 Taxes	25	
9 Car and truck expenses	9		26 Travel, meals, and entertainment:		
10 Commissions	10		a Travel	26a	
11 Depletion	11		b Meals and entertainment		
12 Depreciation and section 179 deduction from Form 4562 (not included in Part III)	12		c Enter 20% of line 26b subject to limitations (see Instructions)		
13 Dues and publications	13		d Subtract line 26c from 26b	26d	
14 Employee benefit programs	14		27 Utilities and telephone	27	
15 Freight (not included in Part III)	15		28a Wages		
16 Insurance	16		b Jobs credit		
17 Interest:			c Subtract line 28b from 28a	28c	
a Mortgage (paid to banks, etc.)	17a		29 Other expenses (list type and amount):		
. Other	17b				

The U.S. Internal Revenue Service form for reporting profit or loss from a business or profession.

A public stenographer may show a gross income of $19,000 on the Form 1040 tax return. Is that the amount on which taxes must be paid? No, there are expenses: office rental ($4,800), telephone ($600), electricity ($350), answering service ($450), advertising ($500), and post office box ($60). The Internal Revenue Service indicates which items can be deducted from gross income to arrive at net income.

The stenographer's items come to a total for expenses of $6,760. These items can be deducted from the gross income figure to give a net income of $12,240. That represents the taxable income, the figure used in the tax tables to find the tax. It also serves as the base for figuring the social security tax.

Depreciation

You have just become acquainted with operating expenses and ways of taking them into account in figuring profits. Some kinds of expenses are obvious. You pay rent, for example, on an office or store, and you enter that amount regularly in your books (your records of all income and expenses).

Some expenses are not so regular or obvious. If your store has a delivery truck, you probably have it serviced or repaired from time to time. Other expenses are "hidden;" these can include supplies, like stationery, that you need to carry on your business. Still other expenses involve the use of equipment. The expense of renting equipment, such as a computer, is obvious. You pay rental on a regular basis. But how do you figure the expense on a computer that you own?

The answer is *depreciation,* a loss in value over a period of time. Items such as computers, vehicles, and manufacturing equipment depreciate; all rank as *fixed assets* because they remain intact as a unit over months or years. While a supply of stationery will dwindle, a computer remains a computer. The computer, however, is much less useful (and valuable) at the end of its lifetime than it was when you bought it new. Either it has worn out or it has become obsolete because new generations of computers have appeared. In either case, the computer may have some leftover value, or scrap value.

The amount of depreciation taking place over time can be described by an equation.

Depreciation = Cost − Scrap Value

Typically, depreciation is thought of as occurring over the lifetime of a piece of equipment, not all at once. Who wants to think of a computer as suddenly having only scrap value? You may have purchased it only a few months ago. On the other hand, you could not realistically picture all depreciation as occurring at the end of the useful life of a piece of equipment. If you traded the item in while it remained useful, no business would give you the price you paid for it, but you would receive a reasonable payoff for it.

There are several ways to figure value of equipment for tax purposes. Property placed in service after 1980 is generally depreciated using the Accelerated Cost Recovery System (ACRS). But you have a choice of the method used for property placed in service before 1981 or property not depreciable under ACRS. One method, the *straight-line method,* spreads the depreciation evenly over the expected lifetime of the equipment. The *units-of-production method* does the same but is based on the use you make of an item rather than on its age. Two other methods, the *declining-balance method* and the *sum-of-the-years'-digits method,* allow you to depreciate a larger amount in the first year or two. These methods enable you to take a larger deduction from your gross income, reducing your tax bill.

Whatever method you use, certain terms are important. The *rate of depreciation* is the percentage by which an item depreciates in a given year. The *amount of depreciation* is the absolute amount for a year or quantity of use rather than a percentage. *Book value* is the item's value in a particular year—at any time from purchase to scrapping or trading. *Accumulated depreciation* is the sum of the amounts of depreciation for any number of years or quantity of use until the time of scrapping.

The straight-line method

Say your business has purchased a computer for $7,000. You can figure that the computer has 5 years of expected life; at the end of that time it will have a scrap value of $1,000. How much will it have depreciated? The answer is $6,000.

You decide to calculate yearly depreciation by the straight-line method. This equation shows you how to figure it.

Annual Depreciation = Rate of Depreciation
× Total Depreciation

Over 5 years, the value will depreciate $\frac{1}{5}$ in 1 year, so the annual rate is 20 percent. If the total depreciation is $6,000, this is the annual depreciation.

20% × $6,000 = $1,200

By this figuring, the book value of the computer will decline from $7,000 to $5,800 in 1 year. The rate and amount of depreciation, along with book value and accumulated depreciation, are shown in the table. Note that the sum of the book value and accumulated depreciation for any given year always equals the original cost.

Year	Rate of depreciation	Amount of depreciation	Book value	Accumulated depreciation
0			$7,000	
1	20%	$1,200	$5,800	$1,200
2	20%	$1,200	$4,600	$2,400
3	20%	$1,200	$3,400	$3,600
4	20%	$1,200	$2,200	$4,800
5	20%	$1,200	$1,000	$6,000

The units-of-production method

Like the straight-line method, the units-of-production method figures depreciation in a way that is directly proportional to the "age" of the item. But the method takes into account the amount of use. For example, you might depreciate your car on an annual basis and yet may drive it only 10,000 to 15,000 miles annually. Your delivery truck may travel twice that far in a year. Is it fair to depreciate the truck as you would a car if the truck is getting double the use? And you may use other items rarely, or at irregular intervals. What is their depreciation?

Clearly, the units-of-production method makes sense for many items. You can figure total depreciation as cost minus scrap value. You would not, however, calculate the depreciation rate on an annual basis but according to this equation.

$$\text{Depreciation Rate} = \frac{\text{Total Depreciation}}{\text{Units of Useful Life}}$$

Here, depreciation rate is not expressed as a percent but as dollars per unit of use.

Say your delivery truck costs $10,000 and has a scrap value of $1,000. If it has an estimated life of 100,000 miles, what is its depreciation rate? First figure its total depreciation, $9,000. Then divide by the units of useful life.

$$\$9,000 \div 100,000 \text{ mi.} = \$.09/\text{mi.}$$

Now suppose your truck has traveled 27,000 miles. You can instantly calculate its depreciation.

**Amount Depreciated = Depreciation Rate
× Units Used**

So the depreciation equals this amount.

27,000 mi. × $.09/mi. = $2,430

The book value of the truck at 27,000 miles is cost minus the depreciation, or $10,000 − $2,430 = $7,570.

Note that whatever method you use to figure depreciation, the book value never goes below the scrap value. You can never claim so much of a deduction for depreciation that you reduce the scrap value. Sometimes, however, the scrap value may be zero. In that case the total depreciation can't exceed the cost of the item. Here it is in algebra.

**Depreciation = Cost − Scrap Value; but if
Scrap Value = 0, then
Depreciation = Cost**

The declining-balance method

The declining-balance method allows you a larger amount of depreciation in the first year or two. Sometimes called the double-declining-balance method, it differs from the straight-line method in the following ways.

First, you don't figure total depreciation by subtracting scrap value from cost. You ignore scrap value and calculate total depreciation according to the expected life of the item in combination with factors discussed below.

Second, the depreciation for a particular year does not come to some proportion of total depreciation, as in straight-line depreciation. Rather, you figure depreciation on the balance, or book value, established at the end of the preceding year. Hence the name "declining balance"; the balance goes down each year.

Third, the amount of depreciation is substantially higher in the first year because the rate of depreciation is higher. The Internal Revenue Service will permit the first-year depreciation rate to run as high as twice the rate applying under the straight-line method.

How does declining-balance depreciation work? Of course, you want to depreciate the delivery truck that cost your business $10,000 at the highest rate possible. Recall that for a 5-year life, the straight-line depreciation rate would be 20 percent. Using the declining-balance rate, you can depreciate up to 40 percent. You figure that the truck depreciates $4,000 in the first year, leaving a book value or balance of $6,000.

How much does the truck depreciate in the second year? Multiplying the balance of $6,000 by the depreciation rate of 40 percent, you get a second-year depreciation of $2,400, leaving a new value of $3,600.

In the third year, 40 percent of the previous balance gives a depreciation of $1,440. You now have a balance of $2,160. The course of depreciation over 5 years is compared for the declining-balance and straight-line methods in this table.

	Straight-line method		Declining-balance method	
Year	Depreciation	Balance	Depreciation	Balance
0		$10,000		$10,000
1	$1,800	8,200	$4,000	6,000
2	1,800	6,400	2,400	3,600
3	1,800	4,600	1,440	2,160
4	1,800	2,800	864	1,296
5	1,800	1,000	518.40	777.60

Obviously, the declining-balance method permits faster depreciation at the beginning. It also allows you to deduct a larger amount from your original cost. You might say you obtained a higher "yield" in taxes saved on your investment, just by using this method of accounting.

The sum-of-the-years'-digits method

This method, like the declining-balance method, permits a fairly large initial depreciation. However, like the straight-line method, it looks at the difference between initial cost and scrap value. The depreciation rate is expressed as a special fraction. The numerator depends on the year being computed. For example, for a 5-year expected life, the numerator for the first year would be 5; for the second year, 4; for the third year, 3; for the fourth year, 2; and for the fifth year, 1. The denominator would be the sum of these digits: $5 + 4 + 3 + 2 + 1 = 15$. Thus the depreciation rates for the first through the fifth years, respectively, would be $\frac{5}{15}$, $\frac{4}{15}$, $\frac{3}{15}$, $\frac{2}{15}$, and $\frac{1}{15}$.

In the truck example, the total depreciation would be as follows.

$$\text{Cost} - \text{Scrap Value} = \$10,000 - \$1,000$$
$$= \$9,000$$

You then multiply this figure by the appropriate fraction. For the first year, the annual depreciation would be $\frac{5}{15} \times \$9,000 = \$3,000$. Simplifying the fraction, you note that it equals $\frac{1}{3}$, and $\frac{1}{3}$ of $9,000 obviously equals $3,000.

Similarly, the depreciation for the second through the fifth years decreases to $2,400, $1,800, $1,200, and $600. The yearly balances, or book values, according to this method, the straight-line method, and the declining-balance method are shown in the table.

Book value

Year	Straight-line	Declining-balance	Sum-of-digits
0	$10,000	$10,000	$10,000
1	8,200	6,000	7,000
2	6,400	3,600	4,600
3	4,600	2,160	2,800
4	2,800	1,296	1,600
5	1,000	777.60	1,000

As you can see, the sum-of-digits method has an advantage over the straight-line method but not over the declining-balance method. The book values are higher in all years for the sum-of-digits method than for the declining-balance method. That rule does not always hold, however. As the table of comparison on the next page shows, where expected life is longer, the cumulative percentage of depreciation for the sum-of-digits method is higher than for the declining-balance method.

Calculator Shortcuts

Many handheld calculators have a feature that is especially useful in carrying out computations in business math, the ability to carry out a series of identical calculations with a minimum of key pressing.

This is what is called the *constant function.* Your calculator may have a constant switch or button. If it does, you're in luck. If it doesn't, it may still have the constant function. If you're not sure about this, you will want to look in your calculator operating manual. Then adapt this shortcut to the instructions for your own machine.

Comparative depreciation table for 25-year life

Year	Straight-line Annual %	Straight-line Cum. %	Declining-balance Annual %	Declining-balance Cum. %	Sum of digits Annual %	Sum of digits Cum. %
1	4.00	4.00	8.00	8.00	7.69	7.69
2	4.00	8.00	7.36	15.36	7.38	15.08
3	4.00	12.00	6.77	22.13	7.08	22.15
4	4.00	16.00	6.23	28.36	6.77	28.92
5	4.00	20.00	5.73	34.09	6.46	35.38
6	4.00	24.00	5.27	39.36	6.15	41.54
7	4.00	28.00	4.86	44.22	5.85	47.38
8	4.00	32.00	4.46	48.68	5.54	52.92
9	4.00	36.00	4.10	52.78	5.23	58.15
10	4.00	40.00	3.78	56.56	4.92	63.08
11	4.00	44.00	3.48	60.04	4.62	67.69
12	4.00	48.00	3.19	63.23	4.31	72.00
13	4.00	52.00	2.94	66.17	4.00	76.00
14	4.00	56.00	2.71	68.88	3.69	79.69
15	4.00	60.00	2.49	71.37	3.38	83.08
16	4.00	64.00	2.29	73.66	3.08	86.15
17	4.00	68.00	2.11	75.77	2.77	88.92
18	4.00	72.00	1.94	77.71	2.46	91.38
19	4.00	76.00	1.78	79.49	2.15	93.54
20	4.00	80.00	1.64	81.13	1.85	95.38
21	4.00	84.00	1.51	82.64	1.54	96.92
22	4.00	88.00	1.39	84.03	1.23	98.15
23	4.00	92.00	1.28	85.31	.92	99.08
24	4.00	96.00	1.17	86.48	.62	99.69
25	4.00	100.00	1.08	87.56	.31	100.00

Say you want to carry out a series of operations with one number. For example, you want to add the number 3 to a variety of other numbers. You *could* carry these out separately, going through the complete cycle each time.

Instead, all you have to do is this.

| 2 | + | 3 | = | 5 | | 10 | = | 13 |

You have eliminated ⊞ and ③ in the shortened method. If you do 10 of these additions, in the last 9 you will eliminate 2 steps each time, or 18 steps altogether.

Here's how you do it for many calculators. The first time you do an addition, be sure you add *last* the number to be used over again. Then all you have to do on the next addition is to key in the new number. It works with subtraction, multiplication, and division on most calculators, too. Suppose you are calculating a 25 percent profit margin on a number of products. You would key in the cost of the first item, then multiply it by 25 percent for the first and last time. After that, all you need to key in is the cost of the other items and the equal sign.

Here's one that's even shorter. You are computing straight-line depreciation on your delivery truck. Say it depreciates $1,500 each year. The cost is $10,000 and the scrap value is $1,000; so total depreciation will be $9,000 over 6 years.

First subtract $1,500 from $10,000, leaving $8,500. Now, instead of doing it the old way—subtracting $1,500 from $8,500—all you do is press the equal key repeatedly until you get down to $1,000.

Key:

| 10,000 | − | 1,500 | = | = | = | = | = | = |

Readout:

| 10,000 | − | 1,500 | 8,500 | 7,000 | 5,500 | 4,000 | 2,500 | 1,000 |

Now doesn't that cut things down to size? Repeating all operations each time would take 24 steps. The shorter way requires only 9 steps.

Basic Accounting Ideas

Little by little, business math becomes accounting. You can, obviously, use accounting in your family finances, to keep books, for example. But more directly, accounting provides business with information. The persons running any business need to know whether it is making a profit. If it is not, they need to know why not. Just as important, a variety of people have to deal with a business. Customers have to know whether they are being charged unreasonable prices. Bankers have to know whether the business is a good credit risk. The government has to know it has received the appropriate tax payments. Potential investors have to know whether the company is a good prospect for an investment.

Accounting, in short, serves as a tool for checking on your company's financial health. You've already learned how to assess the financial health of your family in "Money Math." The same basic ideas that were used there apply also to businesses.

Some concepts are basic. Where you might speak of net worth in family or personal finances, you could in business use the term *capital,* or *equity*. Similarly, extending the idea of personal savings to the business situation, you could speak of net income.

Like the family, business employs methods of summarizing and analyzing. Two such accounting reports are, respectively, the *balance sheet* and the *income statement*. Both types of documents are put together on a regular basis, quarterly, semiannually, or annually. The quarterly report is typical. In addition, in order to compile these reports and the computations on which they are based, the business makes measurements and then records them regularly, sometimes daily.

You know about some of these measurements and records. They include gross and net income and the various expenses—like labor and depreciation—that change gross income into net income. Now consider how these elements can be compiled to provide a clearer overall picture of a business.

Balance sheets

The balance sheet shows the state of a business at a particular time. A kind of financial statement, the balance sheet has three elements: assets, liabilities, and capital. An "accounting equation" describes the relationship among the three.

Assets − Liabilities = Capital

This equation, transposed, may read this way.

Assets = Liabilities + Capital

Thus assets, on the left side of the equation, are "balanced" by the sum of liabilities (a negative) and capital on the right. Typically, a balance sheet actually has a left side and a right side, just as the equation has: assets on the left side; liabilities, capital, and their sum on the right. Inspecting a balance sheet, you should check first for the totals of the left and right sides. They should be equal; the statement should *balance*.

What are these elements—assets, liabilities, capital? *Assets* include everything that belongs to a business, or everything a business owns or controls. Assets have a definite value that can be measured. *Liabilities* are the debts of the business to others, or the claims that others have against assets. One would hope that creditors and others do not have claims against *all* of the business's assets.

Capital represents that portion of the assets on which no others have claims. Thus, assets are the grand sum of two kinds of assets: those subject to claims by others and those under the exclusive control of the business—liabilities and capital, respectively. This clarifies the accounting equation: Assets = Liabilities + Capital.

Assets

You have seen assets classified in one way already, as liabilities and capital. Liabilities and capital both belong on the right side of the balance sheet. On the left side you would use a different way of classifying assets. Typical categories might include cash, equipment, vehicles, supplies, accounts receivable, prepaid rent, and prepaid fire insurance.

These assets fall into two major categories, current assets and fixed assets. *Current assets,* or liquid assets, include cash as well as assets that can be converted into cash within a relatively short time, usually within a year. Types of current assets are notes receivable, accounts receivable, merchandise inventory, unused supplies, and prepaid expenses such as rent or insurance. *Fixed assets* generally do not convert so readily to cash. They can include land, buildings, trucks, or equipment.

Liabilities

Like assets, liabilities fall readily into two categories: current liabilities and long-term liabilities. *Current liabilities* entail obligations that are due within a year. These include notes payable, wages payable, payroll taxes due, and property taxes due. *Long-term liabilities* will not fall due during the current year. An

X-Y-Z companies

Comparative Balance Sheets
December 31, 1989 and 1988 (in $1,000's)

ASSETS	DECEMBER 31, 1989		DECEMBER 31, 1988	
Current assets				
1. Cash	$ 320		$ 375	
2. Marketable securities	195		138	
3. Accounts receivable (net)	200		250	
4. Inventories	240		200	
5. Prepayments	5		7	
6. Current assets		$ 960		$ 970
Long-term investments				
7. Common stock of Caldwell Corporation		70		20
Fixed assets				
8. Land	900		900	
9. Plant & equipment (net)	600		490	
10. Total fixed assets		1,500		1,390
Intangible assets				
11. Trademarks		15		20
12. Total assets		$2,545		$2,400
LIABILITIES & STOCKHOLDERS' EQUITY	DECEMBER 31, 1989		DECEMBER 31, 1988	
Current liabilities				
13. Accounts payable	$ 220		$ 190	
14. Notes payable	160		151	
15. Accrued expenses	66		69	
16. Taxes payable	35		30	
17. Total current liabilities		$ 481		$ 440
Long-term liabilities				
18. Bonds payable		380		340
19. Total liabilities		861		780
Stockholders' equity				
20. Preferred stock ($10 par)	100		100	
21. Common stock ($1 par)	1,000		1,000	
22. Paid-in capital in excess of par	90		90	
23. Total contributed capital	1,190		1,190	
24. Retained earnings	494		430	
25. Total stockholders' equity		1,684		1,620
26. Total liabilities and stockholders' equity		$2,545		$2,400

example would be mortgage payments due after the current year.

The previous page's comparative balance sheets for X-Y-Z companies show a detailed breakdown for all three components. Current liabilities have increased by 9.3 percent [($481 − $440) ÷ $440] in one year. Bonds payable, the only long-term liability, have increased by 11.8 percent ($40 ÷ $340).

Capital

Accountants deal with capital as equity or net worth. If the company is a corporation, its equity becomes *stockholders' equity*. This represents more than whatever is left over after liabilities are subtracted from assets. It can be described in positive, tangible terms such as *stock* and *retained earnings*. Capital represents resources that can be used as the company sees fit.

If you had a company that was a proprietorship, you could withdraw money to pay personal expenses. Your company could *invest* its capital (savings) in another company. Is there any evidence that the company detailed in the balance sheet has done that at any time? Yes, line 7 shows that the company has a long-term investment in another corporation. Moreover, the value of that investment has grown 250 percent in one year [(70 − 20) ÷ 20]. That growth means an increase in the company's capital.

Transactions

A balance sheet constitutes a business "snapshot" or "profile," one made on a particular day. The day on the table happens to be December 31, but it could be any other day. In fact, a company's balance sheet can be drawn up daily, 365 times a year; daily records would make that possible.

If you had a series of such daily pictures for a company you owned, you could put together a "moving picture" of your business. Each day, different transactions would occur. One day, perhaps, you would pay the premium of $100 on the fire insurance policy that gives the business three months of protection. In this transaction, you have exchanged one kind of asset, cash, for another kind of asset, insurance. You have made no net change in assets and thus no change in liabilities or capital. On another day, you purchase

$4,000 worth of merchandise on credit. The asset of merchandise, on the left side of the equation, is balanced by a $4,000 debt on the right side. If you have paid cash, the $4,000 worth of goods would have been balanced by a corresponding decrease in the asset of cash, as with the insurance premium.

Income statements

Balance sheets are important. But they generally tell about your company as of a single day, or a selected few days of the year. Issued on a quarterly basis, the balance sheet gives you an overview of the total assets, liabilities, and capital that have accumulated since the end of the quarter before.

x-y-z companies

**Income statement
for the year ending December 31, 1989 (in $1,000s)**

1. Sales		$1,000
2. Less: Cost of goods sold		620
3. Gross margin on sales		$ 380
Less: Operating expenses		
4. Selling expenses	$84	
5. Administrative expense	67	
6. Depreciation expense	40	
7. Amortization expense	5	
8. Total operating expenses		196
9. Operating income		$ 184
10. Less: Interest expense		14
11. Pretax income		$ 170
12. Less: Income tax on operations		68
13. Income before extraordinary items		$ 102
14. Plus: Extraordinary gain	$ 5	
15. Less: Tax on gain	2	3
16. Net income		$ 105
17. Earnings per share of common stock		
18. Income before extraordinary items		$ 102
19. Extraordinary items		3
20. Net income		$ 105

Income statements give a broader picture. They make summaries of transactions that have occurred between one balance sheet date and the next. The balance sheet usually shows the picture on the last day of a quarter; the income statement covers the entire quarter.

Income statements show how much revenue a company has taken in during a quarter or a year; they serve as a measure of net income, or net profit. You already know how to compute this. Now you know just how important that computation was: it gave one of the two major kinds of financial statements.

This income statement traces the math "production line" used in deriving net income. First, you would subtract the cost of goods from sales to obtain gross margin (or profit). Then deduct operating expenses, or overhead. Note the depreciation expense, which you know how to figure. Assuming that this is a straight-line depreciation computation, is it reasonable to assume that this entry was necessarily the same as the previous year? No, this year's depreciation expense may in part reflect some new fixed asset.

Investments

The information provided by balance sheets and income statements can help you make investing a more exact process. You can take different items of information from these documents, either alone or in certain combinations, to evaluate how well a company is doing. Stockholders have a vital interest in knowing such facts. Usually, stockholders can update their assessments each quarter, when their company issues a financial report. Potential investors, creditors, and competitors should be just as interested.

One way of analyzing a company's performance is to examine selected individual measures. A more useful technique may be to compute ratios that combine two or more of these measures by dividing one by the other. For obvious reasons this is called *ratio analysis.* The table on the following page is a summary of financial indicators for one company.

One ratio, the *current ratio,* indicates current assets divided by current liabilities (*see* line 7 of the table). Both of these quantities appear on the balance sheet shown earlier for the x-y-z companies. The ratio indicates the ability of the company to meet its present debts. Ideally, the ratio should equal 2 or more. In the case of the company shown on that balance sheet, it was 2.20 in the first year and exactly 2 in the second year. Can you locate the figures used in computing this ratio? For the first year, they were 970 ÷ 440; for the second, 960 ÷ 481.

Financial indicators for Teltone Company

Ratio or indicator	Formula	Result 1989	Result 1988	Industry average	Evaluation
Profitability					
1. Earnings per share	Earnings available for common stockholders / Average number of shares outstanding	$0.105	$0.085		Good
2. Payout ratio	Dividends per share / Earnings per share	38.10%	0.00%	42.00%	Low
3. Profit margin	Net profit after taxes / Net sales	10.50%	6.60%	7.42%	Good
4. Return on assets	Operating profit / Average total assets	7.44%	6.35%	6.75%	Good
5. Rate of return on equity	Net profits after taxes / Average total stockholders' equity	6.36%	5.81%	5.03%	Good
Liquidity					
6. Net working capital		$479 million	$530 million		Investigate
7. Current ratio	Current assets / Current liabilities	2.00X*	2.20X*	2.00X*	Satisfactory
8. Acid-test ratio	Cash + marketable securities + receivables / Current liabilities	1.49X*	1.73X*	1.60X*	Slightly low
Efficiency					
9. Inventory turnover ratio	Cost of goods sold / Average inventory	2.82X*	2.81X*	2.75X*	Satisfactory
10. Average collection period	Net sales / 360 = sales per day	$2.78	$2.07		
	Average accounts receivable / Sales per day	80.94 days	80.65 days	80.53 days	Satisfactory
11. Fixed asset turnover	Net sales / Total average assets	0.69	0.73	0.74	Low
Leverage					
12. Long-term debt as percentage of total capital	Long-term debt / Total capital	18.4%	17.3%	32.00%	Too low
13. Debt coverage	Profits before interest and taxes / Interest	13.14X*	10.10X*	11.95X*	Good
14. Cost of long-term debt	Interest / Long-term debt average	3.89%	5.21%	6.71%	Good

*X = times.

A second ratio, the *quick ratio,* or *acid test ratio,* is expressed in this formula.

$$\frac{\textbf{Current Assets } - \textbf{ Inventory}}{\textbf{Current Liabilities}}$$

The quick ratio resembles the current ratio but measures a company's capacity to meet current debts without selling off inventory. You can usually consider a ratio of 1 or higher as desirable; but some accountants view 1.6 as more desirable.

Some common types of ratios, with information on how they serve as business measures, appear here.

Common ratio types, with business applications.

Financial ratio	Significance
Working capital (= current assets − current liabilities)	A measure of the available funds to carry on day-to-day operations.
Net income ÷ working capital	Provides an indication of management's ability to turn working capital into profit.
Net sales ÷ working capital	Provides a measure of management's efficiency in utilizing working capital. Too high a ratio, however, may indicate a shortage of working capital. Normal ratio indicates amount of working capital needed for a given level of sales.
Net sales ÷ inventory	Provides an indication of merchandising efficiency and quality of the inventory.
Fixed assets ÷ net worth	A measure of creditors' protection. The higher this ratio, the less is the owner's contribution to current assets.
Current liabilities ÷ net worth	Provides a measure of a firm's protection to its short-term creditors.
Total liabilities ÷ net worth	Provides an indication of the relative positions between owners and creditors and is a measure of financial strength.
Inventory ÷ working capital	An additional measure of liquidity and inventory balance, normally varies between .75 and 1.00 in most industries.
Current debt ÷ inventory	Shows how much the firm relies on selling its inventories in order to meet its obligations.

Adaptation of Table 32.1 from BUSINESS MATHEMATICS, 2nd Edition by Richard S. Thorn. © 1980 by Richard S. Thorn. Reprinted by permission of Harper & Row, Publishers, Inc.

Selected business ratios

Line of business	Current assets to current debt (times)	Net income on net sales (percent)	Net income on tangible net worth (percent)	Net income on net working capital (percent)	Net sales to tangible net worth (times)	Net sales to net working capital (times)
Retailing						
Clothing & furnishings,	4.48	4.62	13.64	16.08	4.43	5.25
men's & boys'	**2.71†**	**2.47**	**7.52**	**8.96**	**3.30**	**3.71**
	1.91	1.11	2.87	3.37	2.26	2.63
Discount stores	2.29	3.00	20.80	28.56	10.30	14.54
	1.86	**1.87**	**14.16**	**18.70**	**6.95**	**8.85**
	1.46	1.04	7.69	9.78	4.84	5.81
Family clothing stores	4.93	3.46	11.09	14.62	4.42	5.44
	2.78	**1.79**	**6.33**	**7.38**	**3.09**	**3.57**
	1.99	0.70	2.03	2.20	2.02	2.18
Furniture stores	5.74	4.86	11.20	11.94	4.72	5.03
	3.07	**2.16**	**6.01**	**6.33**	**2.49**	**2.71**
	1.79	0.69	2.01	2.05	1.60	1.65
Gasoline service	3.48	6.55	16.40	40.80	4.56	10.53
stations	**2.31**	**2.73**	**8.57**	**18.65**	**3.38**	**7.43**
	1.44	1.14	4.24	8.85	2.12	4.40
Motor vehicle dealers	2.56	1.82	13.37	20.15	11.40	15.95
	1.96	**0.94**	**7.51**	**9.97**	**8.07**	**11.20**
	1.59	0.47	3.74	5.19	4.83	6.79
Wholesaling						
Beer, wine &	3.23	2.01	14.54	22.87	10.39	13.67
alcoholic	**2.04**	**1.18**	**7.40**	**12.17**	**7.14**	**9.59**
beverages	1.53	0.43	3.73	5.38	5.39	6.63

Adaptation of Table 32.2 from BUSINESS MATHEMATICS, 2nd Edition by Richard S. Thorn. © 1980 by Richard S. Thorn. Reprinted by permission of Harper & Row, Publishers, Inc.
*Not available.   †The figure in boldface is the median ratio.

How do different businesses compare on these ratios? Studies have shown relatively broad variations. Of more than 200 retailers of men's and boys' clothing and furnishings covered in one report (*see* table above), on the ratio of current assets over current debts, the "scores" ranged from 4.48 to 1.91. From one area of business activity to another, the variations may be far broader.

Collec- tion period (days)	Net sales to inventory (times)	Fixed assets to tangible net worth (percent)	Current debt to tangible net worth (percent)	Total debt to tangible net worth (percent)	Inventory to net working capital (percent)	Current debt to inventory (percent)	Funded debts to net working capital (percent)
*	4.9	4.4	24.2	56.1	71.6	34.4	10.2
*	**3.6**	**10.9**	**52.7**	**106.2**	**108.9**	**56.5**	**23.5**
*	2.8	21.4	87.7	160.6	146.7	84.7	54.3
*	7.3	11.5	61.8	91.3	108.2	58.7	16.7
*	**5.6**	**27.5**	**97.4**	**142.7**	**161.2**	**76.8**	**41.9**
*	4.2	50.4	154.8	206.4	228.8	98.9	74.8
*	5.3	5.1	23.0	70.5	67.6	34.9	15.6
*	**3.9**	**13.2**	**51.7**	**95.9**	**94.6**	**57.8**	**39.6**
*	3.1	37.6	82.4	189.0	119.7	108.7	57.0
57	6.6	3.8	20.4	47.2	32.2	55.5	9.1
111	**4.8**	**9.2**	**46.3**	**98.2**	**60.2**	**90.2**	**20.0**
209	3.7	22.0	105.6	165.2	106.5	143.7	41.5
*	20.9	18.9	19.1	50.0	34.3	61.6	20.1
*	**10.7**	**46.3**	**34.8**	**79.6**	**64.3**	**114.9**	**58.2**
*	6.1	71.1	69.2	138.3	131.4	256.8	119.4
*	11.1	8.3	42.1	87.4	84.2	66.5	9.0
*	**8.1**	**18.4**	**77.4**	**117.5**	**130.2**	**79.9**	**33.0**
*	5.9	41.1	119.5	183.4	183.9	95.8	74.2
11	17.9	4.9	29.4	78.5	67.2	57.6	10.5
22	**9.3**	**15.2**	**65.0**	**141.2**	**100.8**	**94.5**	**34.4**
30	6.0	44.6	139.7	212.0	160.0	140.6	55.8

You can evaluate a particular business by computing ratios for it and then comparing its ratios to those
for the industry the business belongs to. Suppose you
are interested in investing in a certain discount store
chain. The current ratio for that chain for a given year
might be 1.96; the *median* ratio—the ratio that falls at
the midpoint of all the ratios collected—for this type of
business is 1.86. You conclude that the company is
better than average on this score.

You try another test. Say profit margin (net income over net sales) is 1.75 percent. The median profit margin ratio for the industry is 1.87 percent. You conclude that the company could improve on this score.

Budgets

You are already familiar with the idea of family budgeting. You know how to use only as much of your financial resources as you have to and how to accumulate as much in savings as you can. The same idea applies in business. You need to know where you are going. You need to use the resources you have to generate the most revenue you can. You need to control your business through advance planning.

Budgets can give you the controls you need. Generally, you prepare them according to a yearly profit plan. The final budget limits the spending of each department or profit center. You can allow some cost or expense overruns, but if you permit too many, you may lose control of your financial situation. If your budget serves as a substitute for a general ledger, you can post actual monthly expenditures against budgeted accounts. Your budget then serves a dual purpose.

Financial planning for a business by means of a budget may raise the question whether the cost of an operation is justified by the outcome. In other words, is it profitable? Does the expected profit exceed the expected expense, and by how much?

You can analyze a business in different ways. One way is to analyze the profitability of different products. What you are doing is comparing cost with profit. If a product doesn't sell, it doesn't produce a profit. Common sense tells you that you don't want to keep a line that is not profitable.

Suppose you buy $1,000 worth of shirts. You mark them up 50 percent over cost. If you sell all the shirts, your gross sales will total $1,500. But you want to know the break-even point so that you will know when you start to turn a profit on the transaction. To break even, you need to sell $1,000 worth, or $\frac{2}{3}$ of the items.

When you take inventory, you find that *more* than $\frac{1}{3}$ of the original lot purchased is still in stock, so you didn't break even. You decide not to buy more of that particular line of shirts, especially since you know that other lines are doing much better than breaking even.

In manufacturing, you will no doubt face the budgeting problem of cost versus results, or *cost-effectiveness*. You can measure costs in terms of time consumed, numbers of workers involved, salaries paid, and materials used up. All of these factors clearly mean dollars and cents.

Suppose you find a process that takes $\frac{1}{4}$ less time to turn out the same number of items. If you save 25 percent in time, in theory you should save 25 percent in financial cost. (Some variables may affect that equation.)

You can express your manufacturing problem as a ratio: Income ÷ Cost. If you reduce your costs by 25 percent, you have income ÷ .75 (cost). You are multiplying the ratio by 1 ÷ .75, which equals 1.33. This means that the ratio has improved by $\frac{1}{3}$. Looking at the problem another way, you have found out how to produce $\frac{1}{3}$ more items in the same amount of time.

You have a third alternative to express this. You might say that you have freed up 25 percent of the time and/or financial resources used in this process to be used elsewhere in the company, to become part of the company's capital, or to lower the liabilities.

Flexibility like this is one of the many benefits of developing sound skills in business math. Add to these the efficiency and speed that come from knowing what information you need, how to get it, and what to do with it, and any business you own will have a good chance at running smoothly and profitably.

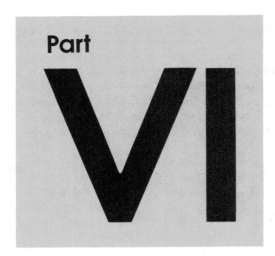

Part

VI

Math Powerhouse

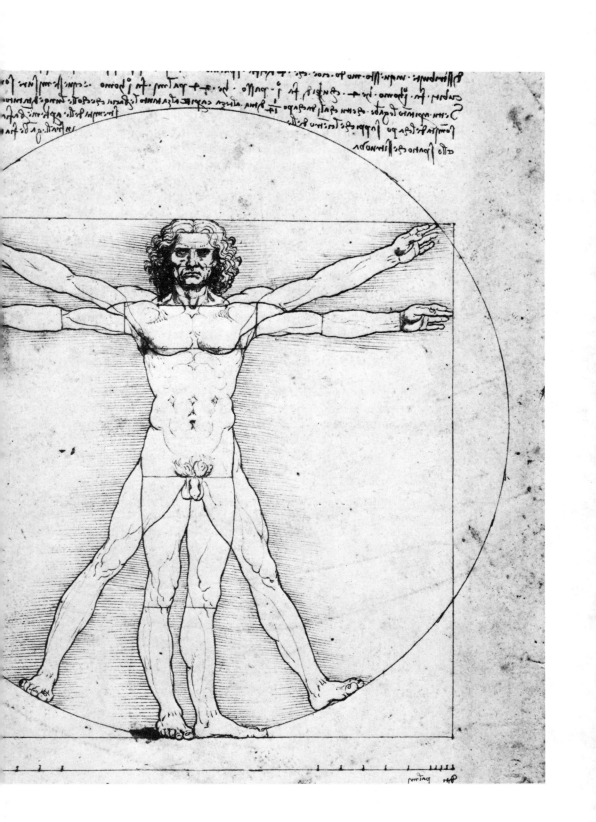

There are many aids to mathematics understanding. When put together, they provide a real powerhouse of information for studying math. Part VI assembles many math aids in one place to provide you with just such a powerhouse.

Mathematics history is a rich source and useful starting point for understanding math. For this reason, Part VI opens with a discussion of math history and of famous mathematicians who contributed to the development of math over the centuries. You will be surprised at how old math is and at how many familiar names you find among the mathematicians.

A number of schools nationwide are using mathematics competitions to improve students' math skills and increase their interest in math. If you are involved in a school math league or would like to start one, you will be interested in the second section of this part. The third section is of interest to all who want to learn math well. The discussion on math reading found there summarizes the useful advice for reading math properly that was given throughout this publication. A list of excellent math books also appears. Use these references for independent reading in math. Each reference is annotated, or described, so that you will be able to select an appropriate reference for your needs.

A series of aids for math computation ends the powerhouse. These include a list of math symbols, including Greek letters used as symbols in mathematics. A math glosssary defines key terms. Arithmetic operations and other mathematical operations are summarized. Finally, math formulas and math tables end the part. ∎

(Preceding photo) Leonardo Da Vinci used math to plan masterpieces in studies such as Vitruvian Man.

You have read about many mathematicians in the first five parts of this publication. The following material will help you put these mathematicians into *historical perspective;* that is, you will see how their work corresponded to other mathematical work going on at the time. A list of important dates will furthermore help you to see at a glance the sequence of mathematical development since early times.

Math Milestones and Mathematicians

Ancient times

Before the time of recorded history, people learned to count such things as the animals in their herds and flocks. They probably first used their fingers or pebbles to help keep track of small numbers. They learned to use the length of their hands and arms and other standards of measure. And they learned to use regular shapes when they molded pottery and chipped stone arrowheads.

By 3000 B.C., the peoples of ancient Babylonia, China and Egypt had developed a practical system of mathematics. They used written symbols to stand for numbers and knew the simple arithmetic operations. They used this knowledge in business and government. They also developed a practical geometry helpful in agriculture and engineering. For example, the ancient Egyptians knew how to survey their fields and to make the intricate measurements necessary to build huge pyramids. The Babylonians and Egyptians had even explored some of the fundamental ideas of algebra. But this early mathematics solved only practical problems. It was applied, rather than pure, mathematics.

The Greeks and the Romans

Between 600 and 300 B.C., the Greeks took the next great step in mathematics. They inherited a large part of their mathematical knowledge from the Babylonians and Egyptians. But they became the first people to separate mathematics from practical problems. For example, they separated geometry from practical applications and made it into an abstract exploration of space. They based this study of points, lines, and figures, such as triangles and circles, on logical reasoning rather than on facts found in nature. Thales of Miletus (c. 640–546 B.C.), a philosopher, helped begin this new viewpoint of geometry. The philosopher Pythagoras

(c. 580–c. 500 B.C.) and his followers explored the nature of numbers. In geometry, the Pythagoreans developed the famous theorem that bears their name, the Pythagorean Theorem. Thales, Pythagoras, and many other Greek mathematicians built up a large body of geometrical knowledge. Euclid (c. 300 B.C.), one of the foremost Greek mathematicians, organized geometry as a single logical system. His book, *The Elements,* remains one of the basic works in studying mathematics.

The Greeks also advanced other branches of mathematics. As early as 450 B.C., Greek mathematicians recognized *irrational numbers* such as the square root of 2. About 370 B.C., Eudoxus of Cnidus (c. 400–355 B.C.), a Greek astronomer and mathematician, formulated a surprisingly masterful definition of proportions. Archimedes (287?–212 B.C.), the leading mathematician of ancient times, devised processes that foreshadowed those of integral calculus. Archimedes made many other contributions to mathematics and physics. The Greek astronomer Ptolemy (c. A.D. 150) helped develop trigonometry. Diophantus (c. A.D. 275), a Greek mathematician, worked on numbers in equations. He earned the title of the father of algebra.

Although the Romans constructed many impressive buildings, they showed little interest in pure mathematics. Roman mathematics dealt largely with practical matters such as business and military science.

The Middle Ages

After the fall of Rome in A.D. 476, Europe saw no new developments in mathematics for hundreds of years. But the Arabs preserved the mathematical tradition of the Greeks and Romans. Mathematicians in India developed zero and the decimal number system. After A.D. 700, the Arabs adopted these inventions from the Indians and used the new numbers in their mathematics. The Arabs also preserved and translated many of the great works of Greek mathematicians. They made important contributions of their own. For example, the mathematician Al-Khowarizmi (c. 820) organized and expanded algebra. The word *algebra* comes from an Arabic word in the title of one of his books on the subject.

After 1100, Europeans began to borrow the mathematics of the Arab world. For example, European merchants started to use the decimal number system. Also,

Important dates

c. 300 B.C.	Euclid organized geometry as a single system of mathematics.
c. 225 B.C.	Archimedes invented processes that foreshadowed those used in integral calculus.
c. A.D. 275	Diophantus helped found algebra.
c. 820	Al-Khowarizmi helped organize algebra as a branch of mathematics.
1614	John Napier published his invention of logarithms, an important mathematical aid.
1637	René Descartes published the first work on analytic geometry.
1640	Pierre de Fermat founded the modern theory of numbers.
1654	Pierre de Fermat and Blaise Pascal established the mathematical theory of probability.
c. 1675	Sir Isaac Newton and Baron von Leibniz, working independently, invented calculus.
1733	Leonhard Euler began a series of publications on calculus that started modern mathematical analysis.
c. 1830	János Bolyai and Nikolai Lobachevsky, working independently, invented non-Euclidean geometry systems.
1843	Sir William Hamilton invented a system of algebra that differed in many ways from traditional algebra.
1854	Georg Riemann invented a non-Euclidean geometry later used in the relativity theory.
1910–1913	Alfred North Whitehead and Bertrand Russell published *Principia Mathematica,* which tries to develop mathematics from logic.
1915	Albert Einstein announced his general theory of relativity.
1950	Einstein announced a major revision of his unified-field theory.
1970's	Mathematical models became widely used to study systems and problems in business, industry, and science.

European scholars began to study Arab works on algebra and geometry. Leonardo Fibonacci (c. 1200), a leading European mathematician of the Middle Ages, contributed to algebra, arithmetic, and geometry.

The Renaissance

The Renaissance, from the 1400's to the 1600's, produced many great advances in mathematics. The exploration of new lands and continents called for better mathematics for navigation. The growth of business demanded better mathematics for banking and finance. The invention of printing brought the appearance of hundreds of popular arithmetic textbooks. Many of the computation methods used today date from this period, such as the procedure for doing a long multiplication problem.

Interest also grew in pure mathematics. Michael Stifel (1487–1567), Nicolò Tartaglia (c. 1500–1557), Girolamo Cardano (1501–1576), and François Viète (1540–1603) pioneered in algebra. Viète introduced the use of letters to stand for unknown numbers. These mathematicians also helped develop trigonometry. Nicolaus Copernicus (1473–1543), the astronomer who defended the theory that the universe had the sun at its center, contributed to mathematics through his work in astronomy.

The 1600's brought many brilliant contributions to mathematics. John Napier (1550–1617), a Scottish mathematician, invented logarithms. Two Britishers, Thomas Harriot (1560–1621) and William Oughtred (1574–1660), worked out new methods for algebra. The astronomers Galileo (1564–1642) and Johannes Kepler (1571–1630) expanded mathematical knowledge through their studies of the stars and planets. Gérard Desargues (1593–1662) helped expand geometry through his study of sections of cones. René Descartes (1596–1650) invented analytic geometry and aided many other branches of mathematics. Pierre de Fermat (1601–1665) founded the modern numbers theory. Blaise Pascal (1623–1662) and Fermat invented the mathematical theory of probability. Then, toward the end of this period, Sir Isaac Newton (1642–1727) and Baron von Leibniz (1646–1716) invented calculus. The invention of calculus marked the beginning of modern mathematics.

1700's

The 1700's saw wide applications of new calculus. Abraham de Moivre (1667–1754) used calculus to contribute to the study of probability. Brook Taylor (1685–1731) helped develop differential calculus. Colin Maclaurin (1698–1746) also helped with calculus. But one of the greatest contributors to calculus was Leonhard Euler (1707–1783), a Swiss mathematician. Euler worked in almost every branch of mathematics. His contributions to calculus reached into so many fields that many mathematicians call him the founder of modern mathematical analysis. Count Lagrange (1736–1813) used calculus for the study of forces in physics. Gaspard Monge (1746–1818) applied calculus to geometry.

1800's

The 1800's brought further application of calculus throughout mathematics. The Marquis de Laplace (1749–1827) used calculus in physics, particularly in astronomy. Jean Baptiste Fourier (1768–1830) used it for the study of heat in physics. Adrien Marie Legendre (1752–1833) also worked with calculus and contributed to the theory of numbers. But the early work in calculus often rested on shaky theoretical foundations. As a result, many disturbing paradoxes appeared. The great achievements in mathematics in the 1800's included rebuilding the theoretical foundations of calculus and mathematical analysis. Four mathematicians—Baron Cauchy (1789–1857), Karl Friedrich Gauss (1777–1855), Georg Friedrich Riemann (1826–1866), and Karl Theodor Weierstrass (1815–1897)—helped carry out this important work.

Another outstanding advance of the 1800's was the invention of non-Euclidean geometry by János Bolyai (1802–1860) and Nikolai Lobachevsky (1793–1856). During the same period, Arthur Cayley (1821–1895) and Sir William Rowan Hamilton (1805–1865) invented new systems of algebra. These discoveries liberated geometry and algebra from their traditional molds and did much to shape present-day mathematics.

1900's

The invention of new systems of algebra and geometry and the revision of the theoretical foundations of calculus had far-reaching effects on mathematics. In the 1900's, mathematicians began to explore the foundations of mathematics itself. Many philosophies of mathematics appeared, as well as attempts to give mathematics a basis in logic. Luitzen Brouwer (1881–1966), Georg Cantor (1845–1918), David Hilbert (1862–1943), Bertrand Russell (1872–1970), and Alfred North Whitehead (1861–1947) made important studies of the foundations of mathematics. The work of Albert Einstein (1879–1955) opened a whole new area for mathematical research.

New developments in science required a tremendous expansion of applied mathematics. Such fields as electronics, nuclear physics, and the exploration of space have used new inventions from pure mathematics to solve problems. For example, electronic computers use systems of mathematics designed by mathematicians. Also, mathematical models have been formulated to study many kinds of systems, including underground petroleum reserves and worldwide weather patterns. The models consist of mathematical equations that describe the relations between the parts or processes of a system. Computers are used to solve these equations.

Math Competitions at School

While math is enjoyable in itself and has many practical uses, another dimension is added when math is combined with serious competition. In the schools, math competitions have been built around academic games or written tests that present mathematical problems. If there are no mathematics competitions available in your school or school district, you may be interested in establishing a math league. Two academic games are described below so that you can become acquainted with them. Discussion of written math competition follows.

Academic games

The world of higher mathematics has contributed academic games that are both fun to play and instructive for the players. The games, like athletics, make no distinctions among students except in their ability to play. The competitions thus bring students of many different backgrounds together. Chicago and Detroit are two cities with active math leagues.

Competitions take place within schools and between schools. Small teams are usually formed at different ability levels. At the end of each round of play, the best student on a team may be moved to the next higher ability level, while the student who has done the worst may slip back to the next lower ability level.

Wff 'n Proof and *Equations* are two academic games that are used in school competitions. Wff 'n Proof was the first game based on higher mathematics that was introduced into schools. Developed by University of Michigan Law Professor Layman Allen, the essence of Wff 'n Proof is formal logic—but not the kind of logic that was used by the ancient Greeks or the medieval logicians. Instead, Wff 'n Proof is based on modern symbolic logic that uses reverse Polish notation, which was discussed in detail in Part II, Section

4. A key concept in logic is the *well-formed formula,* often abbreviated to *WFF* or *wff* (and pronounced "wiff").

The idea of wff can also be used in arithmetic. For example, you would know something was wrong if you saw the following in a math textbook: $4 - \times 17$. As stated, $4 - \times 17$ is not a wff. The rules of arithmetic do not permit you to use a subtraction sign before a times sign. The same kind of rules hold in logic.

Reverse Polish notation is well-suited to the game of Wff 'n Proof because it uses no parentheses. This makes it possible to form more wff's than you would be able to do if parentheses were used as extensively as they are in other notations for symbolic logic. The symbols of reverse Polish notation are capital letters for operators and lower-case letters for sentences. For example, N stands for negation, so Np is a wff that means "not the sentence p." Similarly, K means "and," so the wff Kpq is interpreted as "the sentence p and the sentence q." Other symbols are A for "or," E for "equivalence," and C for "if . . . then." Notice that the logical operators are written *before* the sentences on which they operate, so Cpq means "if p then q."

Students play in teams of one or more. They receive cubes like dice that have the symbols for playing Wff 'n Proof. The dice are randomly presented to the players.

A team constructs a wff from the dice and must survive a challenge from opponents. Points are made when a challenging team can show that the sequence of symbols is not a wff.

The second challenge of the game is to match one wff with another, usually simpler, one. For example, assume that the dice show N, N, K, A, C, K, p, p, r, q, q. A player on one team selects Kpq as a wff and challenges the other team to use the remaining dice to make a wff that means exactly the same as Kpq. If the other team is to win, they must come up with a wff such as NNKpq, which has the same logical meaning as Kpq. Translating from reverse Polish notation, the first team chose a wff that means "p and q." The other team came up with the correct response, "It is not the case that p and q," in which the double negative transforms back into the positive. Most moves in the game would be more complicated than this simple example.

Since proof in this part of symbolic logic consists largely of finding such equivalent wff's, Wff 'n Proof is good practice for symbolic logic. But Dr. Allen, the inventor, claims that it is also good practice for reasoning. He has research studies that show that enough exposure to Wff 'n Proof boosts scores on IQ tests. In fact, Wff 'n Proof is regularly used as a teaching tool at the University of Michigan Law School to train prospective lawyers in the fine points of logic.

The game Equations was modeled after Wff 'n Proof and has proved to be much more popular in high schools and even in middle schools. In Equations, the dice have numbers and operational symbols on them. A roll of the dice may produce 2, 4, 3, 6, +, ×, and so forth. Again, one student chooses something that the opposing team must duplicate with the remaining dice. For example, the student could choose (from the dice shown above) 6. The other team could produce 2×3 to score points. Wff's are implied in this game, although they need no emphasis, since it is easier to recognize a wff in arithmetic than a wff in reverse Polish notation.

Although the previous example was very simple, in actual games the math becomes very involved, requiring exponents and complex combinations of operations to find an expression that has the selected value. It may be required that specific numbers or operations be used to form the result, or that specific numbers or operations be excluded from possible use. As in Wff 'n Proof, challenges are an important part of the game of Equations.

Written tests as competitions

In 1950, the Metropolitan New York Section of the Mathematical Association of America (MAA) started a competition for high-school students that has since become nationwide under the sponsorship of the MAA, the National Council of Teachers of Mathematics (NCTM), and other groups. Instead of games, students are given problems to solve on a written test. The best of these students move on to the U.S.A. Mathematical Olympiad, where more problems are given. The contests have proved to be successful at attracting students' interest. Since 1957, the number of students participating in this program has increased roughly tenfold.

About 150 of the students who earn higher than a specified score on the first test of 30 questions are asked to participate in the Olympiad, where only five problems are posed.

Students' solutions are not scored as only right or wrong. Instead, a panel evaluates the quality of each solution, so that the score on an individual problem can range from 0 to over 21 points. Since 1974, the highest-scoring students from the U.S.A. Mathematical Olympiad have been asked to participate in the International Mathematical Olympiad, where the United States has consistently performed very well.

Many math competitions, including the U.S.A. Mathematical Olympiad, are sponsored in part by Mu Alpha Theta, the National High School and Junior College Mathematics Club, which is itself cosponsored by the NCTM and MAA. Mu Alpha Theta, which accepts only members with sufficient math backgrounds and good grades, holds a national convention and sponsors a magazine for math clubs. There are now about 1300 chapters of Mu Alpha Theta in the United States.

Tips on how to read mathematics

Math Reading

Why do you like or dislike mathematics? Chances are your answer to this question is directly related to your success or lack of success in mathematical problem solving. For many people the lack of success in mathematics is rooted in a poor understanding of content as they read mathematical material. This lack of understanding could be psychological—failure to completely concentrate when reading new material. Or it could be technical—failure to compute enough examples to see what the content is all about. However, in either case the way the material is read is a key to learning what the page is all about. Thus, in order to have clear understanding, a reader must be able to use different techniques of reading. For example, sometimes it is necessary to reread a section and search for specific facts before doing any practice exercises. At other times it may be necessary to reread the same material for content review—for the purpose of relating new content to older, more familiar content. This technique can be useful when you need to incorporate new material as a part of a larger whole. Following is a list of procedures that can help improve your mathematical reading skills. To read with better understanding you should:

1. Use a variety of materials, such as pencil and paper. It is a good idea to decide on the materials you will need before you begin. You can do so by skimming the page or lesson for that information first.
2. Know the meaning of mathematical words and symbols used.
3. Watch for situations that identify the meaning of key terms and symbols.
4. Analyze precisely what is being discussed or given in a problem. Make a list of key ideas and try to see various relationships. Drawing a diagram or a chart can often help you see the facts more clearly.
5. Study all examples and work through every sample exercise on your own. By reading the examples carefully and then reworking the sample exercises yourself you can often discover new ideas. Check the work, both as you go along and at the end of the exercise.
6. Think through the solutions of all sample problems. Try to imagine what is happening as certain computations are carried out. Write the work carefully, indicating as briefly as possible what steps are being performed, so that you can understand the work if it is necessary to reread it.
7. Realize that mathematicians are not always consistent in terminology or symbols, so you must be prepared to discern the writer's meaning.
8. The root, prefix, and suffix of mathematical words usually give valuable hints that may help you find the meaning of a term.
9. Exercise patience. Remove any artificial barriers, such as a self-imposed time limit for reading the discussion or for solving a problem. Give yourself time to read and reread a page so you can focus your thoughts on what must be done. Remember that the language of mathematics contains many compact "sentences"—so reading too rapidly may prove to be a handicap.
10. Realize that mathematical ideas are explained in different ways. This sometimes means that you must change directions or look for patterns as you read.

Sources of mathematical reading materials

The following list contains suggested sources for further mathematical reading. Some sources provide general mathematical information while others provide specific strategies for dealing with difficult areas in mathematics, such as problem solving.

Some of the listings are for books and periodicals that can be obtained from the National Council of Teachers of Mathematics (NCTM) at 1906 Association Drive, Reston, Va., 22091. Many of these books and periodicals may be available at your local public or school library. Local teachers also may have suggestions for further reading sources.

Periodicals

The Arithmetic Teacher, National Council of Teachers of Mathematics (NCTM), Reston, VA
Published monthly September–April, grades K–8.

The Computing Teacher, Computing Center, Eastern Oregon State College, LaGrande, OR
Published bimonthly.

Focus on Learning Problems in Mathematics, Center for Teaching/

Learning Mathematics, Framingham, MA
Published four times a year: Jan., April, July, Oct.

The Mathematics Teacher, NCTM, Reston, VA
Published monthly September–April, grades 7–12.

Scholastic Math, 902 Sylvan Avenue, Englewood Cliffs, NJ 07632.
Published biweekly September–May.

Books

Aufmann, Richard N., and Vernon C. Barker. *Basic College Mathematics: An Applied Approach*. 2d ed. Boston: Houghton Mifflin Company, 1982.
A flexible text designed for college students enrolled in basic mathematics courses.

Averbach, Bonnie, and Orin Chein. *Mathematics: Problem Solving Through Recreational Mathematics*. San Francisco: W. H. Freeman & Co., 1980.
Easy-to-read book that approaches problem solving through puzzles and games.

Bell, Katherine W., and Reta G. Parrish. *Computational Skills with Applications*. Lexington, MA: D. C. Heath and Co., 1975.

Complete review of computational skills along with real-life applications.

Buxton, Laurie. *Mathematics for Everyone*. New York: Schocken Books, 1985.

This book shows the evolution of various mathematical principles and demonstrates their use in daily living.

Carman, Robert A., and Marilyn J. Carman. *Basic Mathematical Skills: A Guided Approach*. 2d ed. New York: John Wiley & Sons, Inc., 1981.

A write-in text designed for college students who need help with basic arithmetic skills.

Charles, Randall. *How to Evaluate Progress in Problem Solving*. Reston, VA: NCTM, 1987.

This book gives valuable suggestions on how to solve mathematical problems and how to evaluate your improvement.

Cummins, Jerry, and Gene Kuechmann. *Programming in BASIC*. Columbus, OH: Charles E. Merrill Publishing Co., 1983.

An introductory text to computer programming in BASIC that guides hands-on experience with many varied computers for data processing.

Edwards, C. H., Jr. *Calculus and the Personal Computer*. Englewood Cliffs, NJ: Prentice-Hall, 1986.

This book presents ways that basic computer techniques can be used to solve area computations, logarithms, and trigonometric problems.

Goozner, Calman. *Arithmetic Skills Worktext*. 2d ed. New York: AMSCO School Publications, Inc., 1988.

Complete coverage of the fundamentals of arithmetic computations along with their applications.

Gowar, Norman. *An Invitation to Mathematics*. New York: Oxford University Press, 1979.

An easy-to-read book that provides a historical description of mathematics from numbers through basic calculus.

Growney, Joanne Simpson. *Mathematics in Daily Life: Making Decisions and Solving Problems*. New York: McGraw-Hill Book Company, 1986.

This text demonstrates how complex mathematics problems that occur in daily life can be analyzed and solved using familiar mathematical processes.

Hill, Shirley. *Education in the 80's: Mathematics*. Washington, D. C.: National Education Association of the United States, 1982.

Text discusses the state of mathematics in the curriculum at the beginning of the decade, and makes predictions for the future. The author discusses subjects including the effect of computer and calculators on math, and the role of women in mathematics.

Jacobs, Harold R. *Mathematics: A Human Endeavor*. 2d ed. San Francisco: W. H. Freeman & Company, 1982.

Text designed especially for people who fear mathematics.

Johnston, C. L. *Essential Arithmetic*. 5th ed. Belmont, CA: Wadsworth Publishing Company, Inc., 1988.

A college text designed for students who need extensive help with basic arithmetic skills.

Lial, Margaret L., and Charles D. Miller (ed.). *Mathematics with Applications in the Management, Natural, and Social Sciences*. 4th ed. Glenview, IL: Scott, Foresman and Co., 1987.

Introduces the mathematical ideas needed by students of management, social science, and biology.

Miller, C. D., and V. E. Heeren. *Mathematics: An Everyday Experience*. 2d ed. Glenview, IL: Scott, Foresman and Co., 1980.

Detailed development of some of the main areas of contemporary mathematics, as well as an appreciation for how mathematics is used in real-life contexts.

Saunders, Brigitte. *Mathematics Workbook for SAT*. New York: Arco Publishing Co., 1980.

Provides help for persons studying for the Scholastic Aptitude Test.

Smith, Karl J. *Mathematics: Its Power and Utility*. 2d ed. Monterey, CA: Brooks/Cole Publishing Company, 1986.

Text introduces concepts of algebra, percentage, the metric system,

statistics and graphing, and the usage of calculators and computers. The book is designed for those people who did not take college math courses and need to freshen up on math skills needed in daily living. The use of cartoons injects humor.

Spencer, Donald D. *Computers in Number Theory*. Rockville, MD: Computer Science Press, 1982.

Introduces computer programming using number theory examples.

Steinke, Don C. *Thirty Days to Metric Mastery for People who Hate Math*. Vancouver, WA: House of Charles, 1981.

Enjoyable book giving historical background and helpful hints on learning to use the metric system.

Student Calculator Math. Dallas, TX: Texas Instruments, Inc., 1980.

This book defines various calculator function and symbol keys. It gives step-by-step instructions on using the calculator to solve algebraic, trigonometric, and statistical problems. A section of games and puzzles is included.

Weiss, Sol. *Helping Your Child With Math*. Englewood Cliffs, NJ: Prentice-Hall, 1986.

Of use to parents and teachers, this is a sourcebook of learning theory, teaching strategies, activities, and games.

Math Symbols

$+$	plus or add, as in $a + b$; positive, as in $+a$
$-$	minus or subtract, as in $a - b$; negative, as in $-a$
$\pm$	plus or minus
$\times$; $\cdot$	times or multiply
$\div$	divide
$-$; $/$	divide, such as $\frac{a}{b}$ or a/b
$=$	equals, is equal to
$\neq$	does not equal, is not equal to
$<$	is less than
$>$	is greater than
$\leq$	is less than or equal to
$\geq$	is greater than or equal to
$<>$	is not equal to, is less than or greater than
$\approx$	is approximately equal to
$\overset{?}{=}$	is it equal to?; asks question, does not state fact
$:$	is to, as in proportions, $a:b$ as $c:d$, which means $\frac{a}{b} = \frac{c}{d}$
$\ldots$	between numerals or letters, shows omission of some numerals or letters at the end of a series or sequence shows "and so on"
$\sqrt{}$	positive square root
$\sqrt[n]{}$	nth root
$!$	factorial
a^b	exponent, use a as a factor b times
a_b	subscript, for descriptive discrimination
$\%$	percent
$\|\ \|$	absolute value
$\subset$	is a subset of
$\supset$	contains as a subset
$\in$	is an element of

°	degree symbol
‖	parallel, is parallel to
⊥	perpendicular, is perpendicular to
~	similar, is similar to
≅	congruent, is congruent to

—	line segment, as in $\overline{AB}$
⟷	line, as in $\overleftrightarrow{AB}$
⟶	ray, as in $\overrightarrow{AB}$
∠	angle, as in ∠A or ∠ABC
m∠	measure of angle
⌐	right angle; is perpendicular to

⊙	circle
⌒	arc, as in $\overset{\frown}{A\,B}$
△	triangle
□	square
▭	rectangle
▱	parallelogram
⏢	trapezoid

(x,y)	coordinates of a point in a plane
(x,y,z)	coordinates of a point in space
∴	therefore
$	dollar sign
¢	cent sign

( )	parentheses, shows order of operations
[ ]	brackets, shows order of operations
{ }	braces, shows order of operations; also shows members of a set, when empty shows empty set

Math Glossary

In the following glossary, italics (e.g., *sum*) indicate terms that have their own entries in the glossary.

A

addend One of the numbers that is combined in an addition problem.

addition facts The *sums* of each possible pair of *addends* from 0 + 0 to 9 + 9; there are one hundred addition facts.

algorithm A procedure for solving a mathematical problem in a finite number of steps.

alphanumeric system This is the system used on many maps. The vertical *coordinates* are numbered, and letters identify the horizontal coordinates.

arc A portion of the circle that connects the two endpoints of a *chord*.

area The number of square units equal in measure to the surface of a region.

arithmetic sequence A number sequence that is obtained by adding the same number.

axiom In geometry, an assumed statement that is applicable to the entire field of study.

B

binary numeration system Unlike the decimal number system, which uses ten digits, the binary system uses only two digits: 0 and 1.

C

cathode-ray tube (CRT) A CRT is a vacuum tube with a screen like that of a TV set. The CRT display enables the operator to check the data being entered into the computer.

chord A *line segment* that connects two points on a circle.

circumference The distance around a circle.

complex fraction A *fraction* in which the *numerator* and the *denominator,* or both, is a *fraction* or a *mixed numeral.*

composite numbers *Whole numbers* that are not *prime numbers.*

cone A three-dimensional figure that has a closed curve for a base and a surface that comes to a point.

congruence Two figures that are the same size and the same shape.

conic section A group of curves that are formed by passing a *plane* through a *cone.* Conic sections include curved lines, circles, parabolas, ellipses, and hyperbolas.

constant A number that has a fixed value.

coordinate axes Two perpendicular lines; the point at which the lines intersect is the starting point of the system.

coordinates Any of a *set* of numbers used to specify the location of a point on a line, on a surface, or in space.

cosecant The trigonometric function that for an acute angle is the *ratio* between the length of the hypotenuse and the length of the opposite side.

cosine The trigonometric function that for an acute angle is the *ratio* between the length of the adjacent side and the length of the hypotenuse.

cotangent The trigonometric function that for an acute angle is the *ratio* between the length of the opposite side and the length of the adjacent side.

counting numbers A whole *set* of numbers—1, 2, 3, 4, 5, and so forth—that can go on indefinitely.

customary units The measurement system that is most often used in the United States.

D

decimal numeral Another way to write a *fraction* that has a *denominator* of 10, 100, or 1000, and so on.

denominator The bottom number of a *fraction*.

diameter Any *chord* that contains the center of a circle.

difference The number that is obtained as a result of subtracting the *subtrahend* from the *minuend*.

differential equation This mathematical equation is an expression of natural laws that describe the rates of change of quantities.

digital computer The most common type of computer. Digital computers use the digits of the *binary numeration system*.

dividend In division, the number being divided into.

division facts Division in which the *divisor* and *quotient* are *whole numbers* not larger than 9; there are 90 division facts.

divisor In division, the number being divided by.

E

equation An open sentence that uses the equal symbol. An equation is a quick way of saying that the symbols before and after the equal sign represent the same number.

equivalent fractions Fractions that name the same number.

even number A number that is two times a *whole number*.

exponent A notation in which a non-zero *whole number* is used to indicate the number of times the base number is used as a *factor*.

F

factor In a multiplication problem, one of the two numbers being multiplied. Also, the factors of a number are the numbers that when multiplied together give the original number (e.g., 3 and 4 are factors of 12).

factoring A method used to determine a *square root* or *factors*.

Fibonacci sequence A sequence of numbers in which every number after the second number is equal to the *sum* of the two preceding numbers.

finite set A *set* with a definite number of members.

formula A way of expressing a rule by using algebraic symbols and operations.

fraction A way of showing a relationship between two numbers— the number of parts and the number of wholes.

G, H

geometric sequence Each term of a sequence that is obtained by always multiplying the previous term by the same number.

greatest common factor (GCF) The largest *factor* that is an exact *divisor* of two or more numbers.

I, J, K

improper fraction When the *numerator* of a *fraction* is equal to or greater than the *denominator*.

infinite set A *set* with an infinite, or endless, number of members.

input equipment This equipment transforms instructions and data into a code understandable to a computer.

inverse operation The relationship between addition and subtraction and between multiplication and division; opposite mathematical functions.

irrational numbers Numbers that are not *rational*.

L

latitude The number that measures how far north or south one is from the equator.

least common multiple (LCM) The smallest number other than zero that is a multiple of several numbers.

like fractions *Fractions* that have the same *denominator*.

linear equation An algebraic equation that represents lines.

line segment The shortest distance between two points.

longitude The number that measures how far east or west one is from the zero, or prime, meridian.

M

mainframe The largest kind of computer. Mainframes may control a telephone switching network or serve as a data base for a major government agency.

main memory The main memory in a computer receives and stores data and instructions from an input device or an auxiliary storage unit.

mean An average; to find the mean, all the values are added and the *sum* is divided by the number of *addends*.

median The value that is in the middle of the data *set* when the data are put in order from highest to lowest.

meridians The north-south imaginary lines on a globe.

metric system A measurement system used by all the major countries in the world except the United States.

microcomputer A small computer system that can range from desktop size to pocket size.

minicomputer A large, high-performance computer.

minuend In subtraction, the larger number being subtracted from; this number is sometimes called the sum.

mixed numerals A number represented by a *whole number* and a *fraction*.

mode The value that occurs with the highest frequency in a data *set*.

multiplicand The number that is being multiplied.

multiplication facts The facts for which both *factors* are nine or less; there are one hundred multiplication facts.

multiplier The number that does the multiplying.

N

numerator The top number of a *fraction*.

O

odd number A number that is one more than an *even number*.

output equipment Serves as a communication link between the computer and the user; it translates the computer's electrical signals into a form comprehensible to the user.

P

parallels The east-west imaginary lines on a globe.

percent A Latin word meaning "per hundred."

perimeter The distance around a geometric figure.

pi The *ratio* of the *circumference* of a circle to its *diameter*. Pi is a constant value.

place value The value of the location of a digit in a numeral.

plane A figure in which two lines either intersect or are parallel.

polygon A closed, many-sided figure in which the *line segments* do not cross.

polyhedron A three-dimensional figure formed by the union of *polygons*; the polygons intersect only at the edges.

postulate An assumption that is not general but is used particularly in geometry.

power The number of times as indicated by the *exponent* that a number occurs as a *factor* in a *product*.

prime number A whole number greater than one that has no *factors* other than one and itself.

prism A special kind of *polyhedron* that consists of figures that have a pair of opposite sides that are parallel.

product The number that is obtained as a result of multiplying two *factors*.

proper fraction When the *numerator* of a *fraction* is smaller than the *denominator*.

properties The characteristics of a figure, or shape.

proportion A statement that two *ratios* are equal.

pyramid A three-dimensional *polyhedron* that has a *polygon* for the base and triangular sides that meet in a point.

Q

quadrant Each of the four regions of a *plane* that has been divided by the two *coordinate axes*.

quadratic equation An equation in one *variable* for which at least one term involves the *square* of the variable.

quadrilateral A four-sided figure.

quotient The number resulting from the division of one number by another.

R

radius Any segment that connects the center of the circle to a point on the circle (plural: radii).

ratio The *fraction* that is formed when two quantities are compared by an indicated division.

rational numbers The *set* of numbers that consists of the *fractional* numbers and their opposites.

ray In geometry, part of a line that includes one endpoint and extends infinitely in one direction.

real numbers The union of *rational numbers* and *irrational numbers*.

remainder The number that results when the division of *whole numbers* is not exact.

repeating decimal The *quotient* that results when a *remainder* of zero occurs in the *divisor*.

S

secant The trigonometric function that for an acute angle is the *ratio* between the length of the side opposite and the length of the adjacent side.

set In mathematics, a collection of numbers.

sine The trigonometric function that for an acute angle is the *ratio* between the length of the opposite side and the length of the hypotenuse.

sphere The space version of a circle; a *set* of points all at a fixed distance from a given point.

square The *product* of a number multiplied by itself.

square root A *factor* of a number that when *squared* gives the number.

statistics The science of collecting and using facts.

subset A *set* each of whose elements is an element of another set.

subtraction facts The *whole-number* facts from $0 - 0 = 0$ to $18 - 9 = 9$; there are one hundred subtraction facts.

subtrahend In subtraction, the smaller number that is to be taken away, or subtracted.

sum The number that is obtained as a result of combining the *addends* in an addition problem.

T

tangent The trigonometric function that for an acute angle is the *ratio* between the length of the side opposite and the length of the adjacent side.

terminating decimal The *quotient* that results when a *remainder* of zero occurs in the *divisor*.

theorem The results of a geometry problem that have been proved or that must be proved.

U

unlike fractions *Fractions* that have different *denominators*.

V

variable A number associated with a *set*; any element of the set may be used to replace the variable.

W, X, Y, Z

whole numbers The *counting numbers* and zero taken together.

Δ   Delta. Used to represent the difference, or change, between two numbers.

μ   Mu; micro. Used to represent a millionth of a quantity or also the arithmetic mean.

π   Pi. Constant of proportionality between the diameter and the circumference of a circle. Pi represents an irrational number. Two frequently used numerical approximations are $\frac{22}{7}$ and 3.14.

Σ   Sigma (capital). Represents summation of terms.

σ   Sigma (lower case). Represents standard deviation.

θ   Theta. Represents the measure of an unspecified angle.

Addition of real numbers

Arithmetic Operations

Addition is an undefined binary operation. That is, addends are always combined two at a time and results are obtained from data contained in the addition table found on page 827. The table should be memorized for success and efficiency in performing addition.

Properties of addition

Closure: For all real numbers a and b, there is a real number c, such that
$$a + b = c$$

Identity: There is a real number 0, such that
$$a + 0 = 0 + a = a$$

Associativity: For all real numbers a, b, and c:
$$(a + b) + c = a + (b + c)$$

Inverse: For every real number a, there is a real number $-a$, the additive inverse, such that
$$a + -a = -a + a = 0$$
Note: the additive inverse of 0 is 0. Zero is neither positive nor negative.

Commutativity: For all real numbers a and b:
$$a + b = b + a$$

Addition of rational numbers

For all real numbers a, b, c, and d, $b \neq 0$, $d \neq 0$:

for like denominators: $\dfrac{a}{b} + \dfrac{c}{b} = \dfrac{a + c}{b}$

for unlike denominators: $\dfrac{a}{b} + \dfrac{c}{d} = \dfrac{ad + bc}{bd}$

Addition of integers

For all real numbers a and b:

$$+ a + \, +b = + \, (a + b)$$
$$- a + \, -b = - \, (a + b)$$
$$+ a + \, -b = - \, (b - a), \text{ if } b > a$$
$$+ a + \, -b = + \, (a - b), \text{ if } a > b$$

Multiplication of real numbers

Multiplication is an undefined binary operation. That is, factors are always multiplied two at a time and results are obtained from data contained in the multiplication table found on page 827. The table should be memorized for success and efficiency in multiplication.

Properties of multiplication

Closure: For all real numbers a and b, there is a real number c, such that
$$a \times b = c$$

Identity: There is a real number 1, such that
$$a \times 1 = 1 \times a = a$$

Associativity: For all real numbers a, b, and c:
$$(a \times b) \times c = a \times (b \times c)$$

Inverse: For every real number a, except zero, there is a number $\dfrac{1}{a}$ such that
$$a \times \dfrac{1}{a} = \dfrac{1}{a} \times a = 1$$

Commutativity: For all real numbers a and b:
$$a \times b = b \times a$$

Distributivity: Multiplication distributes over addition. For all real numbers a, b, and c:
$$a(b + c) = ab + ac$$

Multiplication of rational numbers

For all real numbers a, b, c, and d, $b \neq 0$, $d \neq 0$:

$$\frac{a}{b} \times \frac{c}{d} = \frac{ac}{bd}$$

Multiplication of integers

For all real numbers a and b:

$$(+a) \times (+b) = +(ab) \qquad (+a) \times (-b) = -(ab)$$
$$(-a) \times (-b) = +(ab) \qquad (-a) \times (+b) = -(ab)$$

Subtraction of real numbers

Subtraction is a defined operation. It is defined as the addition of the additive inverse of a number. For all real numbers a and b:

$$a - b = a + (-b)$$

Further, for all real numbers a, b, and c:

$$a - b = c \text{ if, and only if, } a = b + c$$

For success in subtraction, it is necessary to be in command of the 100 addition facts. For more efficiency in subtraction, the subtraction table on page 828 should be memorized.

Subtraction of rational numbers

For all real numbers a, b, c, and d, $b \neq 0$, $d \neq 0$:

for like denominators: $\dfrac{a}{b} - \dfrac{c}{b} = \dfrac{a - c}{b}$

for unlike denominators: $\dfrac{a}{b} - \dfrac{c}{d} = \dfrac{ad - bc}{bd}$

Subtraction of integers

For all real numbers a and b, first rewrite the subtraction as the addition of the additive inverse, then add the integers.

$$(+a) - (+b) = (+a) + (-b)$$
$$(+a) - (-b) = (+a) + (+b)$$
$$(-a) - (-b) = (-a) + (+b)$$
$$(-a) - (+b) = (-a) + (-b)$$

Division of real numbers

Division is a defined operation. It is defined as multiplication by the multiplicative inverse. For all real numbers a and b, $b \neq 0$:

$$a \div b = a \times \frac{1}{b}$$

Division by zero is not defined. Further, for all real numbers a, b, and c, $b \neq 0$:

$$a \div b = c \text{ if, and only if, } a = b \times c$$

For success in division, it is necessary to be in command of the 100 multiplication facts. For more efficiency in division, the division table given on page 829 should be memorized. For any numbers a, b, c, and d, $b \neq 0$, $c \neq 0$, $d \neq 0$:

$$\frac{a}{b} \div \frac{c}{d} = \frac{a}{b} \times \frac{d}{c} = \frac{ad}{bc}$$

Other Operations, Properties, and Laws

Exponents

$$a^0 = 1, a \neq 0$$
$$a^1 = a$$
$$a^2 = a \cdot a$$
$$a^3 = a \cdot a \cdot a$$

$$a^m \cdot a^n = a^{(m+n)}$$

$$a^m \div a^n = a^{(m-n)}$$

$$(a^m)^n = a^{(mn)}$$

n factors

$$a^n = \overbrace{a \cdot a \cdot a \cdot \ldots \cdot a}$$

$$a^{-m} = \frac{1}{a^m}$$

Factorials

$$1! = 1$$
$$2! = 2 \cdot 1$$
$$3! = 3 \cdot 2 \cdot 1$$
$$4! = 4 \cdot 3 \cdot 2 \cdot 1$$

$$n! = n(n-1)(n-2) \ldots 1$$

Average (arithmetic mean)

For two items, a and b: $\dfrac{a + b}{2}$

For n items, $x_1, x_2, \ldots , x_n$:

$$\overset{\displaystyle n \text{ addends}}{\overbrace{\dfrac{x_1 + x_2 + \ldots + x_n}{n}}}$$

Trichotomy law

For all real numbers a and b, there are exactly three possibilities:

$$a < b \quad a > b \quad a = b$$

Properties of equality

For all real numbers a, b, and c:

Reflexive: $a = a$
Symmetric: If $a = b$, then $b = a$
Transitive: If $a = b$ and $b = c$, then $a = c$

Geometric formulas

Math Formulas

Note: The variables that occur in formulas stand for the measures of various parts of geometric figures. For instance, s may represent the measure of a side even though the explanation is simply listed as $s \rightarrow$ side.

Perimeter formulas

Rectangle	$P = 2l + 2w$	$l \rightarrow$ length; $w \rightarrow$ width
Square	$P = 4s$	$s \rightarrow$ side
Triangle	$P = a + b + c$	$a, b, c \rightarrow$ sides of triangle
Circle (called circumference)	$C = \pi d$ or $2\pi r$	$d \rightarrow$ diameter $r \rightarrow$ radius

Area formulas

Rectangle	$A = lw$	$l \rightarrow$ length; $w \rightarrow$ width
Square	$A = s^2$	$s \rightarrow$ side
Parallelogram	$A = bh$	$b \rightarrow$ base $h \rightarrow$ altitude to base, b

Trapezoid $\quad A = \frac{1}{2}h(b_1 + b_2)$ $\qquad b_1, b_2 \rightarrow$ bases; $h \rightarrow$ altitude to bases, b_1 and b_2

Triangle $\qquad A = \frac{1}{2}bh$ $\qquad b \rightarrow$ base $h \rightarrow$ altitude to base, b

Circle $\qquad A = \pi r^2$ $\qquad r \rightarrow$ radius of circle

Volume formulas

Cube $\qquad\qquad\qquad V = s^3$ $\qquad s \rightarrow$ side
Prism or cylinder $\quad V = Bh$ $\qquad B \rightarrow$ area of base
$h \rightarrow$ altitude to base

Pyramid or cone $\qquad V = \frac{1}{3}Bh$ $\qquad B \rightarrow$ area of base
$h \rightarrow$ altitude to base

Sphere $\qquad\qquad V = \frac{4}{3}\pi r^3$ $\qquad r \rightarrow$ radius

Miscellaneous geometric formulas

Pythagorean Theorem
$$a^2 + b^2 = c^2 \qquad a, b \rightarrow \text{sides of right triangle;}$$
$$c \rightarrow \text{hypotenuse}$$

Sum of measures of angles of triangle
$$m\angle A + m\angle B + m\angle C = 180 \qquad m \rightarrow \text{measure}$$
$$A, B, C \rightarrow \text{angle names}$$

Sum of measures of angles for polygon with n sides
$$\text{Sum} = (n - 2) \times 180 \qquad n \rightarrow \text{number of sides}$$

Measure of an angle of a regular polygon with n sides
$$m\angle A = \frac{(n - 2) \times 180}{n} \qquad m\angle A \rightarrow \text{measure of angle}$$
$$n \rightarrow \text{number of sides}$$

Coordinate geometry formulas

Note: (x_1, y_1) are coordinates of A; (x_2, y_2) are coordinates of B.

Distance between two points, A and B
$$d = \sqrt{(x_2 - x_1)^2 + (y_2 - y_1)^2}$$

Slope of a line through points A and B

$$m = \frac{\Delta y}{\Delta x} \text{ or } \frac{y_2 - y_1}{x_2 - x_1} \qquad m \rightarrow \text{slope}$$

General equation for a line through points A and B

$$y - y_1 = \frac{y_2 - y_1}{x_2 - x_1}(x - x_1)$$

Point-slope form for a line through A and B

$$y - y_1 = m(x - x_1) \qquad m \rightarrow \text{slope}$$

Slope-intercept form for a line through A and B

$$y = mx + b \qquad b \rightarrow y\text{-intercept}$$

Intercept form for a line through A and B

$$\frac{x}{a} + \frac{y}{b} = 1 \qquad a \rightarrow x\text{-intercept}$$

General linear equation

$$Ax + By + C = 0. \ A + B \neq 0$$

General equations for conics

Circle
$$(x - h)^2 + (y - k)^2 = r^2$$
center at (h,k) and r is radius

Parabola
$$(y - k)^2 = 4a(x - h)$$
vertex at (h,k) and opens sideways

$$(x - h)^2 = 4a(y - k)$$
vertex at (h,k) and opens up or down

Ellipse
$$\frac{(x - h)^2}{a^2} + \frac{(y - k)^2}{b^2} = 1$$
center at (h,k) with horizontal major axis

$$\frac{(y - k)^2}{a^2} + \frac{(x - h)^2}{b^2} = 1$$
center at (h,k) with vertical major axis

Hyperbola $\dfrac{(x - h)^2}{a^2} - \dfrac{(y - k)^2}{b^2} = 1$

center at (h,k) and opens sideways

$$\dfrac{(y - k)^2}{a^2} - \dfrac{(x - h)^2}{b^2} = 1$$

center at (h,k) and opens up and down

Trigonometric formulas

Note: These ratios and relations are for the right triangle illustrated. The letters a, b, and c represent the
measures of the sides of the triangle.

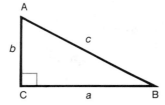

For $\angle A$, a is the opposite side, b is the
adjacent side, and c
is the hypotenuse.

sine A	$\sin A = \dfrac{a}{c}$
cosine A	$\cos A = \dfrac{b}{c}$
tangent A	$\tan A = \dfrac{a}{b}$
cotangent A	$\cot A = \dfrac{b}{a}$
secant A	$\sec A = \dfrac{c}{b}$
cosecant A	$\cos A = \dfrac{c}{a}$

$$\sin A = \dfrac{1}{\csc A} \qquad \csc A = \dfrac{1}{\sin A}$$

$$\cos A = \dfrac{1}{\sec A} \qquad \sec A = \dfrac{1}{\cos A}$$

$$\tan A = \dfrac{1}{\cot A} \qquad \cot A = \dfrac{1}{\tan A}$$

$(\sin A)(\csc A) = 1$
$(\cos A)(\sec A) = 1$
$(\tan A)(\cot A) = 1$

$$\tan A = \frac{\sin A}{\cos A}$$

$\sin^2 A + \cos^2 A = 1$ (called trigonometric form of the Pythagorean Theorem)

$\tan^2 A + 1 = \sec^2 A$
$1 + \cot^2 A = \csc^2 A$

$$\frac{\sin A}{a} = \frac{\sin B}{b} = \frac{\sin C}{c}$$ (called Law of Sines)

$a^2 = b^2 + c^2 - 2bc \cdot \cos A$ (called Law of Cosines)

$b^2 = a^2 + c^2 - 2ac \cdot \cos B$

Algebraic equations

Products of polynomials (a and b are variables)

$(a - b)(a + b) = a^2 - b^2$
$(a + b)^2 = a^2 + 2ab + b^2$
$(a - b)^2 = a^2 - 2ab + b^2$

Quadratic equations

General equation

$ax^2 + bx + c = 0, a \neq 0$

Solution to general equation

$$x = \frac{-b \pm \sqrt{b^2 - 4ac}}{2a}$$

$b^2 - 4ac$ is called the discriminant; it reveals the nature of the roots (solutions).

$b^2 - 4ac \geq 0$ roots are real
   If $b^2 - 4ac$ is a perfect square, then roots are rational.
   If $b^2 - 4ac$ is not a perfect square, then roots are irrational.

$b^2 - 4ac = 0$ roots are equal
$b^2 - 4ac < 0$ roots are complex

Statistical formulas

Average deviation

$$\frac{1}{n} \sum_{i=1}^{i=n} |x_i - \bar{x}|$$

$i \rightarrow$ counter
$n \rightarrow$ number of items
$X \rightarrow$ data point being considered
$\bar{X} \rightarrow$ average X-value (mean)

Standard deviation

$$\sigma = \sqrt{\frac{1}{n} \sum_{i=1}^{i=n} |X_i - \bar{X}|^2}$$

Permutations

For n items taken n at a time with no repetitions

$$_nP_n = n!$$

For n items taken r at a time with no repetitions

$$_nP_r = \frac{n!}{(n - r)!}$$

Combinations

For n items taken r at a time with no repetitions

$$_nC_r = \frac{_nP_r}{r!}$$

Miscellaneous formulas

Distance Formula $d = rt$ $d \rightarrow$ distance;
$r \rightarrow$ rate;
$t \rightarrow$ time

Simple Interest $I = PRT$ $I \rightarrow$ interest;
$R \rightarrow$ rate;
$P \rightarrow$ principal;
$T \rightarrow$ time

Temperature (Fahrenheit and Celsius)

$$F = \frac{9}{5}C + 32 \qquad C = \frac{5}{9}(F - 32)$$

$$\text{Relative Error} = \frac{\text{Greatest Possible Error}}{\text{Actual Measure}}$$

Addition facts

+	0	1	2	3	4	5	6	7	8	9
0	0	1	2	3	4	5	6	7	8	9
1	1	2	3	4	5	6	7	8	9	10
2	2	3	4	5	6	7	8	9	10	11
3	3	4	5	6	7	8	9	10	11	12
4	4	5	6	7	8	9	10	11	12	13
5	5	6	7	8	9	10	11	12	13	14
6	6	7	8	9	10	11	12	13	14	15
7	7	8	9	10	11	12	13	14	15	16
8	8	9	10	11	12	13	14	15	16	17
9	9	10	11	12	13	14	15	16	17	18

Multiplication facts

×	0	1	2	3	4	5	6	7	8	9
0	0	0	0	0	0	0	0	0	0	0
1	0	1	2	3	4	5	6	7	8	9
2	0	2	4	6	8	10	12	14	16	18
3	0	3	6	9	12	15	18	21	24	27
4	0	4	8	12	16	20	24	28	32	36
5	0	5	10	15	20	25	30	35	40	45
6	0	6	12	18	24	30	36	42	48	54
7	0	7	14	21	28	35	42	49	56	63
8	0	8	16	24	32	40	48	56	64	72
9	0	9	18	27	36	45	54	63	72	81

Subtraction facts

Notice that the table for subtraction facts does not look like the addition and multiplication tables. However, it is used the same way. To find the difference between two numbers, find the number in the top row, then go down that column until you reach the row for the number you are subtracting (number at the left). The number appearing in the intersection of the column and the row is the difference. The table also contains some differences that are not basic facts. The basic facts have differences less than ten.

−	18	17	16	15	14	13	12	11	10	9	8	7	6	5	4	3	2	1	0
0	18	17	16	15	14	13	12	11	10	9	8	7	6	5	4	3	2	1	0
1	17	16	15	14	13	12	11	10	9	8	7	6	5	4	3	2	1	0	
2	16	15	14	13	12	11	10	9	8	7	6	5	4	3	2	1	0		
3	15	14	13	12	11	10	9	8	7	6	5	4	3	2	1	0			
4	14	13	12	11	10	9	8	7	6	5	4	3	2	1	0				
5	13	12	11	10	9	8	7	6	5	4	3	2	1	0					
6	12	11	10	9	8	7	6	5	4	3	2	1	0						
7	11	10	9	8	7	6	5	4	3	2	1	0							
8	10	9	8	7	6	5	4	3	2	1	0								
9	9	8	7	6	5	4	3	2	1	0									

Division facts

The division table gives the dividend in the top row and the divisors in the left-hand column. Notice that some boxes for the intersection of columns and rows contain no numbers. This is because the number at the left will not evenly divide the number at the top of that column. Further, the table is separated into parts for easier reading. The table also contains some quotients that are not basic facts. The basic facts have quotients less than ten.

÷	81	72	64	63	56	54	49	48	45	42	40	36	35	32	30	28
9	9	8		7		6			5			4				
8		9	8		7			6			5			4		
7				9	8		7			6			5			4
6		12				9		8		7		6			5	
5									9		8		7		6	
4		18	16		14			12			10	9		8		7

÷	27	25	24	21	20	18	16	15	14	12	10	9	8	7	6	5	4	3	2	1	0
9	3					2						1									0
8			3				2						1								0
7				3					2					1							0
6			4			3				2					1						0
5		5			4			3			2					1					0
4			6		5		4			3			2				1				0
3	9		8	7		6		5		4		3		2			1				0
2			12		10	9	8		7	6	5		4	3		2		1			0
1	27	25	24	21	20	18	16	15	14	12	10	9	8	7	6	5	4	3	2	1	0

Equivalents—Percent, decimal, fraction

Percent	Decimal	Fraction	Percent	Decimal	Fraction
5%	.05	$\frac{1}{20}$	50%	.50	$\frac{1}{2}$
$6\frac{1}{4}$%	.0625	$\frac{1}{16}$	60%	.60	$\frac{3}{5}$
$8\frac{1}{3}$%	$.08\overline{3}$	$\frac{1}{12}$	$62\frac{1}{2}$%	.625	$\frac{5}{8}$
10%	.10	$\frac{1}{10}$	$66\frac{2}{3}$%	$.6\overline{6}$	$\frac{2}{3}$
$12\frac{1}{2}$%	.125	$\frac{1}{8}$	70%	.70	$\frac{7}{10}$
$16\frac{2}{3}$%	$.1\overline{6}$	$\frac{1}{6}$	75%	.75	$\frac{3}{4}$
20%	.20	$\frac{1}{5}$	80%	.80	$\frac{4}{5}$
25%	.25	$\frac{1}{4}$	$83\frac{1}{3}$%	$.8\overline{3}$	$\frac{5}{6}$
30%	.30	$\frac{3}{10}$	$87\frac{1}{2}$%	.875	$\frac{7}{8}$
$33\frac{1}{3}$%	$.3\overline{3}$	$\frac{1}{3}$	90%	.90	$\frac{9}{10}$
$37\frac{1}{2}$%	.375	$\frac{3}{8}$	100%	1.00	$\frac{10}{10}$
40%	.40	$\frac{2}{5}$			

Customary units

Dry measure

2 pints (pt) = 1 quart (qt)
8 quarts   = 1 peck (pk)
4 pecks   = 1 bushel (bu)

Liquid measure

2 cups (c) = 1 pint
2 pints   = 1 quart
4 quarts   = 1 gallon (gal.)

Linear measure

12 inches (in.) = 1 foot (ft)
36 inches   = 1 yard
3 feet   = 1 yard
5280 feet   = 1760 yards = 1 mile (mi)
$16\frac{1}{2}$ feet   = $5\frac{1}{2}$ yards = 1 rod
320 rods   = 1 mile

Area

144 square inches (in.^{2}) = 1 square foot (ft^2)
9 square feet   = 1 square yard (yd^2)
43,560 square feet   = 160 square rods (rd^2)
160 square rods   = 1 acre
640 acres   = 1 square mile (mi^2)

Volume

1728 cubic inches (in.^{3}) = 1 cubic foot (ft^3)
27 cubic feet   = 1 cubic yard (yd^3)
231 cubic inches   = 1 gallon
1 cubic foot   = $7\frac{1}{2}$ gallons
1 cubic foot   = .8 bushel

Metric system

Prefixes in the metric system

Prefix	Symbol	Multiples
kilo-	k	1000
hecto-	h	100
deka-	da	10
deci-	d	0.1
centi-	c	0.01
milli-	m	0.001

Length

10 millimeters (mm)	= 1 centimeter (cm)
10 centimeters	= 1 decimeter (dm)
100 millimeters	= 1 decimeter
10 decimeters	= 1 meter (m)
100 centimeters	= 1 meter
1000 meters	= 1 kilometer (km)

Area

100 square millimeters (mm^2)	= 1 square centimeter (cm^2)
10,000 square centimeters	= 1 square meter (m^2)
10,000 square meters	= 1 hectare (ha)

Volume

1000 cubic millimeters (mm^3)	= 1 cubic centimeter (cm^3)
1000 cubic centimeters	= 1 cubic decimeter (dm^3)
1,000,000 cubic centimeters	= 1 cubic meter (m^3)

Capacity

1000 milliliters (ml)	= 1 liter (L, ℓ, l)
1000 liters	= 1 kiloliter (kl)

Mass

1000 milligrams (mg)	= 1 gram (g)
1000 grams	= 1 kilogram (kg)
1000 kilograms	= 1 metric ton (t)

When using metric or customary units the following procedures are generally used:

The same symbol is used for both singular and plural forms.

No period need be used after the symbol, except to end a sentence or when the symbol makes a word, such as in. for inch.

Superscripts, such as cm^2 and ft^3, are used with all symbols for area and volume.

Customary units are not mixed with metric units.

A prefix is not used without a unit—for example, use kilogram, not kilo.

For a compound unit that is a quotient use a slash to form the symbol. For example, meters per second should be written, m/s.

Metric–Customary conversions

This table can help change customary measurements into or out of metric units. To use it, look up the unit you know in the left-hand column and multiply it by the number given. Your answer will be approximately the number of units in the right-hand column.

When you know:	Multiply by:	To find:
Temperature		
degrees Fahrenheit	$\dfrac{5}{9}$ (after subtracting 32)	degrees Celsius
degrees Celsius	$\dfrac{9}{5}$ (then add 32)	degrees Fahrenheit

When you know:	Multiply by:	To find:
Length and distance		
inches	25	millimeters
feet	30	centimeters
yards	0.9	meters
miles	1.6	kilometers
millimeters	0.04	inches
centimeters	0.4	inches
meters	1.1	yards
kilometers	0.6	miles
Surface or area		
square inches	6.5	square centimeters
square feet	0.09	square meters
square yards	0.8	square meters
square miles	2.6	square kilometers
acres	0.4	hectares
square centimeters	0.16	square inches
square meters	1.2	square yards
square kilometers	0.4	square miles
hectares	2.5	acres
Volume and capacity		
ounces (fluid)	30	milliliters
pints	0.47	liters
quarts	0.95	liters
gallons	3.8	liters
milliliters	0.034	ounces (fluid)
liters	2.1	pints
liters	1.06	quarts
liters	0.26	gallons
Weight and mass		
ounces	28	grams
pounds	0.45	kilograms
short tons	0.9	metric tons
grams	0.035	ounces
kilograms	2.2	pounds
metric tons	1.1	short tons

Trigonometric functions of angles

Degrees	Sin	Cos	Tan	Cot	Sec	Csc	
0	.0000	1.0000	.0000	. . . .	1.0000	. . . .	90
1	.0175	.9998	.0175	57.2900	1.0002	57.299	89
2	.0349	.9994	.0349	28.6363	1.0006	28.654	88
3	.0523	.9986	.0524	19.0811	1.0014	19.107	87
4	.0698	.9976	.0699	14.3007	1.0024	14.336	86
5	.0872	.9962	.0875	11.4301	1.0038	11.474	85
6	.1045	.9945	.1051	9.5144	1.0055	9.5668	84
7	.1219	.9925	.1228	8.1443	1.0075	8.2055	83
8	.1392	.9903	.1405	7.1154	1.0098	7.1853	82
9	.1564	.9877	.1584	6.3138	1.0125	6.3925	81
10	.1736	.9848	.1763	5.6713	1.0154	5.7588	80
11	.1908	.9816	.1944	5.1446	1.0187	5.2408	79
12	.2079	.9781	.2126	4.7046	1.0223	4.8097	78
13	.2250	.9744	.2309	4.3315	1.0263	4.4454	77
14	.2419	.9703	.2493	4.0108	1.0306	4.1336	76
15	.2588	.9659	.2679	3.7321	1.0353	3.8637	75
16	.2756	.9613	.2867	3.4874	1.0403	3.6280	74
17	.2924	.9563	.3057	3.2709	1.0457	3.4203	73
18	.3090	.9511	.3249	3.0777	1.0515	3.2361	72
19	.3256	.9455	.3443	2.9042	1.0576	3.0716	71
20	.3420	.9397	.3640	2.7475	1.0642	2.9238	70
21	.3584	.9336	.3839	2.6051	1.0711	2.7904	69
22	.3746	.9272	.4040	2.4751	1.0785	2.6695	68
23	.3907	.9205	.4245	2.3559	1.0864	2.5593	67
24	.4067	.9135	.4452	2.2460	1.0946	2.4586	66
25	.4226	.9063	.4663	2.1445	1.1034	2.3662	65
26	.4384	.8988	.4877	2.0503	1.1126	2.2812	64
27	.4540	.8910	.5095	1.9626	1.1223	2.2027	63
28	.4695	.8829	.5317	1.8807	1.1326	2.1301	62
29	.4848	.8746	.5543	1.8040	1.1434	2.0627	61
30	.5000	.8660	.5774	1.7321	1.1547	2.0000	60
31	.5150	.8572	.6009	1.6643	1.1666	1.9416	59
32	.5299	.8480	.6249	1.6003	1.1792	1.8871	58
33	.5446	.8387	.6494	1.5399	1.1924	1.8361	57
34	.5592	.8290	.6745	1.4826	1.2062	1.7883	56
35	.5736	.8192	.7002	1.4281	1.2208	1.7434	55
36	.5878	.8090	.7265	1.3764	1.2361	1.7013	54
37	.6018	.7986	.7536	1.3270	1.2521	1.6616	53
38	.6157	.7880	.7813	1.2799	1.2690	1.6243	52
39	.6293	.7771	.8098	1.2349	1.2868	1.5890	51
40	.6428	.7660	.8391	1.1918	1.3054	1.5557	50
41	.6561	.7547	.8693	1.1504	1.3250	1.5243	49
42	.6691	.7431	.9004	1.1106	1.3456	1.4945	48
43	.6820	.7314	.9325	1.0724	1.3673	1.4663	47
44	.6947	.7193	.9657	1.0355	1.3902	1.4396	46
45	.7071	.7071	1.0000	1.0000	1.4142	1.4142	45
	Cos	Sin	Cot	Tan	Csc	Sec	Degrees

Squares, cubes, roots, and reciprocals

n	n^2	n^3	$\sqrt{n}$	$\sqrt{10n}$	$\dfrac{1}{n}$
1	1	1	1.0000	3.1623	1.0000
2	4	8	1.4142	4.4721	.5000
3	9	27	1,7321	5.4772	.3333
4	16	64	2.0000	6.3246	.2500
5	25	125	2.2361	7.0711	.2000
6	36	216	2.4495	7.7460	.1667
7	49	343	2.6458	8.3666	.1429
8	64	512	2.8284	8.9443	.1250
9	81	729	3.0000	9.4868	.1111
10	100	1,000	3.1623	10.0000	.1000
11	121	1,331	3.3166	10.4881	.0909
12	144	1,728	3.4641	10.9545	.0833
13	169	2,197	3.6056	11.4018	.0769
14	196	2,744	3.7417	11.8322	.0714
15	225	3,375	3.8730	12.2475	.0667
16	256	4,096	4.0000	12.6491	.0625
17	289	4,913	4.1231	13.0384	.0588
18	324	5,832	4.2426	13.4164	.0556
19	361	6,859	4.3589	13.7840	.0526
20	400	8,000	4.4721	14.1421	.0500
21	441	9,261	4.5826	14.4914	.0476
22	484	10,648	4.6904	14.8324	.0455
23	529	12,167	4.7958	15.1658	.0435
24	576	13,824	4.8990	15.4919	.0417
25	625	15,625	5.0000	15.8114	.0400
26	676	17,576	5.0990	16.1245	.0385
27	729	19,683	5.1962	16.4317	.0370
28	784	21,952	5.2915	16.7332	.0357
29	841	24,389	5.3852	17.0294	.0345
30	900	27,000	5.4772	17.3205	.0333
31	961	29,791	5.5678	17.6068	.0323
32	1,024	32,768	5.6569	17.8885	.0313
33	1,089	35,937	5.7446	18.1659	.0303
34	1,156	39,304	5.8310	18.4391	.0294
35	1,225	42,875	5.9161	18.7083	.0286
36	1,296	46,656	6.0000	18.9737	.0278
37	1,369	50,653	6.0828	19.2354	.0270
38	1,444	54,872	6.1644	19.4936	.0263
39	1,521	59,319	6.2450	19.7484	.0256
40	1,600	64,000	6.3246	20.0000	.0250
41	1,681	68,921	6.4031	20.2485	.0244
42	1,764	74,088	6.4807	20.4939	.0238
43	1,849	79,507	6.5574	20.7364	.0233
44	1,936	85,184	6.6332	20.9762	.0227
45	2,025	91,125	6.7082	21.2132	.0222
46	2,116	97,336	6.7823	21.4476	.0217
47	2,209	103,823	6.8557	21.6795	.0213
48	2,304	110,592	6.9282	21.9089	.0208
49	2,401	117,649	7.0000	22.1359	.0204
50	2,500	125,000	7.0711	22.3607	.0200

n	n^2	n^3	$\sqrt{n}$	$\sqrt{10n}$	$\dfrac{1}{n}$
51	2,601	132,651	7.1414	22.5832	.0196
52	2,704	140,608	7.2111	22.8035	.0192
53	2,809	148,877	7.2801	23.0217	.0189
54	2,916	157,464	7.3485	23.2379	.0185
55	3,025	166,375	7.4162	23.4521	.0182
56	3,136	175,616	7.4833	23.6643	.0179
57	3,249	185,193	7.5498	23.8747	.0175
58	3,364	195,112	7.6158	24.0832	.0172
59	3,481	205,379	7.6811	24.2899	.0169
60	3,600	216,000	7.7460	24.4949	.0167
61	3,721	226,981	7.8102	24.6982	.0164
62	3,844	238,328	7.8740	24.8998	.0161
63	3,969	250,047	7.9373	25.0998	.0159
64	4,096	262,144	8.0000	25.2982	.0156
65	4,225	274,625	8.0623	25.4951	.0154
66	4,356	287,496	8.1240	25.6905	.0152
67	4,489	300,763	8.1854	25.8844	.0149
68	4,624	314,432	8.2462	26.0768	.0147
69	4,761	328,509	8.3066	26.2679	.0145
70	4,900	343,000	8.3666	26.4575	.0143
71	5,041	357,911	8.4261	26.6458	.0141
72	5,184	373,248	8.4853	26.8328	.0139
73	5,329	389,017	8.5440	27.0185	.0137
74	5,476	405,224	8.6023	27.2029	.0135
75	5,625	421,875	8.6603	27.3861	.0133
76	5,776	438,976	8.7178	27.5681	.0132
77	5,929	456,533	8.7750	27.7489	.0130
78	6,084	474,552	8.8318	27.9285	.0128
79	6,241	493,039	8.8882	28.1069	.0127
80	6,400	512,000	8.9443	28.2843	.0125
81	6,561	531,441	9.0000	28.4605	.0123
82	6,724	551,368	9.0554	28.6356	.0122
83	6,889	571,787	9.1104	28.8097	.0120
84	7,056	592,704	9.1652	28.9828	.0119
85	7,225	614,125	9.2195	29.1548	.0118
86	7,396	636,056	9.2736	29.3258	.0116
87	7,569	658,503	9.3274	29.4958	.0115
88	7,744	681,472	9.3808	29.6648	.0114
89	7,921	704,969	9.4340	29.8329	.0112
90	8,100	729,000	9.4868	30.0000	.0111
91	8,281	753,571	9.5394	30.1662	.0110
92	8,464	778,688	9.5917	30.3315	.0109
93	8,649	804,357	9.6437	30.4959	.0108
94	8,836	830,584	9.6954	30.6594	.0106
95	9,025	857,375	9.7468	30.8221	.0105
96	9,216	884,736	9.7980	30.9839	.0104
97	9,409	912,673	9.8489	31.1448	.0103
98	9,604	941,192	9.8995	31.3050	.0102
99	9,801	970,299	9.9499	31.4643	.0101
100	10,000	1,000,000	10.0000	31.6228	.0100

Index

L

Large-scale integrated circuit
 (LSI), 130
Latitude, 707
Law of Cosines, 552–55.
 See also Trigonometry
Law of Sines, 549–52.
 See also Trigonometry
Law of Trichotomy, 428–29
Learning disabilities, 73–74
Learning styles, 71–73
 environment, 73
 physical, 73
 sociological factors, 73
Least common multiple (LCM),
 229–31
Leibniz, Gottfried Wilhelm,
 111, 800
Leonardo of Pisa, 208
Liabilities
 current, 783
 long-term, 783
Life insurance
 endowment, 748
 limited-payment policy, 748
 straight, 748
 term, 747
Lighting, 647–49
Linear equations, 498–518
Linear measure. *See* Measurement
Lines, 276–77.
 See also Parallel lines;
  Perpendicular lines
 cevians, 293
 graphing in a plane, 499
 horizontal, 502–3
 intersecting, 287
 in a plane, 287–88
 skew, 320
 slope, 499–504
 in space, 319–20
 transversal, 287
 vertical, 502–3
Line symmetry, 17
Liquid measure. *See* Measurement
Lobachevskian geometry, 485–86
Lobachevsky, Nikolai, 485–86, 801
Logic, 471, 476–79, 596–97, 803–4.
 See also Geometry
 algebraic, 114–15
 arithmetic, 113–14
 calculator, 112–17
 reverse Polish, 115–17
Long division, 38, 39–41, 173–74.
 See also Division
Longitude, 707

Lukasiewicz, Jan, 116
Lumen, 648

M

Mainframe, 130
Main memory, 132–33
Maps, 697–707
 alphanumeric system, 701, 704
 calculating distance, 704–5
 gridiron, 698–99
 making, 702–3
 mileage, 705
 neighborhood, 703
 orienteering, 702–3
 road, 704–5
 squared, 699–701
 zero point, 698
Matching model, 604
Math anxiety, 64, 107–108
Mathematical Association
 of America, 804–5
Mathematical models, 599–600
 addition, 601–2
 division, 605–8
 multiplication, 603–5
 subtraction, 602–3
Mathematics
 and animals, 589–90
 beginning, 13–27
 business, 757–93
 competition, 802–6
 consumer, 720–34
 definition, 588
 good habits, 68–74
 history of, 797–801.
 *See also specific disciplines
  and nationalities*
 important dates, 799
 money, 719–56
 necessity of, 109–110
 nutrition, 690–95
 objections to, 108–110
 tables, 827–37
 for traveling, 696–718
 uses of, 28–29
Mathematics education.
 See also Curriculum; Tests
 concept versus technique, 51
 goals of, 50–51
 history of, 54–61
Mayan mathematics, 614
Mean, 441, 451, 452–53, 821
Measurement, 17–18, 33, 35, 37,
 333–73
 angles, 42, 372
 area, 353–65, 831

World Book Encyclopedia, Inc. offers a wide range of educational and reference materials, including a video—"How to Study." This 45-minute VHS tape combines the appeal of television with an easy-to-use formula for developing successful study habits. For more information on World Book's "How to Study" video, as well as our wide selection of educational and reference books, please write:
World Book Encyclopedia, Inc.
P.O. Box 3405, Chicago, Illinois 60654-9980